PARKY

MY AUTOBIOGRAPHY

PARKY

MY AUTOBIOGRAPHY

MICHAEL PARKINSON

HODDER &
STOUGHTON

First published in Great Britain in 2008 by Hodder & Stoughton
An Hachette Livre UK company

1

Copyright © Michael Parkinson 2008

The right of Michael Parkinson to be identified as the Author
of the Work has been asserted by him in accordance with the
Copyright, Designs and Patents Act 1988.

A CIP catalogue record for this title is available from the British Library

Hardback ISBN 978 0 340 96166 7
Trade paperback ISBN 978 0 340 97680 7

Typeset in Minion by Ellipsis Books Limited, Glasgow

Printed and bound by Clays Ltd, St Ives plc.

Hodder & Stoughton policy is to use papers that are natural, renewable and
recyclable products and made from wood grown in sustainable forests.
The logging and manufacturing processes are expected to conform to the
environmental regulations of the country of origin.

Hodder & Stoughton Ltd
338 Euston Road
London NW1 3BH

www.hodder.co.uk

*This book celebrates
the memory of my parents, the love of Mary,
the blessing of our sons Andrew, Nicholas and Michael
and the joy of our grandchildren, Emma, Georgina and Ben;
Laura and James; Honey, Felix and Sophia.*

CONTENTS

ACKNOWLEDGEMENTS

My special thanks to Erin Reimer and my son Michael for their dedicated research and intelligent prompting; to Teresa Rudge for her patience and skill in making sense of an untidy manuscript; to Andrew Bullock for his enthusiastic support; and to my former PA Autumn Phillips for causing a much-needed break from writing with a royal wedding! Also to my son Nicholas for finding me a typewriter (and some ribbons) in America thereby frustrating my last feeble excuse for not writing the book; and to Mo, Michael, Dom and the rest of the staff at the Royal Oak in Paley Street for the marvellous sustenance. Finally, warm thanks to Roddy Bloomfield, my editor at Hodder & Stoughton, who has nursed the book through decades of uncertainty.

Then there are the stalwarts who worked hard on the *Parkinson* show but didn't get a mention in the narrative simply because there wasn't the space. They are Graham Lindsay, Gill Stribling-Wright, Christina Baker and Lynda Wood and, in particular, Quentin Mann who, as floor manager, guided me through near on 600 shows and never let me down.

I would also like to thank friends and colleagues who were interviewed for the book and gave so generously of their time: Anthony Howard, Harry Whewell, Michael Frayn, Barrie Heads, Brian Armstrong, Chris Menges, Johnnie Hamp, Leslie Woodhead, Sir Paul Fox, the late Sir Bill Cotton, Cecil Korer, Eve Lucas, Jill Drewett, John Fisher, Kate Greer, Patricia Houlihan, Roger Ordish, Chris Greenwood, Colin McLennan, David Lyle, David Mitchell, Greg Coote, Bea Ballard, George Morton, Jim Moir, Anthony Cherry, Sir David Frost, Steven Lappin and Robin Esser.

Other helpful people and organisations were: Jeff Walden/BBC Written Archives Centre, Stuart Craig/Bishop Simeon Trust, Simon Hoggart, Jarvis Astaire, Mirrorpix, News International Archives, The *Guardian* Newsroom Archive Centre, Parliamentary Archives, The London Library, ITN Source, BBC Motion Gallery, *Desert Island Discs*, ITV Press Office, Cutting it Fine, ABC Library/Australia, National Film and Sound Archives/Australia and the *Daily Telegraph*.

And, finally, looking back at what I have written I am aware I have failed to mention lifelong friends including Carol and Marshall Bellow, of Leeds, and Athol and Jean Carr, who live in Rotherham, whose friendship and loyal support over the years has been a treasured gift to all our family.

Photographic Acknowledgements

The author and publisher would like to thank the following for permission to reproduce photographs:

Robin Anderson / Rex Features, BBC Photo Library, *Daily Express* Pictures, Alan Davidson / Camera Press, Fremantle Media, Jenny Goodall / AFP / Getty Images, Granada Television, ITV / Rex Features, Charles Knight / Rex Features, Kobal Collection / United Artists, John Lyons / Reveille Newspapers Ltd, Ken McKay / Rex Features, *Manchester Evening News*, Harry Myers / Rex Features, Newspix / Rex Features, PA Archive / PA Photos, PIC Photos, Nick Potts / Action Images, Snapper Media / PA Photos, Sport & General / PA Photos, Raymond Thatcher Photography, David Young Photography.

Other photographs are from private collections.

Every reasonable effort has been made to contact the copyright holders, but if there are any errors or omissions, Hodder & Stoughton will be pleased to insert the appropriate acknowledgement in any subsequent printing of this publication.

PREFACE – THE CHOICE

Every morning, when I woke, I could see the pit from my bedroom window. When you couldn't see it you could smell it, an invisible sulphurous presence. It was where my dad worked, where my granddad worked and his dad before him. It was where I expected to end up. I remember thinking it wouldn't bother me, providing I could marry Ingrid Bergman and get a house much nearer the pit gates. Shortly after Vesting Day, when Attlee's government nationalised the mines, we were taken from Barnsley Grammar School to visit a colliery. When I arrived home my father asked me where we had been. I told him. He said, 'That's not a pit, it's a holiday camp.'

He told me to be ready, 4 a.m. the following Sunday, and he would show me what a real coal mine was like. He took me down Grimethorpe Colliery and tipped the wink to his mate on the winding gear that there was a tourist on board. We dropped like a man without a parachute. Big laugh. The rest wasn't so funny. He took me where men worked on their knees getting coal, showed me the lamp he used to test for methane gas, explained how dangerous it was. He showed me the pit ponies. The only time I had seen them before was when they had their annual holiday from their work underground and emerged from the dark, their eyes bandaged against the light.

We stood in front of a seam of coal, black and shiny. 'Let's see if you'd make a miner,' he said. He gave me a pick and nodded at the seam. The harder I hit the coal, the more the pick bounced off the surface. 'Find the fault,' he said, running his fingers across the coal face. He tapped it and a chunk fell out, glittering in his lamplight. We walked back and he said nothing until we reached the pit gates. 'What do you reckon?' he said.

'You won't get me down there for a hundred quid a shift,' I said.

He nodded and smiled. 'That's good,' he said, 'but be warned that if ever you change your mind and I see you coming through those gates I'll kick your arse all the way home.'

This is a story of a child who did as he was told.

1

PIT VILLAGE

My father used to love coming to the show, although he was never quite sure that what I was doing was a proper job. He wanted me to be a professional cricketer. Just before he died he said to me: 'You've had a good life, lad.' I said I had. 'You've met some fascinating people and become quite famous yourself,' he said. I nodded. 'What is more, you've made a bob or two without breaking sweat,' he said. I agreed. 'Well done,' he said. 'But think on, it's not like playing cricket for Yorkshire, is it?' That may well be true, but once or twice it got pretty darned close.

From the script of the final *Parkinson Show* recorded at the London Studios, 6 December 2007

When I was born in 1935 my father wanted me called Melbourne Parkinson because we had just won a Test match there. My mother, a woman of great common sense, put her foot down. Her winning argument was that my father could have his way if she could pick a second name. He was agreeable until she told him that she wanted me called Gershwin after her favourite composer. They settled for Michael.

1

I was born on a council estate in Cudworth, a mining village in the South Yorkshire coalfield. In those days it was nicknamed 'Debtors' Retreat' and my dad told me the rent collectors walked around in pairs. He was a miner at Grimethorpe Colliery. Every day he would walk three miles to his place of work, spending eight hours underground getting coal. He was paid seven shillings a shift.

The year after I was born a dispute at the pit ended, as disputes did in those days, with a lockout. The management simply closed the pit gates until the miners, having learnt their lesson, went back to work. Fed up with the mining industry, seeking a less uncertain career, father borrowed a fiver from a relative and went to Oxford to get a job on the new Morris Motors car assembly line. The day after the interview, walking around Oxford waiting to see if he had been accepted, he felt a terrible longing for his native landscape, so he came home. A week later a letter arrived telling him the job was his if he wanted it.

My mother, Freda, was in favour of a move. She had been born in Oxford. Her father was killed in France in the First World War. She arrived in Yorkshire not out of choice but by chance. After her husband's death, my grandmother would visit a local hospital where the casualties of war were left outside in their wheelchairs awaiting anyone kind enough to take them for a walk. One day she took Fred Binns for a spin. He had been invalided out of the army after being wounded on the Western Front. Lodged in the back of his shoulder was a spectacular lump of metal, which surgeons deemed too risky to remove. Later on, when he became my grandmother's second husband and took her family back to his native Yorkshire, he would allow me, as a Christmas treat, to feel the shrapnel in his back.

'How did it happen?' I'd say. 'That would be telling,' he would reply, the longest sentence I ever heard him speak and the only time he ever mentioned the war.

My mother always said she wasn't really a Yorkshire woman, more a transplant. Living in a pit village, being married to a miner, was not how she had imagined her life. In an unfinished family history, which she started writing after the death of my father, she explains her frustration:

> My older brother Tom was a bright boy. He won a scholarship to Grammar School. My parents borrowed £100 from a local money lender to send him there. They paid 66 per cent interest. They were still paying it off when I was pulled out of school to look after my mother who was unwell. I wanted to be a designer. I had a flare for making clothes. I dreamed of a life in a street of doctors and professional people. I imagined marrying a teacher.

Throughout her life she never lost her belief that she had been thwarted in her ambitions, that she was unfairly cheated of an opportunity to prove her talent. But I don't want to portray her as a bitter person, as someone soured by disappointment. Quite the opposite. She channelled her ambitions through her son, found great joy and fulfilment in her grandchildren and, most of all, never had occasion to doubt the profound and enduring love of a good man.

Even though she said she would never marry a miner, she reckoned without John William Parkinson. He was ten years older than my mother and the best friend of her brother. She was twelve when she first became aware of him. He was one of sixteen children, ten of whom survived infancy.

His father, Sammy, was a miner, like his dad before him. And, like his dad, Sammy was a black-backed miner. These men believed that excessive washing of the back weakened the muscles needed to take the weight of a collapsing seam. They washed their backs once a week, no more.

I remember seeing my granddad with his strange discoloured back, sitting in the tub in front of the fire while his wife and daughters took turns to fill it from a brick-built copper in the corner of the room. Before pithead baths sons would follow fathers into the water in order of seniority. Women and children witnessed the ritual. Modesty was not something the working class could afford. When pithead baths eventually arrived and his sons started using them, Sammy stuck by his home ritual. Even a serious accident when he was buried in a fall and suffered severe injuries didn't change his attitude. When they dug him out he had deep lacerations to the top of his head. In later life, when his hair turned white, the scars showed through like veins in a leaf.

Sammy's father signed the parish register with a cross. Sammy wrote in a fine copperplate hand. He had left school at twelve and was largely self-taught. He was the first literate member of his family. He wrote clearly and he was particularly adept with numbers, a talent he put to use in a daily attempt to beat the bookies with a complicated series of multiple bets. He bet in tanners and would send me to the bookie's runner who lived two doors away. He was a tiny man of dark hue whom I took to be a West Indian until I realised his colour was caused by the fact he never washed. My granddad said he was the sort who kept coal in the bath.

His office was the public telephone kiosk down the street, from where he would phone the bets he had taken to his boss, who lived in a nice house with a tennis court. Later, when I became a journalist

4

and before we had a phone of our own, I used to have to follow him into the phone booth. I would wear gloves to handle the receiver, holding it as far as possible away from my ear while bellowing through the mouthpiece, which I had covered with a cloth. It was said he was the most successful bookie's runner of the lot because the police never raided his house. They were scared of what they might catch.

Sammy's wife, my grandma, was a tall and bony woman, missing most of her teeth and deaf as a post. She was also short-sighted, which enabled her husband to cheat her during their daily game of dominoes. He would put threes against fives, twos against sixes, and she'd cry, 'I don't know how he keeps on winning.'

She didn't say much apart from that. Her deafness imprisoned her in a silent and solitary world. She rarely went out and spent her life wearing pinafores.

She worshipped my father who was the main breadwinner of the family. He lived at home until he was nearly thirty, still tipping up his wages and being given spending money back. The family was trying to pay off what they had borrowed to survive the general strike. They were enslaved by poverty.

One of my father's sisters, Aunt Lavinia, rarely moved from the front room where she would sit all day watching the street through lace curtains. Sometimes I would sit with her. One day a local girl, heavily pregnant, walked by. Lavinia watched her passing and said to herself, but loud enough for me to hear, 'She should have it sewn up.' I didn't know what she meant but it sounded drastic.

Sammy never took his family on holiday. He lived to his mid-seventies and never visited London. He went once to Leeds, walking the thirty miles there and back to see Bradman play. His only other excursion was a bus trip to Blackpool with the local working-men's club. The story goes he was so disappointed with the local beer he had one pint and started walking home.

He worked at the pit for sixty years or more, ending up with my father as his boss. In the drastic winter of 1947 when the pit lane was blocked with snow drifts, only about four men managed the three-mile walk to Grimethorpe Colliery. Sammy Parkinson was one of them. I knew he was my father's father but I couldn't make the connection. As a child I could not understand how a man as vigorous as my father, as full of life and laughter, could have sprung from such an environment.

John William Parkinson – he preferred Jack and I was always Jack's lad – had a talent for ignoring misery or circumnavigating poverty. He would say: 'If you don't have money, you never miss it.' He didn't care. Once he was rid of his teeth – in those days you had them removed as soon as possible because they were too expensive to keep – and had a set of pearly gnashers there was no stopping him.

My mother remembers him as a dandy, wearing double-breasted tight jackets, Oxford bags with twenty-six-inch bottoms, patent leather shoes with pointed toes and a trilby hat with a snap brim. He was good-looking with wavy brown hair, blue/grey eyes and an athletic figure. My mother noticed that whenever he went out on a double date with her brother he always ended up with the prettier girl. He was a good dancer, taking lessons at Madame Woodcock's Emporium of Dance in Barnsley. It was here he learnt the scandalous new form of dancing, which involved holding your partner close and dancing cheek to cheek.

My mother was present at a local dance hall when John William Parkinson and a partner (who my mother in her book describes as 'no better than she ought to be') danced with bodies so passionately entwined that the other dancers stopped and became spectators. My father smooched his partner around the dance floor, timing things so that the dance finished as he foxtrotted through the door and into the night. 'Just like Fred Astaire,' my mother observed. The room was aghast at such wanton behaviour. My mother was smitten.

She was even more beguiled when she heard from her brother Tom of an encounter involving his future mother-in-law. Tom had asked my father to make up a foursome with his bride-to-be and her sister Gertie who, in spite of her name, was a looker. They finished their evening back at the girls' home where their mum, a formidable woman with a posh accent, afraid Gertie might be mixing in the wrong company being escorted by a miner, began asking my father about his prospects.

My father answered with amused good nature until the mother asked the direct question: 'Tell me, young man, do you have any money in the bank?' Whereupon my father replied: 'I ought to have, missus, seeing I've never taken any out.'

Some time later a group of them went to the cinema. My mother sat between my father and her current boyfriend, a grammar school boy with ambitions to be a teacher. She found herself slipping her hand into my father's and realising he was the man she wanted to marry. He told her he had loved her since the day he first saw her and had waited for her to grow up until he declared his love. In her book my mother notes that while she found the notion of him waiting for her to be romantic, having seen him dance, she had no doubt he'd had 'a bloody good time while waiting'.

Much later, when my father was trying to tell me about sex, a lecture that involved birds' nests and sparrows' eggs, I asked him what kind of sex education he had received. He said the local vicar, who was also the captain of his first cricket team, had warned him that inappropriate touching of his willy would make it fall off.

Mother, on the other hand, relates in her book that she was told if she kissed a boy more than twenty times she would automatically become pregnant – which might explain why I was born twelve months after they were married in 1934, and maybe why, as Mother says, it was a complete surprise to both of them.

2

JACK'S LAD

Aside from World War Two breaking out, the other significant event of 1939 was that we moved house. We left 'Debtors' Retreat' four hundred yards behind and moved into what the locals sarcastically termed 'Millionaires' Row'. It earned the title because it housed one or two white-collar workers, including a surveyor and the council's finance officer. We moved next door to the local sanitary inspector, which pleased my mother.

Maurice Bennett was the sort who liked to know everything about his neighbours. He was a tall, beaky man who loved peering over the garden wall, making your business his. That was fine by my father, who loved a natter. Indeed, if he couldn't find anyone to talk to, he would often converse with himself. All was well until Maurice Bennett, neighbour, became Mr Bennett, council official.

In those days miners were given a free ton of coal each month as part of a pay deal. It was an excessive amount for a small grate in a council house, so my father would load our shed and then distribute what was left over to people who didn't get the concessions, mainly pensioners. One day, as I was helping my dad shift the ton of coal, Maurice Bennett stopped by.

'Now then, John Willy,' he said, which was his first mistake. No one called my father John Willy without getting his ear chewed off.

'Jack,' said my dad. 'The name is Jack.'

'Well, Jack lad,' said Mr Bennett, 'it has come to my attention that you are distributing coal to people in the vicinity who don't get the free ton. I must point out that this is against regulations. I don't want to report you so we'll just say this is friendly advice.'

My father seemed to take the rebuke in untroubled fashion. 'Thank you for the warning,' he said. Mr Bennett left to get the bus to work. My father said nothing until we came to loading the last two barrowloads of coal. 'This way,' he said, and went down the Bennetts' garden path and filled his coal shed with an illegal load.

'Let's see him explain that lot away,' said my father.

Mr Bennett never mentioned it again.

Our other neighbours were really strange. One woman suffered from a form of religious mania and would sit all day in the bath while her husband poured jugs of water over her. She thought she was being baptised in the river Jordan.

We celebrated our move with our first family holiday. We went to the newly opened Butlin's Holiday Camp at Skegness. He didn't know it at the time but when Billy Butlin devised his all-action holidays he had my father in mind. My dad entered and won the wheelbarrow race, the tennis tournament, the hundred-yard dash, the three-legged race, the knobbly knees contest, the high jump, the snooker final and was doing well in the table-tennis competition until I ruined his chances of a clean sweep. My parents had left me with a babysitter and I had walked away and become lost. My earliest childhood memory is of sitting on the counter of a café being fed ice creams by a blonde woman and seeing my mother and father coming through the door to collect me. According to my mother, I told my rescuers that she had run away from me.

My father forgave me but he couldn't forgive Adolf Hitler. With war imminent, we cut our holiday short and returned home early so that he might be better prepared to repulse Adolf's ambitions.

First he joined the local fire-fighting unit and, armed with a bucket and a hand pump, demonstrated how he had been taught to rescue us in the event of our house being hit by an incendiary bomb. The nearest the Luftwaffe came to Cudworth was fifteen miles away when it bombed Sheffield. His training might have come in handy ten years later when our house accidentally caught fire but on that occasion he simply picked up the burning sofa and bundled it through the living-room window. I know because I was standing behind him when he did it.

Our Anderson shelter set the standard for the rest of the street. Not only did my father bury it deep in our garden but he camouflaged the top with earth and grass. Flying over it, the German pilots must have thought it was a giant mole hill.

When the sirens sounded, Dad would march us down the shelter where we would sit with gas masks on, awaiting our fate.

One day he brought a canary into our sanctuary. They were used down the pit to test for methane gas. The first night there was a panic because the bird closed its eyes and my father thought the end had come. In fact, it was having a nap. From that point on, my father sat making noises through his gas mask, rattling the cage to keep the bird awake and alert. The next night, we found it lying stiff in the bottom of its cage. My father put it in a box and we buried it on top of the shelter. He said it had died fighting Hitler. My mother said she'd had enough of all the nonsense and she was sick of spending her evenings with a gas mask on. So our air-raid shelter became a relic of the war until we dismantled it and discovered the curved sheet metal made wonderful, if lethal, sledges in the bitter winter of 1947.

This was not the end of my father's personal feud with Adolf. He pinned a huge map over the fireplace to trace the course of the Allied advance through Europe. Every day we would listen to the BBC News and in red crayon mark the boundaries of the latest success. In many ways, in spite of my father's obsession with Hitler, the war passed us by. Miners were not required to join up. They were essential workers, therefore our village was comparatively untouched by the sorrow of war.

My own view was that the fighting wouldn't last much longer because we had John Wayne on our side. Aged eight or nine I was already a veteran movie-goer. Our cinema was called the Rock, which we always said had something to do with the seats. My first cinema memory is of my father being warned by the management that unless he improved his behaviour he would be kicked out. At the time he was falling into the aisle, helpless with laughter at Laurel and Hardy.

He loved comics. I grew up on Chaplin, Lloyd, Keaton, Ben Turpin, Wheeler and Wolsey, Abbott and Costello. He took us to the theatre to see a comedy double act called Collinson and Breen. It must have been wartime because they were dressed in army uniform. It was my mother's birthday and we celebrated with a box at the Theatre Royal, Barnsley. It was the first time I had visited the theatre and I remember the plush reds and golds. But most of all I remember the deckchairs. Our box had three of them and we sat, as if on Bridlington beach, watching the turns.

My mother, a good-looking woman and at her best for the occasion, attracted the attention of the taller comic of the double act, who kept giving her saucy winks. She loved the attention but Dad became restless. As they took their bows the tall one started blowing kisses in my mother's direction. This was too much for the old man who would have undoubtedly made it on stage for a punch-up had it not been for his deckchair collapsing as he struggled to get at the leering comic. I've had better nights in the theatre since, but none more dramatic.

During my childhood, theatre was a rare treat – mainly panto with Norman Evans, Nat Jackley and strapping-thighed principal boys. Cinema, on the other hand, became my second home and the source of all my aspirations. It was here I decided I wanted to be a journalist. I'd still marry Ingrid Bergman and we'd live in a house next to Barnsley Football Club.

I went to the movies with my mother four nights a week and with my mates on Saturday for the children's matinee, when I would scour the dustbins outside the cinema for scraps of film. In those days, if the movie broke down, as it often did, the projectionist would make a crude edit and bung the leftover bits in the bins. I once found about six inches of a Charlie Chaplin film and kept it in my pocket for many years, feeling its smooth texture, dreaming of Hollywood.

My mother used to knit her way through movies. She had a gift for designing knitwear. She would create a pattern while watching a film and then come home, write it down and send it off to Stitchcraft, a company specialising in knitting patterns. She was paid three quid a design. I learned to type, as soon as my fingers could cope, by setting down her patterns on a battered old Corona. The first line I ever typed was 'KI,PI,K2TOG . . .'

She continued her career for many years, one of her patterns being modelled by a young Roger Moore, and a Fair Isle pullover

13

she created was worn by Paul McCartney. More importantly, what she taught her son, who sat by her side in the cinema, to the gentle sound of clicking needles, was that it is possible to earn a living while having a good time.

As we waited for the war to end our sheltered life was disturbed by the arrival of Auntie Florrie and Uncle Harry from London. They had been bombed out of their flat in King's Cross. Harry hated being away from his beloved London. He went back almost straight away. Florrie stayed and eventually took charge of a hostel for evacuees at Rogerthorpe Manor, an old and neglected country house surrounded by damp and bowed trees that looked like graveside mourners.

It held a strange fascination for me, particularly as some of the inhabitants were as mysterious as the house they lived in. In the main these were the soldier-husbands of the occupants, who came on leave or sometimes because they had been invalided out of the army. One such casualty sat all day, cross-legged, wearing only a loin cloth, looking out of the window. I was nine or ten at the time and I remember standing in the doorway of his room, staring at him, waiting for a move. After a while his back trembled, I heard a sound and realised he was weeping.

On another occasion, a soldier on leave from combat in the desert asked me to show him the way to the village shop where he wanted to buy cigarettes. When we arrived there the shopkeeper said he hadn't any. Cigarettes were in short supply in wartime and he was clearly keeping them for his regulars. The soldier reached over the counter, took him by the shirt front and said, 'Mister, I hope you're telling the truth.' He came away with twenty Woodbines. On the way back, a car backfired and the soldier dived to the pavement, flattening himself against the concrete. When he got to his feet he apologised. He was trembling.

When next I marked the Allied advance on our map, I remembered that soldier, although it was not until a few years later I really understood what had happened.

3

CUDWORTH, YORKSHIRE AND ENGLAND

When I was five I experienced two important events. I went to school for the first time and my father took me to see Barnsley FC play at Oakwell. When I returned from the first day of formal education and was asked what I thought, I replied, 'It was all right but I don't think I'll bother any more.' Similarly, when asked at half-time my opinion of watching Barnsley, I said, 'It's all right but can I go home now?' Whereas I can believe my assessment of school was to prove both sensible and perceptive, I never stopped thanking my father for keeping me at Oakwell.

Snydale Road Junior School was a doddle. I loved reading so they put me in charge of the library. I maintained order by employing Horace Copley as my sidekick. Horace had thumped me in the playground. Horace thumped everyone at school just in case anyone doubted he was the boss. With Horace at my side the library was a quiet and well-ordered place. Forty years later, when I returned to the school with a film crew for a documentary, a tough-looking kid stuck up his hand in class and said, 'My granddad says he used to beat you up at school.'

I didn't need to say it, but I did. 'Is your granddad called Horace Copley?'

He nodded.

'It's true.'

'Told you!' he said, thumping the child next to him.

I captained the school cricket team, which pleased my father who, since my birth, had been preparing me for the day when I played for Yorkshire. As far as he was concerned it wasn't merely a possibility but a certainty that one day I would wear the White Rose. He drilled me in every spare moment on the basic principles of the game. Play forward, play back, elbow high – show them the full face of the willow, nothing fancy. By the age of eight I had a solid defence and a hatred of getting out.

After school we would play in the street and under the light of a solitary gas lamp as the day faded. Once I batted for a week scoring 2,023 runs before having to declare because my mates wouldn't bowl at me any more. Weekends we would play on a strip of land between Bailey's fish and chip shop and a house owned by a miserable old harpy who kept our cricket balls when they went over her fence. In soccer season she stuck a garden fork in our footballs. We repaid her every Mischief Night by daubing her door handles with dog poo and shoving mice through her letterbox.

In order to raise money to replace our confiscated equipment we devised a means of ensnaring the lunchtime drinkers at the nearby pub on Sundays. As they lurched home at chucking-out time, they would stop and watch our game and offer drunken advice. We would challenge them to bowl me out. Twenty balls for a sixpence. They never refused. They would take off their jackets and come racing in like fighting bulls. What happened as they approached the delivery crease always depended on how many pints they had drunk. When I tell you that these were eight to ten pints a session men, you'll understand that anything was possible. There were those who spun round and ended up delivering the ball in the direction they had approached the crease. Others forgot to let go of the ball and charged past me in drunken flight. One or two delivered a challenge but we were never out of pocket. On a good day we'd make a bob or two.

The drinkers didn't know it but they were, in fact, cricket's first sponsors.

Looking back, I am struck by the freedom I had as a child. When I wasn't playing cricket or soccer I was roaming the village and surrounding countryside as Wilson of *The Wizard*. Wilson was my favourite character from the many comics I read as a child. No one knew his age. He lived in the hills in North Yorkshire on a diet of spring water and berries and would leave his native habitat only to achieve some astounding new feat of athleticism. He ran the first three-minute mile, set the long-jump record with a leap that carried him so far out of the pit they couldn't properly measure it, and won the marathon running in diver's boots. His most spectacular feat was leaping a pit of spears while carrying two buckets of cement in order to quell a native uprising in Oogoboogo Land, or whatever passed as the name of an African country in those innocent days.

All these feats I surpassed in my imagination as I raced through the fields of my youth. Later in life, wondering in print whatever became of the Great Wilson, I was informed he had gone missing over the Channel during the war. He had been the greatest Spitfire pilot of them all with 195 kills but had disappeared on a routine mission over the Channel, just like Glenn Miller.

When I wasn't Wilson I was lying in the long grass watching my dad play cricket. The field, located next to a farmyard, was bounded by sloping wheat fields and when the sun shone on the ripening grain, golden ripples appeared to flow up the hillside. Just visible over the brow of the hill was the pithead gear of Grimethorpe Colliery, just in case we thought we were in Elysium. My father was a fast bowler with an action based on his great hero, Harold Larwood. He was quick and aggressive and never short of a word or two. As a spectator I often wondered what was said when my father engaged the opposition in conversation. Later on, when I played with him, I found out.

My very first senior game for Cudworth was against Grimethorpe, very much a local derby. It was just after the war, I was eleven and we had a new fast bowler, a soldier who had married a local girl. He bowled a first over of real pace and hostility, at the end of which my father said to their opening bat, 'What's tha' reckon, then?'

'By God, Jack, he's quick,' he said.

'He is that but tha' should have seen him before he was gassed,' said my father, a remark which caused so much confusion it won us the match.

The Cudworth team of that time was rich in character. There was George Roberts, our big hitter, who had a tin leg. He wore one pad only, so that when the ball struck his false leg it would make a noise like Big Ben striking.

'How's that?' the bowler would say.

'One o'clock and all's well,' George would reply. He had an eye like a sparrowhawk and would hit the ball into the cornfields and beyond.

His rival as a big hitter was Norman Stewardson, whose bat was bound with a vellum-like sheath and weighed a bit less than a large

19

sledgehammer. If anyone queried the origin of his bat's covering, he would say, 'Kangaroo skin.' When asked where they could find such an implement, he would reply, 'First of all you've got to find your kangaroo.'

My father's partner with the new ball was a tall and handsome man called Jim Baker. He had the longest run-up I had ever seen. He went back so far my father explained to me that they had to cut a hole in the hedge at one end of the field to accommodate him. And of course I believed him. Then there was Jack Berry who bowled leg spin at medium pace and was one of the best club cricketers I ever saw.

I was a last-minute replacement for a senior member who was injured in the pre-match knock-up. They put me in the deep amid the cow slop and the daisies, out of the way. Jack Berry was bowling and the batsman went for a slog and top-edged it in a high and spinning loop to where I was fielding. I remember nothing except diving and the ball sticking in my hand. But what I will never forget is my heroes picking me up and congratulating me and the look of pride on my father's face.

I was eleven years old, playing with the big guys and on my way to grammar school.

4

THE NOBLE ART
OF BEACH CRICKET

'No supermarkets, no teabags, no lager, no Formica, no vinyl, no CDs, no trainers, no hoodies, no Starbucks. Shops on every corner, red telephone boxes, Lyon's Corner Houses, trams, steam trains. Woodbines, Senior Service, Smog. No automatic washing machines, wash every Monday. Central heating rare, chilblains common. Abortion illegal, homosexual relationships illegal, suicide illegal. Capital punishment legal. White faces everywhere. Austin Sevens, Ford Eights. A Bakelite wireless in every home, television almost unknown, the family eating together. Heavy rationing, sides to middle. Make do and mend.'

That is how the historian David Kynaston sums up the immediate postwar years in his excellent book, *Austerity Britain*.

Looking back, my memories of childhood are black and white, now and again sepia. It wasn't until the sixties I started recording in colour.

'Make do and mend' had its virtues. There was a certainty and closeness about life in a pit village that was comforting for the child lucky enough to find its embrace. There was also poverty and oft-times, because of it, drunkenness and violence. There was madness, too. I had a friend whose mother was driven crazy by worry and the physical and mental brutality of her husband. I never saw him beat her – although the consequences were apparent – but on more than one occasion I witnessed his merciless taunting, which would always end with her distressed and weeping, being comforted by her son, my mate.

I used to stand there like a statue, thanking God my parents were not like that. One day, my mate's father walked past me, smelling like a tap room, and, nodding towards his distraught wife and son, said, 'Never get married, lad.' And he ruffled my hair.

I was safe in the perfect cocoon of my home, with my loving parents and an extended family never less than a street away. When my mother started work at the Co-op as a shop assistant in 1943, I was fed and watered by my two sets of grandparents, who lived next door but one to each other. That is if I managed to avoid several aunties living along the route, who, if they saw me passing by, would insist on feeding me. I sometimes had three teas in one afternoon. All my family were rock-solid working-class people, law-abiding, sober (more often than not) and loving.

When the genealogy programme *Whose Life Is It Anyway?* asked if they could research my life, I told them they would find nothing to intrigue them. They smiled, knowingly, and said, 'That is what they all say, but we always find something.' Six weeks later they called. 'You were right,' they said. What they didn't add was, 'You have the most boring background of anyone we have so far researched.' But they didn't have to. I already knew.

Boring it might have seemed to outsiders, but far from it to the child growing up happy and beloved in a warm and secure nest. The time was austere; we had just come through a war, we were underfed and dressed like refugees. The pit village we lived in would never win a beauty contest, and its men did a dangerous and dirty job. Yet, I look back on my childhood there with great affection and no little gratitude. You could say my situation has changed somewhat in the intervening years, but if I could rewrite my life I wouldn't alter a line of my early childhood.

This contentment was due in no small part to my father who, as they said of someone else, was 'born intoxicated'. Life to him was not all underground misery, inhaling coal dust, fouled lungs, a struggle. In my father's view, that part existed only as an interlude between seasonal merrymaking.

Christmas was his favourite. What we used to do for Christmas was share a pig with three or four other families. Throughout the year we would take it in turns to clean and feed it and then, just when we were getting fond of it, my old man and his mates would send for the local gamekeeper, who would slaughter anything for a couple of bob and a pint or two. I can remember standing outside the pig sty – a very small child – tears running down my face at the noise of the carnage inside.

One year someone pinched our pig. They waited until it was fattened and ready for the kill and then spirited it away at dead of night. We never found out who it was but ever after we mounted guard on our pig sty from November onwards, saving it for the slaughter man. Our Christmases really began when the pig was jointed, jellied, pied, sausaged, rissoled, trottered and shared out among the owners.

Looking back, Christmas to my child's mind was a rich stew of smells and sensations. The table groaned for the one and only day of the year under the unexpected weight of food. Men I otherwise saw in their working clothes and pit muck turned up in tight blue suits and Co-op shoes, and aunties with new hair-dos seemed suddenly aware of what they'd kept under their pinafores all year long. The air was heavy with Soir de Paris and the promise of mischief.

The sharpest memories of Christmas in those days are the football matches. It seemed to me that Barnsley never stopped playing football over Christmas and I never missed a match.

Christmas matches were different altogether. In the bus going to the ground, men would be wearing new scarves and gloves and they smoked cigars instead of Woodbines. In the ground the normal smell of stale beer was replaced with a whisky aroma from a thousand miniature bottles, which were produced from inside pockets and offered surreptitiously to the man next door in the way they might proffer a glimpse of a dirty postcard.

In fact, two or three games would be played over the Christmas period and often the players appeared as imbued with the Christmas spirit as the spectators. There was one famous Boxing Day game when one of our team, a man not unknown in certain licensed premises in Barnsley, set the ball down for a free kick and, as he walked steadily backwards to prepare his run-up, collided with the low wall separating the pitch from the spectators, and fell backwards into the crowd. He was caught by spectators who later swore he fell asleep in their arms. Much later, having been revived, he stumbled making a tackle and fell to earth holding his leg. As our trainer ran on to the field someone shouted, 'Don't revive him! Bury the sod!'

Christmas games were derby days – Rotherham United, Sheffield Wednesday, Doncaster Rovers and, best of all, Chesterfield. In those days before crowd segregation, the anticipation of going to a match was in standing next to visiting fans and hearing their take on the game. Playing for Chesterfield at the time were the Capel brothers. Tommy, the really gifted one, was the captain. Chesterfield were awarded a late penalty and Tommy Capel selected his brother to take the kick to win the game. He shot hopelessly wide whereupon one Chesterfield fan standing next to us turned to his companion and said, 'Nepotism. That's what lost us the game, bloody nepotism.'

None of us knew what he meant. We didn't laugh, mainly because we thought it had something to do with incest. It wasn't until we got home and searched the dictionary we got the joke.

The next ritual on my father's calendar was the start of the shooting season. Every year, the mine-owners would gather with a few cronies and shoot our wildlife. They continued the slaughter even after the mines were nationalised. We lived opposite the gamekeeper, a small bow-legged man called Athey Crossley. He was the man who killed the pig for us every Christmas. My father was employed as a beater and from a very early age I went along with him. When I was big enough I was given a pick handle to try to bash the rabbits we startled as we clumped through the countryside towards the guns. The rabbits were ours to eat if we were successful.

It always seemed to me incongruous that we should be walking towards the pithead gear and slag heaps of Grimethorpe Colliery for the amusement of armed men, while deep down, beneath our feet, miners were getting coal. One day, walking through a field of stubble towards the guns, before my dad took me down the pit, I asked him what it was like deep underground.

'Blacker than a crow's arse,' he said, and left it at that.

It was when it came to summer holidays my father's gift for creating drama out of the commonplace flourished in the most spectacular manner. We took our holidays in August, Barnsley

Feast Week, when the whole village upped and went away like some Indian tribe moving reservations. The destination varied. The majority went across the Pennines to Blackpool, the rest headed for the east coast – Cleethorpes, Bridlington, Filey and particularly Scarborough. We were east-coast people because my father only went to seaside resorts where the sands were suitable for beach cricket. Like some inspector of wickets he had, during his time, closely examined the west-coast beaches and found them unfit for play. The east coast, notably Scarborough, Bridlington and Filey, were declared first class.

Thus it was that during my youth, whenever we went on holiday, we resembled some MCC party heading for a three-month tour of the West Indies. We were easily discernible from the rest of the mob at the railway station, being the only family with a full set of stumps strapped to our suitcase. Mother's carrier bag was full of balls and both Father and I carried cricket bats. Indeed, a photograph of the time, taken at Bridlington shortly after our arrival, shows father and son strolling down the promenade, one carrying a Frank Sugg and the other a Gunn and Moore, looking for all the world like Sutcliffe and Holmes walking out to open for Yorkshire at Park Avenue, Bradford.

One of the outstanding features of our holidays was that play started as soon as we stepped off the train and continued through every daylight hour until it was time to go home again. My childhood memories of those days are of burning beaches and large men trying to bowl me out. Misery was rain and shelter in the amusement arcade and the smell of cheap raincoats and human damp. The success of the holiday depended entirely on how much cricket we could get in and, even more important, how many games we won. Here it should be explained to occasional participants of bat and ball on the sands that our version of beach cricket was the equivalent of a five-day Test match between England and Australia, or at least as important as the War of the Roses.

My old man took his cricket very seriously, as befitted a Yorkshireman, team captain and tour organiser. His first job after arrival was to make an immediate recce of the beach to lay claim to the best batting strip. Then he would mark out the wicket and, with my mother acting as wicket keeper, using her coat to stop the ball, he would bowl a few overs at me. This activity invariably attracted onlookers who would be invited to play by my old man in order that he might make a shrewd assessment of their worth. Outstanding talents would be immediately signed on for the coming week, but only if their antecedents matched their ability. Simply stated, he would have anyone playing in his team provided they didn't come from Lancashire. This chauvinism was deliberately designed to stir up tribal warfare and always ended in the highlight of our week, a challenge from a team of Lancastrians who were bitter and disgruntled about being turned down because of an accident of birth.

They never won. The fact was that my father was a magnificent beach cricketer with a profound knowledge of the tactics needed to achieve success in this kind of game. For instance, he won many a game by his keen study of the east-coast tides. The importance of this can be gauged from the fact that in our kind of beach cricket the edge of the sea was always a boundary.

Thus, on a morning with the tide receding, if the old man won the toss, he would put the other side in. By the time they had exhausted themselves trying to hit a six into the fast disappearing sea, the tide would change, and we would have the comparatively easy task of lobbing boundaries into the oggin while their fielders were distracted by the fear of being cut off by the onrushing waves. My dad never lost a game of beach cricket and when the time came to retire from the pit, he devoted his life to coaching his grandchildren in the mysteries of the greatest game. He had spectacular success.

Much later, when I was off working abroad with television, my parents would stay at our house to help Mary with the kids. This was my father's idea of paradise. After one trip he could hardly wait for me to get through the door before inviting me into the garden to see the progress he had made with my middle son, Nicholas, who was ten at the time. Nicholas was a slow bowler and his granddad had already taught him how to spin a ball from leg.

'See how he's come on since you went away,' said my dad, handing me a bat.

My son bowled three respectable leg breaks and then skidded one through to hit my leg.

'That's his top spinner and you are plumb lbw,' said my dad.

'Nonsense, it hit a pebble,' I said.

'You'll see,' said Father.

Next ball was a leg break, or so I thought. Instead it turned the other way and bowled me. I looked at my ten-year-old.

'That was my goggly. Granddad showed me how to do it,' said my son.

My father had a smile that went right round his face and ended at the back collar stud.

Later on John Boorman, the film director, used the incident in his film *Hope and Glory* to symbolise the way some families use the sporting rather than the Gregorian calendar to mark the passing of time.

An irregular part of my father's social calendar was a visit to

London. We sometimes dossed down in Auntie Florrie's cold-water flat, up two flights of stairs above a pie shop, between King's Cross and St Pancras Station. She had returned home after working at Rogerthorpe Manor during the war and been reunited with husband Harry, who had stayed in London and kept on working as a messenger for a newspaper in Fleet Street.

I saw Grub Street for the first time through his eyes, and I saw it as it should be seen, standing outside El Vino's looking down the street and up to Saint Paul's. I didn't realise at the time that it would be, for a short but significant period, my place of work, and it would be a toss up whether El Vino's or the *Daily Express* would have the more significant effect on my career.

It would be untrue to say my father's obsession with a visit to the capital was due to a love of the place. London to him meant three things: Lord's, Wembley and The Oval. He took my mother to London for a couple of days for their honeymoon. She was overwhelmed at the prospect of seeing the city for the first time. She didn't realise there was a Test match in progress and she spent two days at Lord's.

It was a fair introduction to life with Father.

Another time, upon arrival in London, we were whisked to the theatre to see the Ink Spots perform. They were an American close harmony group, popular at the time, and my father's favourite singers. Their big hit was a sentimental song called 'Whispering grass'. 'Why do you whisper green grass? What makes the wind stir you so?'

I can remember the lyric clearly, sixty years on, only because my father sang it every day. Indeed he joined in at the theatre, singing the bass part, which brought him a visit from the manager who threatened to evict him if he didn't stop humming.

Another time my mother, who loved musicals, took us to see

the original production of *Kismet*. She also introduced me to the treasures within the Great American Songbook. She loved the Astaire movies and bought all the recordings of the tunes by Gershwin, Cole Porter, Irving Berlin and Jerome Kern. They were the lullabies of my infancy. By the time I was five of six I knew more Gershwin songs than I did nursery rhymes.

Every year I bought my mother a record for her birthday. It would be by Crosby or Sinatra, singing a classic, or sometimes I'd buy one by Andre Kostalanetz and some massive orchestra playing a selection of Hollywood hits. The only time I displeased her was when I was fifteen or sixteen and I gave her 'All the things you are' played by Charlie Parker. She said she had never heard anything like it.

Nor had I.

5

GRAMMAR SCHOOL SENTENCE

Miss Turpin, my teacher at junior school, had done a remarkable job. My eleven plus results were so good I had been awarded a place in the Express stream at Barnsley Grammar School, which meant we took the School Certificate in four years instead of five. We also had to learn three foreign languages instead of two.

I didn't like the place. For one thing I had been previously taught by women, in the main caring and nurturing. Now I was in an all-male world, instructed by short-tempered brutes who, when all else failed, would try to beat information into you. The specialist at this form of teaching was our German master, Goodman, an angry-looking man whose favoured form of instruction was to emphasise a point by drilling his knuckle into the top of a boy's head. Alternatively, he would raise you to your feet by hoisting you up by your hair. If he considered a boy to be particularly stupid, he would make him stand by the blackboard and belittle him by asking questions he knew he couldn't answer. We had double German on Monday mornings, the prospect of which would turn my bowels to water as I walked to school from the bus station. If there was a particular reason why I disliked grammar school, Goodman was at its source.

They weren't all like that. There was the odd gentle soul. We had a music teacher whose lesson consisted of playing Mozart's piano concertos and 'Eine Kleine Nachtmusik' over and over again. He never analysed, simply listened, his face reflecting the mood of the music. He instilled in me a lifelong love of Mozart and gave me an early introduction to the world of classical music. On the other hand, I can't speak German. There is a lesson there.

An English teacher who was keen on drama cast me as Mrs Cratchit in an adaptation of Dickens' *A Christmas Carol*. My appearance wearing a grey wig and a black dress made out of old black-out curtains was greeted with derision by mates in the audience. They particularly enjoyed my ad lib during the serving of the Cratchits' Christmas dinner when my husband Bob Cratchit forgot his line. I covered with: 'Would anyone like stuffing?' A critic wrote, 'There was much audience sympathy for Mrs Cratchit who last week scored a hat trick for Darfield Road Juniors and whose father is well known in the local cricket circles.'

Best of all the teachers was the sports master, Webb Swift, a large and craggy man who was good enough to play football and cricket at professional level. The first time I came across him he was bowling in the nets to youngsters who were hoping to make the Under-14 team. His first ball to me was a little short of a length and, being young and full of madness, I went for a hook and missed by a mile. It didn't seem that important to me and I was therefore a little taken aback on returning the ball to see the master, hands on hips, staring at the sky. He remained like that for some time, lips moving silently, and then he looked at me.

'What was that?' he asked.

'A hook, sir,' I said.

'Hook?' he said, shaking his head. 'A hook? At your age you shouldn't even know what that means.'

It was the best possible introduction to the man who, for the next four years, was to coach me in the game. He taught in the great Yorkshire tradition, concentrating solely on backward and forward defence play. Any strokes we played that required the bat moving from the perpendicular were better done when he wasn't looking. I once played a late cut for four in a school game when I thought he was in bed with 'flu and, as my eyes followed the ball to the boundary, I saw him standing there, sadly shaking his head at the horror of it all.

For all he was a puritan about cricket, he was a marvellous coach. He turned out a succession of young cricketers who were so well versed in the rudiments of the game that they found the transition from schoolboy cricket to the leagues fairly painless. His one blind spot was a total inability to appreciate the odd exceptional talent that came his way. Everyone had to conform to his basic principles, no matter how rich their natural gifts.

At the time I was at school we had in our team a batsman of remarkable ability. Hector Allsop, who was shaped like a junior Colin Milburn, the rotund Test cricketer, had no time for acquiring defensive techniques. He approached each ball as if it was the last he would ever receive on this earth and, that being the case, he was going to try to split it in two. For a schoolboy he was an exceptional striker of the ball, blessed with a powerful physique, a quick eye and a sure sense of timing. He played some fine innings for the school teams, but no matter how brilliantly he played, he never pleased Webb.

'Defence, Hector lad, defence,' Webb would say, and Hector would put one foot down the track and blast the ball straight for six.

The high point of their relationship occurred in a Masters versus Boys game in which the sports master opened the bowling and Hector opened the batting. He played one of his best innings that day, thrashing the bowling, particularly the sports master's, without mercy. Webb kept the ball pitched up, as he always taught us to do, and Hector kept thumping away.

He had scored about 86 in thirty minutes when he hit over one of Webb's deliveries and was bowled. As he walked towards the pavilion the sports master said triumphantly, 'I warned you Hector lad, that's what fancy play gets you.'

He was the only man on the field, or off it, who remained convinced that Hector had failed. But for all that, he was a good man who taught a lot of boys a proper respect for the most difficult and beautiful of games. He was an important man in my life.

I never recovered from the first unhappy year at Barnsley Grammar. I had been promoted way above and beyond my capabilities. Moreover, halfway through the first term I spent six weeks out of school with rheumatic fever. When I returned I was two inches taller but, sadly, no brighter. I dropped to the A stream, which was easier, but I was still unhappy.

Whenever I try to analyse the reason for my disaffection with the grammar school I remember one free period when we were allowed to read a book of our own choosing. At the time I had discovered American novelists. I devoured the likes of Hemingway, William Faulkner, John Dos Passos and Scott Fitzgerald. I brought to school my own copy of John Steinbeck's *The Grapes of Wrath*. Our presiding teacher was an old and chalky man who taught science and was one of a group brought out of retirement to replace the young men who went to war. He picked up my book and, holding it aloft, asked me to explain to the class what I was reading. I started to speak but he interrupted.

'Tripe,' he said. 'Filthy tripe', and dropped the book in the waste-paper basket.

I once wrote that my time at Barnsley Grammar School did for my education what myxomatosis did for the rabbit. This assessment produced the predictable squawks of protest from those of my contemporaries who had a better time than I did.

The most interesting letter contained a clipping of the group photograph of Barnsley Grammar School's club Express One of 1946/47 with me sitting next to our form master, the formidable Hubert Haigh. I was looking quite happy. It was taken before the rot set in. The letter pointed out that, in spite of my reservations, the school did a good job because ten boys in a class of twenty-four had gone to university, seven to Oxbridge, where two had won blues for soccer and athletics. Among the rest were several captains of industry, not forgetting the misfit who became a TV star.

It didn't change my view and – Webb Swift apart – I regarded Barnsley Grammar School as a waste of time.

The fact is I had already decided what I wanted to be. When my father was captain of the local cricket team we were visited every Monday by a man from the local paper riding a large and sturdy Raleigh bicycle. He would collect a match report from my dad. It seemed to me a wonderful way to spend a day. I wanted a job like that. In fact, I wanted his job.

At the same time, I had seen enough Hollywood movies to realise that there was also a more glamorous side to being a journalist, involving men wearing trilby hats and belted raincoats, with epaulettes. Often these men looked like Humphrey Bogart and bought cocktails for molls who resembled Lauren Bacall. I wanted to be a reporter and I couldn't see anything stopping me. I had always possessed an ability to write, even making a bob or two writing essays for friends at school. In my dafter moments I had practised phoning in imaginary scoops. I would find a public call box, nestle the receiver into my shoulder in the approved manner and dial the operator. When she replied I'd say something like, 'Get me the city desk, doll,' or 'Sister, hold the front page.' They thought at first they were dealing with a nutter. After a while they would simply tell me to bugger off.

Shortly before I took my O levels I was caned by my headmaster, Roche. A large and blustery man with strange eyes, he took his time, keeping you waiting outside his study, making sure you heard the whacks and cries as he beat the bum or hands of some unfortunate boy ahead of you. He had three or four canes he would practise swishing while you stood there wondering how many you might get and what the target might be. Before the beating he told you what he thought of you. He was a man who took his job seriously.

On this occasion he finished his speech by saying, 'Unless you buck up, Parkinson, you will never add up to much.' Then he gave me six on the hand, which meant I couldn't pick up a pen for a day or two. As I left his study, trying hard not to whimper, I remember thinking there wasn't much point in hanging about. He didn't like me and I hated him and what he stood for, so the sooner we parted the better.

I took O levels without doing any work and without caring. I passed in Art and English and departed Barnsley Grammar School shortly after. I was sixteen and already had a job. I was the man on the bike who came to our house for the cricket scores, a junior reporter on the *South Yorkshire Times*.

Many years later I received a letter saying that there was to be a dinner in honour of Mr Roche and, since he had watched my career on newspaper and TV with interest, would I be willing to be a guest of honour? I politely declined.

6

JUNIOR REPORTER

So that was how it started. I bought myself a bike, a drop-handled Raleigh with a Sturmey-Archer three-speed, a pair of metal bike clips, and a trench coat like Bogey wore in all his pictures. I was sixteen years old, working for a local paper and cycling twenty-five miles a day around a cluster of pit villages, interviewing anyone who would stand still for two minutes.

The gap between the glamorous Hollywood image of a news-paperman's life and my own could hardly have been greater and might well have defeated a more sensitive soul. I was oblivious to the discomforts of the job. Indeed, the more I cycled about my area, chronicling the births and deaths of the community, reporting the functions at the local chapels, detailing the doings of the Mothers' Union, the more I became convinced that I *was* Humphrey Bogart.

In homage to my hero, I topped my uniform of trench coat and bicycle clips with a pearl grey, snap brim fedora and further adorned it with a label in the hat band marked 'Press'. I solved the inevitable problem of cycling into a wind while wearing such headgear by making a chinstrap out of knicker elastic, a measure that appeared incongruous but was, in fact, generally speaking, a practical solution. The only drawback occurred if I sped downhill into a fierce wind, when I was in danger of being lifted from my seat as the hat billowed backwards, the elastic threatening to yank my head from my shoulders. On such occasions my fedora must have looked like the arresting parachute on a space shuttle.

Thus attired, from sixteen to nineteen, acned, brilliantined, tireless in limb and imagination, I belted through my pit villages, embracing everyone with my foolish ambition. I bought a typewriter, a battered portable Corona, and every evening would translate the contents of my bulging notebook on to copy paper.

When I had finished I would sometimes read aloud my efforts to my parents. My mother, an avid reader and a woman of great natural style, would nod approvingly at some particularly fine phrase. My father, who liked the court reports best, would supplement the telling of the misadventures of some well-known ne're-do-well with his own assessment, which would be either: 'Not surprised about him. Never could play cricket.' Or, 'Fancy that, I mean he's a good opening bat, that fella.'

The next day I'd present my copy to the senior journalist whose job it was to supervise my work. His name was Stan Bristow and I could not have had a finer teacher. He was a proper journalist, methodical, meticulous and, above all, patient with the vagaries of my prose style, which varied according to the particular author I was reading at the time. Some weeks I would present him with, say, a report of a wedding written in the style of Hemingway: 'It was a good wedding. You could say that about it. It was a very good wedding.' On other occasions he would have to point out that a review of a local drama group's production of *An Inspector Calls* in the style of Dorothy Parker might be unacceptable in the columns of the *South Yorkshire Times*. Thus: '*An Inspector Calls* is a production which begs the question, why did he bother? Come

39

to that, why did we?' – which seemed to me all that needed to be said and sufficiently witty to get me an immediate invite to the Algonquin Round Table – was gently blue pencilled and replaced with a proper review.

About this time I thought I would specialise in showbiz interviews, which, given the area I worked in, would make me the most underemployed journalist in the world. No matter. Instead of interviewing Bob Hope, Bing Crosby, Fred Astaire, Gene Kelly and all that lot, who, as far as we know, had no plans to visit Barnsley, I decided to make stars of the more exotic club acts.

My first victims were a couple called Denis and Sylvana, or some such. He was a dark, slim man who wore make-up all the time. She was blonde, prettily plump and perpetually sad. Together they belted out the popular songs of the day to audiences whose attitude to an entertainer was: 'I won't bother you if you don't bother me.' I don't know what attracted me to them but I do remember that at the time I believed they were the most glamorous, fascinating people I had ever met. Not only did I give them a rave write-up on their debut before two hundred drunks at a local working-men's club, but I invited them home for Sunday lunch. Denis's make-up was a definite obstacle to free-flowing conversation, particularly with my father who, although not a censorious being, had never been confronted by a man wearing mascara and rouge with a mouth full of Yorkshire pudding.

In the main, the job of being a local reporter meant sifting through the minutiae of village life, involving oneself in the daily rituals of a mining community. The dramatic moment was when the siren sounded, meaning there had been an accident at the pit. Then the village paused – the world suspended – while women at home wondered if the victim was their loved one.

One of the most vivid images of my childhood is hearing the siren at Grimethorpe and my mother pausing while ironing and looking out of the window towards the pithead. When you are sixteen or seventeen, grief and loss are hard to imagine, never mind come to terms with. Yet as a junior reporter I soon learned about the sorrow of death and the theatre of mourning.

I worked my nest of pit villages with a good journalist from the *Barnsley Chronicle*, Don Booker. The job we hated was following up reported deaths and getting details of the departed for the obituary page. We developed a quiet, almost unctuous manner, more like undertakers than reporters. We would invariably be invited to view the body, which was always laid out in the spare room, designed it seemed for no other purpose than to be a temporary resting place for the departed. We became experts at viewing dead people and assessing, by the way they had been laid out, which firm was in charge of the funeral arrangements.

We would inspect the rigid, shiny face of the deceased and mutter things like, 'He looks at peace,' while noting the cake frill around his neck, which was most certainly the work of the Co-op undertakers. In the winter, with bad weather and a 'flu epidemic, we would visit four or five such scenes every day.

One day I received a message from head office that a local lad had been killed in an accident abroad. I went to the address to collect the details and my knock was answered by a woman about the same age as my mum. I introduced myself, expecting her to invite me in. Instead, in a puzzled voice, she asked me how she could be of assistance.

'I've come about your son,' I said.

'What about my son?' she said, warily.

I realised there had been a terrible mistake and that I had been informed of her boy's death but she had not. She made me tea. I fetched a neighbour to sit with her. When I left she took my hand and thanked me. I went to our house and stayed in bed for the rest of the day.

That was about the time I started leaving my trilby at home.

Five days I laboured and at weekends I played cricket for Barnsley and football for Darfield Road Juniors. As a footballer I was best described as a centre forward of delicate disposition. I was quick and could score goals but I didn't like getting kicked. Nonetheless, being in the unique position of playing in games I reported, I soon gained a reputation as a forward of great promise. Headlines such as 'Scoring Machine Mike Nets Hat Trick' or 'Promising Parky on Goal Trail Again' on the sports pages of the *South Yorkshire Times* began to interest scouts from Football League clubs.

At one game we had representatives from Wolverhampton Wanderers, Barnsley and Sheffield Wednesday on the touchline checking out this young player, who, if the local rag was to be believed, was another Tom Finney. They left at half-time thinking, no doubt, that the writer was as witless as the player was useless and not realising how right they were. Nothing deterred me or checked the flow of my imagination.

The Rock Cinema became my second home. I paid threepence for a hard, wooden seat in the front row and when the lights went out would drop to the floor and start crawling to the plush seats at the back. If undetected, I would arrive among the courting couples covered in sweet papers, discarded chewing gum and the rest of the detritus of a busy cinema.

If you were caught you were banned for a time, which meant a visit to the cinema in the next village. This one had half a dozen saddles mounted on poles at the back of the stalls. If you were lucky enough to get one, you could ride into the sunset with Hopalong Cassidy, Gene Autry and the rest of the cowboy heroes of the time.

My bike was a limousine, the Monkton Pit canteen the Trocadero, and Karen, the large-busted woman who served the tea and bacon sandwiches, and whom I fancied like mad, was Jane Russell. I had seen Jane in *The Outlaw*. It took me ages to recover. I lived in a state of unfulfilled desire. The movies fuelled my imagination.

In the austere and gloomy fifties, the movies provided our only alternative view of the world. I knew what the New York skyline looked like long before I saw Big Ben and the Houses of Parliament. I knew how Yellow Cab drivers spoke way before I encountered a London cabbie, and when I saw Ingrid Bergman in *Casablanca* I fell in love for the very first time. This was not like Jane Russell. This was love, not lust.

As a teenager, gawky and quite shy of girls, I had an uncertain and tentative initiation into love and romance. Sex seemed out of the question. The general opinion was that sex – whatever that might be – was something that happened only after marriage. There were exceptions and I knew one of them. His name was Don and he owned a motorbike. He was also well built and good-looking and a never-ending source of stories about how he shagged this girl and then another. I didn't doubt him, and his stories tantalised me with a glimpse of what seemed an inaccessible world.

I did my best to remedy the situation. Working on the principle that the best-looking girls wanted to go on stage, I joined the drama group at the local youth club. In my debut I played a dashing cavalry officer in a play called *Captain Carvallo*. Opposite me, playing my romantic interest, was a handsome buxom girl called Tina – another Jane Russell substitute – whom I had long had my eye on. I gave the part my all and much more besides in my efforts to impress the delectable Tina.

We opened at a drama festival and all seemed to go well until the adjudication. The adjudicator said he quite liked what he saw, except he wasn't convinced by the romantic scenes. He summed up his doubts by saying: 'The dashing Captain Carvallo would have been even more dashing and irresistible to his partner – not to mention the audience – had he not been wearing odd socks.'

Goodbye Tina.

I decided to use my persona as Mike Bogart, fearless reporter, to pursue my lustful ambition. Wearing my reporter's outfit, I took a girl called Annie to the Three Cranes Hotel in Barnsley. This was posh. The Three Cranes had the only cocktail bar in Barnsley. Imagining my hero and trying to impress my date, I pushed the trilby to the back of my head and said to the barman, 'Two Manhattans on the rocks, buddy.'

'Tha' what?' he said.

I repeated the order, whereupon he shrugged and turned to his bottles. A few minutes later he handed me two half-pint glasses of what looked like sump oil with a cherry floating alongside a stick of celery. It cost me a week's wages and got me nowhere. She was sick over my shoes on the bus going home.

The search for the willing girl, willing to cure my ignorance, was fruitless but fun and, no matter how urgent it might have seemed, it was very much incidental to a developing conflict in my life, whether to be a journalist or a professional cricketer. My twin heroes at the time were Neville Cardus, who wrote about cricket and music for the then *Manchester Guardian*, and Len Hutton who opened the innings for Yorkshire and England.

My dilemma was perfectly summed up in a cartoon in *Punch* magazine, which showed two children standing next to wickets chalked on a wall. One child was a ragamuffin, the other a bespectacled swot. The one wearing specs says to the other: 'No, you be Neville Cardus today and I will be Len Hutton.'

I wanted to be both.

I was doing well as a junior reporter on the *South Yorkshire Times* and could see a future ahead. At the same time I was playing for Barnsley in the Yorkshire League and competing for a place against some promising young talent. My team-mates included Dickie Bird and Geoffrey Boycott.

7

ALL THAT JAZZ

Brass bands provided the background music for life in a pit village. I grew up listening to the virile sound of the Grimethorpe Colliery Band. Best of all was marching in time to its music at the annual miners' gala. On that day, all the bands in the coalfield turned out, the miners and their families united behind swirling banners bearing messages such as 'Succour the Widows and the Orphans'. It was a time when we declared our independence and our solidarity, as well as the music of our culture.

The first time we marched I sat astride my father's shoulders. The last time was after his death, in the late seventies, and I was a guest of honour. That was during a period of turmoil in the coalfields and it was a very political event. Arthur Scargill was leading his Yorkshire miners, and Michael Foot and Mick McGahey, the deputy leader of the NUM, marched with us in the front line.

I said to Arthur, 'Lot of press photographers around,' indicating the snappers following our progress.

'Mainly Special Branch,' said Arthur. 'After this there'll be a file on you at Scotland Yard.'

I hoped he was kidding.

I judged the Miss South Yorkshire Coalfield contest in Lock Park and when it came to presentation time Arthur said to me, 'I suppose you know what we're going to give you?'

'A miner's lamp?' I said.

'Quite right,' he said. 'But not the tourist version.'

He handed me a battered lamp, one which had spent some time underground. 'This was your dad's.'

My mother decided I should have piano lessons. She had mistaken my love for music for a desire to play it. Or maybe she thought contact with Chopin and Mozart and the like would steer me away from the decadence of my new heroes, Dizzy Gillespie and Charlie Parker.

Miss Green was a wispy lady who had played at the Rock Cinema during the silent era and now taught piano for a living. She had to compete with my mates who would play cricket and football outside our front window. She came to our house every Wednesday and with great patience endeavoured to make me into a piano-player. After eighteen months I could play the first four bars of Handel's 'Largo' (simplified version). I didn't give up. Miss Green just stopped coming.

My lack of talent as a musician did nothing to diminish my enthusiasm as a listener. We had five or six nonconformist chapels in our village and there seemed to be a never-ending production of *The Messiah* shifting from one to the other. Me and my mate Barrie would sit in the wooden bum-numbing pews and stare, transfixed, at the heaving bosoms and jiggling adam's apples of the visiting singers. Even though the performances were enthusiastic rather than memorable, it seemed to me the glory of the music somehow triumphed. It has certainly stayed with me throughout my life.

Barrie treated these occasions as more of a fashion event. After all, where else in a mining village could you find women in long satin dresses and men in tails and starched white collars? Barrie himself was the arbiter of fashion in our village. He was a tall, big lad with soft brown and permanently startled eyes and not a hair out of place, like his great heroes Fred Astaire and Peter May, captain of Surrey and England. He loved dressing up. In a pit village this could cause some consternation among your peers. It didn't bother Barrie.

While we were still in school blazers or duffel coats and chukka boots, he favoured the city gent look; pin-striped suits, waistcoats, patent leather shoes, club ties. Instead of playing football he joined the local hunt and turned up outside our house one day astride a chestnut horse and wearing full hunting pink, accompanied by a gang of snotty, dribbling kids who thought he had arrived from Mars. He seemed oblivious to convention and the misgivings of his fellow men.

He started work at the pits but then he joined the Household Cavalry. While I was doing my National Service and working at the War Office, I was walking past a mounted guard in Horseguards' Parade one day when I heard, from underneath the helmet, a voice say, 'Ayup, Parky, old lad.' It was Barrie.

Some time after leaving the army and working for a while in the drinks business, with an office in Mayfair, he returned to Cudworth and, no doubt finding the contrast difficult to accommodate, was soon occupied inventing the adventures and disguises that ruled his imagination.

He decided to compete in a car race to a vineyard in Burgundy, and to make the trip as Field Marshal Erwin Rommel. He found a second-hand American jeep and persuaded a friend to accompany him dressed as General George Patton.

With General Patton driving and Rommel wearing an iron cross and a monocle, they set off on the first leg of their journey. They were just outside Warrington when they started to feel hungry and stopped for fish and chips. General Patton sat outside while Rommel joined the queue in the chip shop. The rest of the customers tried hard to ignore the fact they had been joined by a German officer speaking English the way Germans did in movies.

Approaching the woman at the head of the queue, Rommel said, 'I'm in ze big hurry. Can I get ze fish and cheeps before you?'

'Of course, love. Are you going anywhere nice?' said the woman.

'I'm off to invade Moscow,' said Barrie.

'Very nice. I hope the weather stays fine,' said the woman.

'Ve are lost. Can you show us ze vay?' asked the Field Marshal.

He and General Patton were waved off by their new-found friends, who advised them to head for London and ask a policeman. They arrived in France on the commemoration of VE Day and were detained for a while by the local gendarmerie. Barrie was one of the most extraordinary characters I have ever encountered, possessing that eccentricity of manner and style that is so peculiarly English.

He told me that the funniest line he ever heard, which summed up the unintentionally surreal humour of working-class communities, was delivered by a friend explaining why he admired Barrie's father. Barrie's dad had a retirement job tending the boiler room at the local cinema. After his death the friend was trying to define to Barrie what he thought about his dad. 'He was a good man,' he said. Then, searching for an example, eventually added, 'He kept them boilers spotless.' We decided, there and then, this was the epitaph we would both settle for.

The only other teenager in our group to challenge Barrie's unconventional dress sense was Freddie Handley. He was another important influence on the way music played a significant part in my life. When we discuss music and teenagers nowadays the two are synonymous. Indeed, the market for popular music is aimed at and dependent upon what young people buy. In the fifties, teenagers were simply a group of people going through an awkward phase, which ended, in the main, at the age of sixteen when the majority would get a job, learn some sense and begin to earn a living.

The fashion at the time was the so-called New Look, which was out of date by the time it reached us. The newest suits for men were demob suits, often characterised by square shoulders and pleated backs. The popular music was what mum and dad played on the gramophone – Al Martino, Perry Como, Eddie Calvert and his Golden Trumpet and Lita Roza enquiring 'How much is that doggie in the window?' These were the chart-toppers. The brash newcomer and American superstar was Guy Mitchell who announced himself with 'She wears red feathers and a hula hula skirt' – a huge hit in 1953. Teenagers were ignored and left to find their own music. And we did.

A major influence on our lives was American Forces Network. Set up by the Americans for their troops in Europe and available – just about – on our primitive radios in Britain, it introduced my generation to jazz. It was on AFN I first heard Louis Armstrong and his Hot Five, Duke Ellington, Woody Herman, Billie Holiday, Ella Fitzgerald, Joe Williams and the like. Then came Dizzy Gillespie and Charlie Parker. They stood music on its head. Listening on AFN was one thing, finding the music they played in record shops in Barnsley quite another. Somehow Freddie Handley found a way.

He produced a stack of records of the new music and hired the bandstand at Lock Park. There, once a week, Freddie and his disciples would meet to listen to this new music played in a bandstand on an old record player. What is more, we would dress up for the occasion. Freddie was the first to wear what later became our uniform – drape jacket, drainpipe trousers and shoes with crepe soles so thick and cumbersome they looked and felt like you were wearing a landing craft on each foot. Hair was short on top, long at the sides, and swept back into a DA (duck's arse). Freddie was the first man in the whole of Barnsley to wear sunglasses at night, and the only man in Yorkshire, outside the odd seller of French onions, who wore a black beret at all times. This, in honour of his great hero, Dizzy Gillespie.

Thus attired, we would stand and listen to the new Be-Bop, only moving to nod our heads to the beat of the music, or give a V sign to the musical morons who would sometimes appear wearing college scarves and bearing signs proclaiming 'Trad Is Best'. I don't know what was happening in the rest of Britain but we felt like pioneers of a new music. We were isolated, even reviled by the rest, but we were certain that what we had discovered was both a new form of musical expression and one that would enrich our lives in future years. And so it proved.

Certainly, in my case, it allowed me during my years in broadcasting the confidence and determination to promote what I believe to be the best in popular music against an ever-rising tide of musical bilge that nowadays swamps radio and, in particular, television. Looking back, I see a remarkable generation of young people who might have been neglected but would not allow themselves to be ignored. In retrospect, what is most admirable is that we made up our own minds about what we wore and listened to and how we behaved.

During my apprenticeship on the *South Yorkshire Times*, I was transferred a few miles down the road to South Elmsall to work for another boss, Arthur Mosley. He was a local entrepreneur and owned a venue called the Miners at Moorthorpe. Every Saturday he would hire a jazz band and, for an extra bob or two, I took tickets on the door. It was a blossoming time for British jazz and I had a front-row seat. I also learned at first hand the strange habits of that peculiar tribe known as musicians.

During the interval I would visit the dressing room and ask what the band required in terms of food and drink. Many of the requests were unprintable as well as unattainable, at least in that part of the South Yorkshire coalfields in the 1950s. But that is how I first met Ronnie Scott, Tubby Hayes, Chris Barber, Jimmy Deuchar, John Dankworth and Cleo Lane and many others. I saw what turned out to be Cleo's debut with the Dankworth band. I remember she was wearing a flimsy blue dress and looked somewhat awkward on stage. But it all changed when she started singing.

It was in the dressing room at the Miners that I first met Benny Green. He was playing in Ronnie Scott's band and was sitting in a corner quietly reading a Penguin Classic. Later on, when I was at Granada Television working as a producer, I worked with Benny on a weekly jazz programme. No one cared more or wrote better about the music he loved than Benny Green. Like John and Cleo, his fastidious, uncompromising promotion of his craft inspired succeeding generations of music lovers and musicians.

The same could be said about Humphrey Lyttelton, another I first came across during my stint as a doorman all those many years ago. None of us could imagine what the passing years would bring. The drummer in Humph's band was a young lad called Stan Greig. Two or three years later we met in Port Said. He was a soldier playing the blues in a bar and I was the youngest captain in the British army. We were both part of a military operation that became known simply as Suez.

8

PRIVATE
PARKINSON

I was deferred from National Service, meaning I entered the service of Her Majesty a year later in order that I might complete my three-year apprenticeship as a junior reporter. It also gave me a year to think about how I might avoid National Service altogether. I didn't fancy two years marching up and down being bullied by sergeant majors, which my colleagues who had already done their time assured me was what happened.

There were others, a minority, who, while not exactly enjoying it, spoke of the benefits of living away from home and expanding the boundaries of their lives. In the forties and fifties the greater part of the population did not travel abroad. None of my family had voluntarily left the country. Only those taken away by the war or National Service had viewed the world outside the acres of their birth.

While the prospect of foreign travel was seductive, I decided I would rather stay at home. How to get out of it? I could go down the pit, but that wasn't even worth considering so long as I was 'Jack's lad' and lived at home. I could become a Quaker, but that wouldn't get me out of National Service, it would merely guarantee I'd drive an ambulance or carry a stretcher. One of my friends said a mate of his had gone to his medical doused in his mother's perfume and wearing a pair of his sister's frilly knickers. The examining officer sent him away for psychiatric examination and the shrink declared him unfit for purpose. I thought seriously about this but decided against it. Two years in the army would be paradise compared to living in a mining village with the reputation of being a 'wrong 'un', as they used to say. In any case, I didn't have a sister.

I had received my call-up papers and was preparing myself for the inevitable when what seemed the perfect get-out occurred. I had gone to Oxford to see an aunt who lived in Summertown in a street smelling of bread and cream cakes from a nearby bakery. A delicious place. I loved walking in the town, watching the cricket in the Parks. It was here, as a child, I had stood at the pavilion gates and watched the mighty Australians play the university. My great hero, Keith Miller, swept past me and as he did so he drew his hand over his hair and I could see he had a comb concealed in the palm of his hand. It was a traumatic moment. I hadn't realised that gods used combs or that heroes possessed human vanity.

Fifty years later I went for lunch with Keith Miller in Australia and in the lift going up to the restaurant he swept his hand over his head.

'Still got the comb in there?' I asked.

I told him how I knew.

'Still got the same comb,' he said.

In 1954 this walk to the Parks had a special significance. I had been ordered to report to Catterick Camp in North Yorkshire in ten days' time. My rail pass was in my pocket. This was to be my last taste of freedom for two years. I was thinking all these things while walking down the High Street when I felt a terrible pain in my side, underneath the rib cage. It felled me.

I lay in the street certain I had been shot. I looked for assistance, but people stepped around me and only one or two bothered to give me even a second look. I assumed they thought I was drunk, a student reveller from yet another all-night party, who ought to be doing National Service. I managed to crawl into a shop and tell the girl I was very ill. She phoned the ambulance and I spent the next three weeks in hospital recovering from a spontaneous pneumothorax.

My nurse, who looked like Vera Hruba Ralston (a Hollywood B movie star who sensibly married the head of a Hollywood studio instead of waiting for me), told me that what had happened was a one in a million chance, that for no reason whatsoever the membrane surrounding the lung punctured and let in air, causing it to collapse. She said I ought to feel flattered because it only happened in young fit males.

The doctor said much the same thing. He stuck a large needle in me to draw off the air and then said it would take a week or two for recuperation during which time I would be taught how to basket weave. I told him I was due to go into the army.

'That's out of the question, at present,' he said.

My heart sang.

'But there's no reason why you shouldn't be fit as a flea in a few months' time,' he added.

So I set about making the most of my basket weaving. My teacher was a pretty girl who looked like Patricia Roc. I became her star pupil. By the time my next army medical was due, I could weave lamp shades as well as baskets. The doctor said I seemed very fit but he didn't want me to join the infantry. He categorised me as 'fit for lines of communication anywhere', which basically meant an office job.

They put me in the Royal Army Pay Corps and sent me for basic training to Devizes in Wiltshire. Putting me in the Pay Corps was a serious piece of miscasting. I could add up, but not without moving my mouth. My results in maths examinations over the years certified me as innumerate. If National Service was brought back today it would be the equivalent of putting Wayne Rooney in the Education Corps.

I started looking around for alternatives and discovered that young journalists were being encouraged to take up PR work in the army. I wrote to the War Office asking for a transfer but in the meantime buckled down reluctantly to the task of becoming a soldier. The records show I became Private Parkinson RAPC, army number 23131269 on 7 July 1955.

Generally speaking, we were a scrawny lot. There were not too many fat children around in those days. When we piled out of the trucks that brought us from the station and assembled on the square, we had that silly bemused look of contestants at the very beginning of shows like *I'm a Celebrity* . . . We were awaiting an indication of whether or not it was going to be a bearable time. We soon found out.

Our sergeant was a Scot with the sharpest crease in his pants I had ever seen. He said his name was Furlingham and he was going to transform the shambles before him into fighting men. Or he was going to die in the attempt. Or, alternatively, or more likely, we were.

We were herded into Nissen huts and I found myself a bunk between a loud jolly lad from Birmingham called Nick and a pale fragile-looking youth called Quint who turned out to be a bed-wetter. His condition was not helped by the bullying he received from the NCOs because he couldn't march. He was one of those unfortunate people whose lack of coordination meant that as his right leg went forward so did his right arm. Instead of looking like a marching soldier he resembled a marionette. At first this amused the NCOs, then it infuriated them. Quint became the target for their anger. There was nothing we could do except try to help him change the sheets when he peed the bed.

He was the only casualty. The rest of us developed our own way of dealing with the abuse, which, generally speaking, involved keeping still and staring straight ahead while some corporal stood two inches from your face and abused you.

'Parkinson, you are a big Yorkshire prick. What are you?' they would say, and you would tell them in a loud and sincere voice.

We knew it would pass – twelve weeks basic training and then a cushy job in an office adding up army pay. We also knew we were just the latest in a long line of young men who had been forced to join up and face the same ritual of abuse. It wasn't personal, except for one instance.

I had my hair cut very short before Devizes because I didn't want scalping by an army barber. Two days into our training we were marched into the regimental barber by a corporal who was himself a National Serviceman but had been made power mad by the stripes on his arm. He was one of Quint's most persistent abusers. When it came to my turn I looked in the mirror and thought he couldn't cut it much shorter. I saw the barber glance at the NCO, who smirked and gave him the wink, whereupon he took the shears down the centre of my head leaving just a stubble. I have always had thick hair and the sight of my shaven head both shocked and angered me. I noted the amusement of my tormentor and vowed to get even.

It was July and a pleasant summer. When we were not marching we played football and cricket and learned how to shoot. In the evenings we pressed our uniforms with hot irons and brown paper, and polished our boots with burnt Cherry Blossom and spit. These were the bullshit days and, we told ourselves, they would soon pass. We were not let out to visit Devizes town. They no doubt thought the locals might recoil at the sight of us.

The only entertainment was a concert in camp. Top of the bill were Denis and Sylvana, the couple I had taken home for Sunday lunch in an attempt to make them into stars. Denis was even more rouged and camp than I remembered. She was still beautiful but a touch wan. Perhaps she was pining for me.

I told my mates I knew them but they didn't believe me. After the show we waited outside for them to appear. I removed my cap so that she might recognise me the better, forgetting I had only a bit more hair than a seal.

'Hello again,' I said when she appeared.

She looked at me, or rather through me, thrust an autographed photo into my hand, and disappeared, leaving behind a whiff of perfume. I never saw her again. For a while, my colleagues referred to me as 'Mr Showbiz'.

We did a series of intelligence tests and a few of us were marked down as potential officers with a chance to attend a War Office Selection Board. We had to have proof of passing at least five O levels. I had two but didn't see why that should stand between me and the chance to wear a better uniform. I said I had five O levels and was awaiting my certificate confirming the fact, but it had been delayed because my parents were skiing in St Moritz. This delayed the reckoning long enough to get me confirmed as a candidate. Thereafter I stalled them with a heartbreaking letter, stating that an elderly aunt, making her way to the post office, with the certificate in her hand, was knocked down by a double-decker bus. She survived being run over but the certificate didn't. I heard no more.

The War Office Selection Board was where I began fully to appreciate the difference between a state education and public school. Faced with a task of getting six soldiers across a wide gorge with only a piece of rope, an empty oil drum and a step-ladder as equipment, I was bemused. The question, it seemed to me, was not so much how but why? For the public schoolboy who had served in the cadet force it was simply an extension of the school curriculum.

I watched and learned.

I soon worked out that what impressed the observers was a confident assertion of authority, a demonstration that no matter how confused he might be, the leader of men gave his orders in a loud and clear voice. The fact that he and his troops ended up in the gorge instead of across it seemed not to matter. It was a clear demonstration of that most famous of all army maxims: bullshit baffles brains.

I passed and was sent to Mons Officer Cadet School in Aldershot. Here I encountered a superior kind of abuse. Our drill sergeant was a fierce north countryman with a habit of marching at your shoulder and delivering, in a low conversational tone, the most unforgettable observations. One day he was drilling us at a fast pace across the square when he came alongside. He said, 'Your marching is horrible, a disgrace to the British Army, an insult to manhood. What is it?'

I repeated his observation.

He continued, 'I am here to tell you that unless it improves I

59

will kick you so hard up the arse that when you return to earth your uniform will be out of date. Do you understand?'

I started laughing. I couldn't help it. I thought I would be in trouble.

Instead, he said, 'I am glad you like my little joke and that you have a sense of humour. You will need it.'

It was at Mons we encountered the spine and strength of the British Army. These were not National Servicemen, crazed with authority, tipsy with power. These were the professional soldiers who, even though they didn't want us in their army, treated training us as a task to be carried out to the best of their ability. They were the men who you relied on. These were the soldiers who, while calling you 'sir', left no doubt who it was running the show. I understood and admired them. What is more they were recognisably creatures from the planet I had known, unlike one or two of my fellow officer cadets and certainly a couple of the officers I encountered at Mons.

I was in a billet with a languid young man who was a son of a member of the aristocracy. He drove a large red sports car and often arrived at the camp gates on Monday mornings accompanied by his 'chauffeur', a blonde with long hair who looked like Veronica Lake in *The Blue Dahlia*. His insouciance was awesome. One morning he arrived late on parade and, upon approaching the regimental sergeant major, a man who positively quivered with authority, smiled, and said, 'Terribly sorry, sergeant major, delayed by tourists outside the Palace.'

My training officer was a captain in a posh regiment. He had a slight Scottish accent delivered in an affected drawl. He didn't like me. He thought I was an imposter and a useless soldier, an opinion confirmed when he asked me to lead my platoon across a ploughed field to attack a copse allegedly hiding a German gun emplacement.

I studied the map, considered the options and decided on a full frontal assault in true up and at 'em style, like Gary Cooper in *Sergeant York*. I hadn't calculated that heavy overnight rain had turned the field into treacle and that by the time we had got halfway to our target the majority of my platoon were too knackered to carry on and those of us who slogged it out were being bombarded with thunder flashes and blank rounds. I made it to the cover of trees and fell down in utter exhaustion.

I was lying there thinking of *All Quiet on the Western Front* and that final scene when they are all dying and Lew Ayres reaches out for the butterfly, when I heard and felt an explosion near my crutch. Then another. I opened my eyes to see my favourite officer standing over me lighting thunder flashes and dropping them between my legs, shouting, 'You are dead, sir, quite dead.'

'I know, sir,' I replied, and lay there thinking what a silly bloody game this was. I was also certain I was about to be kicked out, given the dreaded RTU, returned to unit. In fact, they called me in, said I was a borderline case and gave me a second chance. I was to be held back for another term.

My second spell with the training officer was easier for both of us. He came to accept me as a sign the army was going to pot, as I continued to lead my men with the kind of gung-ho bravado displayed by Errol Flynn when he single-handedly defeated the Japanese Army in *Objective Burma*.

My major problem was getting leave. The totting-up system of offences meant that I was more often than not confined to barracks at the weekends. I wasn't an unruly soldier, merely an untidy one. I decided to concentrate on getting at least one weekend in London. I succeeded to the point where I had only to survive a visit to the adjutant's office to answer some minor offence, and I was up the West End.

I was marched in, double time, by an NCO who halted me side on to the adjutant's desk. All I had to do was a smart right turn, bringing up my left knee and driving my foot down to attention facing the adjutant. He was a cavalry officer with beautifully tailored breeches and a soft barathea jacket. He had sandy hair and a moustache and was the very picture of a man born to lead. The sergeant major gave me the right turn, whereupon my left knee caught the underside of the adjutant's desk and sent a bottle of ink spiralling into the air. It seemed to hang there for a while before tipping its contents over the officer's trousers. All I remember is the sergeant leaning in and whispering into my ear, 'Bang goes your fucking weekend.' And so it proved. I think, in the end, they gave me a commission to get rid of me.

I went back to Devizes to await my posting. The first time I was duty officer I went on a tour of the camp, which included a visit to the barber's shop. The man who had given me the scalping was just finishing for the day. I inspected his premises and found a hair or two. I charged him with having a dirty barber's shop and had him doubling round the square for a long time. He didn't recognise me. He simply thought I was another toffee-nosed public-school shit.

I looked for the corporal but couldn't find him. I'm still looking.

When my posting came through I found I had to report to a Pay Office at Ashton-under-Lyne in Lancashire. I didn't mind that. What did bother me was the thought that I was going to be in charge of working out pay for soldiers and I still couldn't add up. After months of bobbing and weaving I was finally going to get found out. I decided to write again to the War Office, a letter about round pegs and square holes, asking if they were serious about making the best use of journalists by placing them in PR – in which case, I was their man!

9

A CRICKETING
GUINEA PIG

I know I'm not supposed to admire Lancastrians, but I do. One way or another I have spent a good part of my working life in the county and have grown to admire a vigorous tribe of people. They have a dry wit I find appealing, best summed up in the story of Ken Taylor, a fine Yorkshire cricketer, making his debut in a Roses game at Old Trafford in the fifties. In those days there was a gate at the foot of the pavilion stairs manned by an attendant. As Taylor walked out in front of thirty thousand hostiles, the attendant opened the gate and as Taylor passed through said, 'Good luck, young man, but think on, don't be long.' With this advice echoing in his mind, Ken was bowled first ball. As he returned, the attendant opened the gate for him and said, 'Thank you, lad.'

All of which explains why I enjoyed Ashton-under-Lyne. It was my first venture into what my father regarded as enemy territory. When I went home on leave he questioned me closely about the natives and warned me to be on my guard. He thought the people who lived on the wrong side of the Pennines were a tricky lot.

I wasn't there very long. I received a letter from the War Office saying I should report to the Army PR Department in Whitehall. I was given a desk in a large high-ceilinged room, opposite Captain

Johnny Verschoyle. He had silver hair and I think he wore a monocle. If he didn't, he ought to have. He was retired from his regiment and – if it wasn't the Bengal Lancers, it should have been. The archetypal old-school British cavalry officer, he was also a kind and funny man.

I was allowed to wear civvies, which was good news except for the fact that the only clothes I possessed were a pair of grey trousers and a black blazer with the badge of Barnsley Cricket Club on the top pocket. My colleagues all wore smart suits, and Captain Verschoyle was immaculate in waistcoat and regimental tie.

'Which regiment is that, dear boy?' he asked, indicating my blazer badge.

'Barnsley Cricket Club,' I replied.

He lifted an eyebrow. 'We've not had one of those at the War Office for a long time,' he said. I took the kindly hint and bought a second-hand suit.

The captain's attitude to his job was, generally speaking, that enquiries from journalists interfered with his daily battle with the *Daily Telegraph* crossword. After sitting opposite him for about a week, I noticed I took many more calls than the good captain. I would receive twenty or more calls to his two or three. I decided to monitor his system and discovered that when he took a call he would say to the caller, 'Just hang on for a moment, old chap, my other phone is ringing.' Then he would put the receiver in his drawer and close it before returning to the crossword. After about thirty minutes he would replace the receiver. In that time, all his calls had been transferred elsewhere – mainly to me!

I lived at Auntie Florrie's cold-water flat in King's Cross, sleeping on a camp bed in a frozen room. My lodgings could not have been in greater contrast to my place of work. I slept in the slum dwelling where my aunt and her family, like millions of others, lived in the most primitive of circumstances. I watched my auntie washing up in a slimy stone sink on the landing. I watched her daughter, Hetty, a petite attractive girl, who worked at the Kardomah Café, painting her legs with gravy browning to make it look like she was wearing nylons, which she couldn't afford. She added the seam with eyebrow pencil.

I witnessed all this and then went to work in one of the temples of privilege and power, among sleek men in surroundings so polished you could see your face in the table tops. It didn't last long. After a month or two they sent me to Southern Command in Salisbury to work under a splendid Northumbrian, Don Leslie. It was to be the happiest time of my army life.

I fell in love with Salisbury as soon as I saw it. The narrow ancient streets, the white cottages, the low-beamed pubs, the cathedral and its close were a part of England I had never seen before except on picture postcards. I was directed to a beautiful Georgian mansion between Salisbury and Wilton. It was a mess for senior officers and I was the first National Service officer to be billeted there. The next in rank to me was a major.

It was an experiment and I was the guinea pig. I don't know what they were trying to prove. I was never told the nature of the experiment, but I felt like a specimen in a bottle. It was all exceedingly ordered and civilised. I had a batman and my own room. The senior officers treated me with great kindness and understanding but there was a gap between us that even good manners and the best of intentions could not straddle.

Mess dinners were an ordeal. As junior officer present I had to propose the loyal toast and it brought me out in a flop sweat every time. Later, reading in my room, I would hear the clatter of horseplay as my fellow officers indulged in the various rumbustious conclusions to dining-in nights. I didn't mind being excluded. My great fear was that they might come for me.

Weekends they all cleared off home and I was left the sole occupant of the mess. I played cricket for the South Wilts Club whose members included some fine players and one or two formidable drinkers. After one Saturday game, when the pubs closed, I invited a few of my team-mates back for a drink. The mess had an honour system whereby you poured from an open and well-stocked bar and left a chitty informing the mess steward what you had drunk.

I awoke next morning still in the bar, which gave every indication of having been pillaged. The consequence was a bar bill I didn't have a chance of paying during my term of service, never mind straightaway. The officer in charge of the bar called me in and asked for an explanation. I told him what had happened. He said he ought to be more angry than he was, but he understood my discomfort at the situation I had been put in and thought it best if he wrote off the bill and we parted company.

'The experiment didn't quite work, did it?' he said.

They had found me digs in a pub on the Shaftesbury Road. He hoped I'd be happier there. I was.

Don Leslie was a rubicund man of relentless energy and great good humour. He had my father's capacity to see the possibility of delight in whatever he did. He was a gifted leader of men because he wanted everyone to share his joy in the job he was doing. The media loved him. I'm not sure the army shared their enthusiasm. He was too much of a maverick for comfort, yet they could not argue with the advantageous relationship he created with the press. As for me, I had a green Austin saloon from the car pool, a driver, a room in a pub with a large soft bed, and an inspirational boss.

All that was missing was Jane Russell, or Joan Leslie, or Vera Hruba Ralston, or Veronica Lake, or anyone who would have me.

I did find one girl who cuddled me on the riverbank, and as we kissed and canoodled and I was imagining Burt Lancaster and Deborah Kerr in *From Here to Eternity*, we were interrupted by the light from a torch. Behind the beam, a voice said something like, 'I am PC Dixon, and what are you doing?' which I thought was a pretty stupid question. He shifted the beam from my eyes to inspect my partner, and as he did so I could see that what he had in his other hand was not his truncheon. I chased him without much enthusiasm. I wanted to get back as soon as possible to the beach and Deborah in her swimming costume. When I did return, she had gone and I didn't see her again.

Given my social life was just about non-existent, I concentrated on the South Wilts cricket team. We played some decent fixtures but the cricket was very different from playing for Barnsley in the Yorkshire League. I was made aware of the difference when we went to Frome and I batted out time to create a boring draw when we looked like losing. When I returned to the pavilion I was severely bollocked by our skipper who pointed out that my rescue act had cost them at least an hour's drinking time.

They were carefree days. The summer was long and warm; we played in lovely country villages, which seemed, more often than not, to have a Compton or a Wallop in the title. I was playing well, scoring enough runs still to imagine I might one day play professional cricket. I was fit, never in better shape.

One Sunday, playing against a team skippered by Jim Bailey, a former Hampshire player, I scored a century. Jim asked me if I fancied a run-out with the club and ground side at Southampton. I turned up to play with the young pros and, because of my amateur status, had a dressing room all to myself. After sitting in solitary splendour I made my way to the wicket and was bowled first ball by another Hampshire spinner, and a very good one, called C.J. Knott.

I thought that would be it, but Arthur Holt, who was Hampshire coach at the time, invited me back. I made 80 odd and it was suggested I might like to accompany the second team on a tour starting in Bristol and finishing in Kent. This was my big chance. Don Leslie sent me home for a celebratory leave. My father was not in favour of me playing for any county other than Yorkshire and we were in the middle of a dispute when I received a cable saying I had to return to Salisbury immediately.

The consequence was that when I ought to have been playing cricket for Hampshire Seconds I was aboard a landing craft heading for Suez.

10

PROPER JOURNALISTS BEGIN AT SUEZ

I was ordered to join a unit called 4PRS. This was a hastily conceived outfit assembled to deal with the requirements of the world's media if and when we invaded Egypt. Our commanding officer was John Stubbs, a lieutenant-colonel in the Sherwood Foresters. He was a genial man who laughed a lot, mainly at my Yorkshire accent, which he thought hilarious. He descended from fighting man to media nursemaid when he lost an arm in a battle and there were times when you caught him gazing wistfully at nothing in particular, like a man recalling happier times.

His number two was another fighting soldier, Major Charles Macgregor, who had been injured in Korea. He was not much given to introspection and was clearly disgruntled with his new posting. Then there were two captains from the army reserve, one of whom had something to do with publishing. The other worked as a salesman with a drinks company. He was a reluctant soldier with a ruddy face and a short temper. Our team was completed by one other National Service second lieutenant, a young journalist called Robin Esser, who later went on to become editor of the *Sunday Express* and is now the executive managing editor of the *Daily Mail*.

We planned our part in the downfall of Gamal Abdel Nasser in a Lyons tea house in Piccadilly. It soon became apparent that the National Service officers were the ones designated to have daily contacts with the media while the senior officers would play a strategic role. Generally speaking, the political arguments raging at the time passed us by. It is not that the embarking soldier is ignorant of why he is getting on a troopship, it is simply he has other more important things to worry about, like staying alive.

I was both frightened and excited at the prospect of going to war. I wondered, as all men do, what I'd be like under fire. Mainly, I was intrigued at the prospect of travelling to foreign lands. I was twenty and had never been on a plane or left the country of my birth. My mother wrote to me, calling the prime minister, Sir Anthony Eden, a 'warmonger'. My father added a note saying Barnsley was doing well.

We flew to Cyprus in a DC3, which bucked and lurched in such an erratic and frightening manner it gave me a lifelong dislike of flying. We stayed in the Ledra Palace Hotel in Nicosia, which had been the media base during that dangerous time in Cyprus when EOKA was conducting a terrorist campaign against British rule on the island. The hotel was favoured by the media not simply because it was the best hotel but because the concierge, George Savas, was an infallible source of information of the most important kind. If you were heading out of the house, particularly at night, it was prudent to check with Savas. He would ask your destination and then nod or gravely shake his head, which meant there was likely to be an incident in the area to which you were heading. While I was in Cyprus, half of 4PRS, the vehicles and radio vans and their drivers, were camped in Malta, waiting to cross over to Egypt when the action was ready.

Robin was with them when a big story broke in October 1956.

Many of the men in the 3rd Battalion of the famous Grenadier Guards regiment, also camped in Malta, were Z reservists, plucked from their civilian jobs and recalled for the invasion force.

Unfortunately, army pay lagged far behind civilian pay and the reservists' families were left back in the UK struggling to make ends meet and feed the children on a few pounds a week. The reservists themselves were fed up with hanging around in temporary accommodation waiting for the politicians to decide if they were going to fight or not. The pressure on the men was huge and there were open demonstrations and even threats to mutiny.

'Guards Mutiny' – what a headline for Fleet Street!

A plane load of reporters landed in Malta to be met by the only army PR officer on the island at the time – Second Lieutenant Robin Esser.

He provided a coach, suitably equipped with cold beers, towels and swimming costumes, and bussed them, via a pleasant beach, to the headquarters of the regiment on the island. He arranged for the soldiers to explain all their grievances, openly and fully, and sent the reporters and photographers away fully briefed.

A day or so later General Sir Hugh Stockwell, who was in charge of the invasion force, flew in to Malta. He called for the PR officer responsible for what he judged a job well done. When Robin presented himself, in the uniform of the General Services Corps and with one pip on his shoulder, the general looked him up and down and asked, 'What are you?'

'Your public relations officer, sir,' Robin replied. 'I am doing my National Service.' Stockwell, a charismatic soldier with a great sense of fairness, turned to his ADC and asked, 'What rank do these chaps normally have if they are doing this job?'

'Captain, sir,' came the reply.

'Well make him a bloody captain then,' said Stockwell.

'Excuse me, sir,' said Robin. 'But there's another one. My colleague Second Lieutenant Parkinson is in Cyprus organising the advance band of correspondents.'

'Same for him,' said Stockwell to his ADC. 'I want my men properly rewarded.' That was how we became the two youngest serving captains in that force.

It was decided a volunteer media party would accompany the first assault troops and I would accompany them. I don't know how I was given this job. Unlike the correspondents – Cyril Page of ITN, Terry Fincher and Donald Edgar of the *Daily Express*, Hanson Baldwin of the *New York Times* and Seeghan Maynes of Reuters – who all bravely stuck their hands in the air when the colonel asked for volunteers, I had most certainly kept my hands in my pockets.

All we knew was that, while the politicians dithered, a large invasion force was gathering in the Mediterranean and a declaration of war was imminent. I was told to conduct my advance party to Famagusta where we would join a boat to rendezvous with the invasion fleet. I took my colleagues to the quartermaster's store to get them kitted out and when I saw them in their uniforms they looked shambolic. I have never been able to fathom why the uniform of the British Army is so ugly, uncomfortable and ill-fitting. It doesn't approximate to any known human shape or size and is made of material as hairy and intractable as coconut matting. Terry Fincher – who later became a friend and a colleague on the *Daily Express* – was an especially forlorn sight, wearing a blouse the size of a large overcoat and a pair of trousers that kept falling around his ankles.

The only one of the party who looked remotely businesslike was

Cyril Page of ITN. No matter what the turmoil, Cyril always looked smart and groomed. He wore a Canadian army uniform in soft and tailored material. Cyril was a top-class cameraman, fearless without being reckless, a man who survived a lifetime of conflict and who came to know more about operating in a war zone than most of the soldiers he filmed in battle.

We travelled through the night in a taxi. The driver thought we were crazy, a group of men in army uniform, driving across the island in the dark, prime targets for the terrorists. We bribed him to continue his journey but his concern caused me to consider checking our only means of defence, which was my revolver. Then I remembered I had packed it in my kitbag which was strapped to the roof of our vehicle. I decided to keep this information to myself.

We arrived at the dock gates at Famagusta and they wouldn't let us in, saying they had no record of a group of correspondents joining a ship. The duty officer arrived and after a great palaver we discovered our vessel was berthed at Limassol, a port some fifty miles away. I had been given the wrong orders, not that a taxi load of tired and cynical correspondents believed me.

We arrived at our destination at dawn and were ferried out to the *Empire Ken*, a boat that had done long service as an Irish ferry before being converted into a troopship. Soldiers were idling on deck, but there was an expectation around that we were not far from the action. As it was, we cruised the Mediterranean for a couple of days more while the politicians argued about what should happen. On the morning of 6 November we ceased sailing in circles and started a purposeful move south.

We were part of a formidable armada sailing towards the coast of Egypt and it was in that moment I fully realised, for the first time, that I was going to be witness to a war. As Port Said became a line on the horizon, jet fighters started appearing overhead, screeching towards their targets, and we began to see fingers of smoke appearing on the skyline.

They told us to prepare to land and when we were about a hundred yards from shore we were transferred into a landing craft crammed with assault troops. There was tracer both going in and out of Port Said and, as we headed for shore, I looked at the strained faces around me and saw that stoic resolve we Brits have of not making too much of a fuss about things. My fear was contained by a thought I had as I leapt ashore. I realised that instead of a weapon I was carrying my portable typewriter above my head and I wondered what Mum and Dad would think if they received a telegram from the War Office informing them their son had died defending his Remington.

Our destination was a block of flats on the sea front, which was to serve as media headquarters. We arrived in time to see a platoon of commandos working through the building, floor by floor, flushing out snipers. There were a couple of dead soldiers in the well of the building, and large holes in the walls where it had taken a direct hit from shellfire. Even this early in the campaign there was a feeling that Port Said had fallen, the opposition had fled and all that remained to be done was the mopping up.

We didn't have any transport so we went in search of a car and found a large abandoned American saloon. Driving through the streets of Port Said, we saw two young women struggling with heavy suitcases. They said they had been working as dancers in a local nightclub and had become caught up in the war. Their flat had been damaged and now they were homeless. As gallant invaders, we found them an empty apartment nearby and told them we would return with provisions.

It was a day or two before I managed to avoid the curfew and, carrying a large box of food and drink, visited the apartment. The door was opened by the biggest French paratrooper in the world. He looked me up and down, curled his lip at my Pay Corps cap badge, relieved me of my goodies, said 'Merci', grinned and closed the door. Sometime later, I heard some of the journalists talking about a brothel run by two dancers in a nearby building. I didn't inform them who was responsible for providing the business opportunity to the women involved.

The Egyptians surrendered after twelve hours. There was a ceasefire and we sat and awaited the next move. The media group became bored at the lack of attention, frustrated and angry at an almost non-existent communication system that meant, even if they had a story to film, the method of getting it back to base was, even on a good day, useless.

4PRS took a battering. There was also a conflict within the ranks between the journalists, such as Robin Esser and me, who understood the media's frustration, and one or two of the other officers who believed in keeping the media at a safe distance. I was told to keep a tight rein on a reporter from ITN. According to an instruction from London, this man was likely to turn into a hostile and subversive presence. I was required to watch him closely and report any untoward behaviour. The reporter was Robin Day. I followed Mr Day doggedly without seeing or hearing anything that might be termed treasonable. He regarded me as more of a batman than an accompanying officer, treating me with the haughty disdain that was to become his trademark.

Another journalist I was assigned to accompany was Randolph Churchill, son of Winston, who had been employed by a London paper to write an overview of the operation. I was warned he might be irascible and rude. The man I met at El Gamil airport was best described as mellow.

'Where do you want to go, sir?' I enquired.

'Where are the French?' he asked.

'Across the canal in Port Fouad,' I said.

'Let us proceed there ... better cellar,' he said, by way of explanation.

* * * *

The big story was when the United Nations troops arrived as peace-keepers in Port Said. I had four or five photographers in the back of a jeep driven by Corporal Chayevsky. The corporal was an interesting man, a regular soldier who had spent some time in military prison in the Far East for assault. He was my self-appointed driver and bodyguard. He was an East End wheeler-dealer, in the terminology of the day a bit of a wide boy. He didn't like Port Said or its citizens, most of whom turned out to welcome the United Nations troops.

We were following the Blue Berets as they marched through the streets when we were cut off at an intersection by a mob of demonstrators. They ignored us until Chayevsky started nudging forward, sounding his horn. Then they turned and, seeing our isolation, began pressing on the front of the jeep, forcing us to stop. At this moment one demonstrator jumped on to the front of the jeep and began ranting at us. We had a sten gun in the car and I had my .45 revolver in its holster but I reckoned a move to use either might prove provocative, not to mention fatal.

By now we were surrounded and one or two of the locals were working themselves into a lather. The photographers seemed unconcerned. They kept snapping away, apparently oblivious to the danger and unaware that the men they were taking photographs of might turn out to be our lynch mob. I could imagine the caption: 'Last Picture of British Press Party. Army Officer from Barnsley Among the Missing'.

At this point Chayevsky got from behind the wheel and, waving what looked like a starting handle, grabbed the man who was dancing on the bonnet of his jeep and threatened him with serious damage if he didn't 'fuck off'. I imagined this was the point where we were torn to bits. Instead, seemingly nonplussed by Chayevsky's aggression, the mob quietened and watched him get in behind the wheel and start the car. He gently eased it forward and the demonstration parted to let us through.

'That could have gone either way,' I said, when I had stopped shaking.

He nodded. 'Didn't want to use the sten. Might have set them off,' he said, which reminded me. I checked his gun just to see how efficient it might have been. The breech was jammed. It would only have been effective as a weapon if he had thrown it at the mob.

'This bloody gun is useless,' I said.

'I know. That's why I didn't use it,' he said.

I thought of charging him, but then I remembered the starting handle and the look in his eyes, and thought again.

They were frightening and exhilarating times. I was twenty and the youngest captain in the British Army, so the folks at home got to read about this young officer who was forging ahead in a glorious military career and was obviously destined for great things.

What I really wanted was to be one of the journalists I was

looking after. I had served an apprenticeship on local newspapers but the men I was working with now were a different breed. These were proper journalists, like I had seen in the movies – tough, smart, worldly. They were also vastly experienced.

I remember a party thrown for the media by General Stockwell. Medals were worn and Ronnie Monson, a taciturn, grizzled Aussie journalist, turned up wearing more medal ribbons than the general. He had reported wars long forgotten. He had also been one of the first journalists into Belsen, so there was nothing on earth he hadn't seen.

Little did I realise that before long I would be sharing assignments with Sandy Gall, who was then working for Reuters, Denis Pitts, Cyril Page, Terry Fincher and even Robin Day. I began hanging out with them.

The toilets in our apartment block had overloaded the sewage system, which had packed up. Consequently, the block stank and became a health hazard. Many of the journalists were found lodging aboard HMS *Forth,* a former submarine mother ship, now doing duty as a floating NAAFI in the harbour. One night, in the bar, I became embroiled in a dispute with a bar steward who threatened to knife me. I tried to grab him and in the ensuing mêlée was rescued by a couple of drinking companions and taken home.

The next day I was required to explain my actions to a senior officer who said that because the barman was a civilian and not a soldier (in which case I would have been in serious trouble), and because the dispute did not come to blows, and particularly because independent witnesses had heard the man threaten me, he would let me off with a bollocking. He also said he didn't think it wise for me to drink on board in the future, so HMS *Forth* was off limits. This seemed a minor inconvenience until the day arrived when we were withdrawing from Port Said and I was told I was to report to HMS *Forth*, which would be the last ship to leave. Would they leave me on the quayside with the angry approaching mob?

As it was, they changed their minds and put me on a troopship in charge of a convoy of trucks, carrying our office equipment, which, upon return to England, would disband at Mons barracks. Moreover, my driver in the lead truck was Corporal Chayevsky.

I remember looking at the coast of southern England and thinking the boy who left those shores was not the man returning. It was an optimistic, energising feeling. I felt more confident as a citizen and as a journalist. I imagined I had seen my future.

We set off in convoy for Aldershot, me in the front vehicle with Chayevsky. After a while it occurred to me we were on the main road to London. When I pointed this out, Chayevsky said he was making a short detour in order to take a nostalgic look at the place of his birth. I wasn't going to argue. I had a couple of months to serve and I didn't care. We ended up in a street somewhere near West Ham Football Club. I took the advice of my driver and went to a nearby café for a cup of tea.

Upon my return, the convoy looked the same but I had no doubt was a few tons lighter, having been relieved of whatever loot had been hidden away among the office stores. I didn't enquire, but on the drive to Aldershot, Chayevsky asked me if my dear old mum was looking for a new fridge. We parted company at Mons. I never saw or heard of him after that, but often remembered him. He played an important part in my life – he saved it.

At Mons I came across my old training captain. We bumped

into each other in the officers' mess. He appeared not to recognise me and I didn't provide any clues. There was a moment when his eyes seemed to register the three pips on my shoulder and I thought he shook his head in disbelief, but maybe I was imagining things. What I didn't imagine was the reaction of my drill sergeant as we passed each other in camp and saluted.

'Jesus Christ,' he said, when he recognised the young captain he was acknowledging. He had forgotten his advice about needing a sense of humour in the army.

When I was demobbed I informed the *South Yorkshire Times* of my availability and was offered five quid a week and a job in head office in Mexborough. As I was earning fifteen quid a week as a captain in the army I thought I might as well re-enlist. I tried a couple of other newspapers without getting an offer, so I took a job at a local glass works, driving a fork-lift, shifting palettes from one place and stacking them in another. As the new recruit, I was also given the job of a daily visit to the nearby pub where I would fill two buckets with Barnsley Bitter for my workmates to sup. I was told gruesome stories of initiation ceremonies for new male employees, carried out on the night shift by female workers. I looked forward to being seriously interfered with, but nothing happened.

The job served its purpose. It kept me going financially until I could move on. I also experienced the drab and monotonous routine of factory work, a production line of labour stretching from school to retirement without change and without hope of anything better. We had been told in 1946 that things would be different. We assumed we were the masters now. A decade on and it seemed to me that for the vast majority of people in Britain nothing much had changed.

On the other hand, I had seen the alternative, a world beyond the one served by the Barnsley Traction Bus Company. As soon as I could afford the fare, I was off!

11
OPENING FOR BARNSLEY WITH DICKIE BIRD

I was rescued from the glass works by my old colleague, Don Booker. He arranged for me to meet the editor of the *Barnsley Chronicle* and I was hired as a reporter. Arthur Hopcraft, who later went on to a distinguished career as a television playwright and who also adapted John le Carré's *Tinker Tailor Soldier Spy* for television, was a fellow hack. For all he was quiet and reserved by nature, Arthur was easily recognisable as the only man in Barnsley to wear a bow tie to work, which was an oddly flamboyant gesture for one so diffident. He also favoured beige as a feature of his out and about wardrobe, which, in Barnsley at that time, had him singled out as a colourful character. He was a good reporter and a marvellous feature writer with an enviable elegance.

He loved football and went on to write *The Football Man*, one of the best books ever written about the game. There was unspoken competition between us. We would try to outdo each other with fancy phrases, showing off like competing birds of paradise. I was particularly proud of a reminiscence about Barnsley Football Club in which I pointed out that Roy Cooling, a blond and handsome inside forward on Barnsley's books in the days of my youth, had the romantic looks of the young Scott Fitzgerald. I imagined this would display to the general public, and to Mr Hopcraft in particular, that I had a working knowledge of contemporary American literature they might find surprising, and don't get me started on Ernest Hemingway, John Steinbeck and John Dos Passos.

What I wrote was: 'A particular favourite of mine was Roy Cooling, then a young and promising play maker, who bore a distinct resemblance to the young Scott Fitzgerald.' Sadly, my ambitions were frustrated by a subeditor who had never heard of *The Great Gatsby*. He changed my line to 'Roy Cooling . . . who bears a distinct resemblance to Scott of the Antarctic.'

They were good days, ripe with youthful energy, a feeling we were on the springboard of our careers. I was still inspired by those glamorous men I had met in Port Said but, on the other hand, I hadn't entirely given up my ambition to be a professional cricketer.

Playing for Barnsley and opening the innings with Dickie Bird, we once put on nearly 200 together. I scored a century and went to my 100 by hitting a six into the gents' toilet, from where my father emerged holding the ball like some precious gem. He had been hiding while I went through what are called 'the nervous nineties'. From the moment I left Cudworth Cricket Club when I was fifteen or sixteen and joined Barnsley he had given up playing himself to watch every game I played but he couldn't simply stand and watch. He had to contribute. He would position himself behind the bowler's arm alongside the sightscreen and semaphore his mood – happiness, concern, disgust even, to his son.

His most emphatic gesture was reserved for when I went to cut a ball and missed. I loved cutting outside my off stump and wasn't bad at it. My father, however, had been brought up on the Yorkshire coaching manual, which insisted, in the words of the immortal

Preparing the wicket for beach cricket. Scarborough 1938.

About to open the innings with my captain.

Poshed up at Bridlington with Mum, uncles, aunts and cousins. The pretty girl behind me gave me my first kiss.

P980

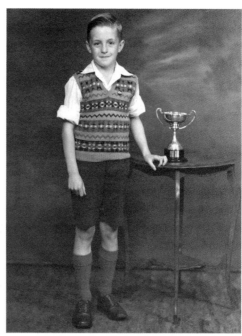

Me and my mum, partners in knitting.

Junior school Victor Ludorum aged ten. I was a runner not a fighter.

Family holiday at Butlins with neighbours. Granny Binns and her husband, Fred, are on my left.

Me in my droopy teenager phase, with Mum, her sister Madge and her children. The child on my lap now weighs 190lbs.

Form E1 at Barnsley Grammar School. I'm front row, third from the left, before the rot set in.

Dreaming of playing for Yorkshire and England.

Teenage hooligans at Filey. Note the hair, first manifestation of my Robert Mitchum phase.

A cricket team assembled and captained by my father to take on all comers.

Basic training in Wiltshire. My trousers were last worn by Ronnie Corbett.

Our billet in Port Said. The shell holes provided the air conditioning.

After twelve weeks basic training this is what you look like. Don't know about the enemy but they sure as hell would frighten their girlfriends.

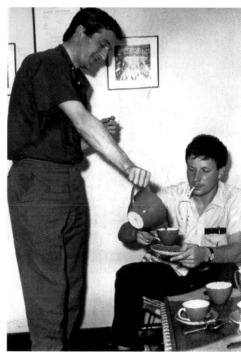

Returning from the Skerries for the *Guardian* in 1959.

Pouring tea for cameraman Chris Menges to celebrate leaving Zanzibar after being arrested in 1964.

My first job as an army PR.

My hero Fred Trueman and the perfect action. Taken in 1960 and still the model for all those who followed with ambitions to bowl fast.

We played together as teenagers in Barnsley. I dreamed of playing for Yorkshire, Geoff Boycott was certain he would – and England, too.

Sir Neville Cardus. I wanted to play cricket like Len Hutton and write like Neville Cardus. I failed but it was fun trying.

Maurice Leyland: 'Never cut until June is out, and even then only when you have thought about it.' What he did if I shaped to cut the ball and missed was a mime Monsieur Marceau would have paid to see. It involved firstly throwing his arms in the air with his face towards the heavens, then putting his head in his hands and shrugging his shoulders as if sobbing with uncontrollable grief. After that, he would stand to attention and, looking in my direction, wave a fist at me.

One day when I was playing and missing quite a lot and my father was giving a command performance, the wicket keeper said to me, 'Does tha' reckon yon bloke's having a fit?'

I said it looked like it.

'Does tha' know him?' he asked.

I shook my head.

'Must be the local nutter,' he said.

I nodded in agreement.

'Poor sod,' he said.

When I first played for Barnsley as a teenager I was so paralysed by fear and the reputation of opposition players I could barely play a shot. My slow play once proved too much for one spectator who, after watching me for about half an hour without much happening, shouted, 'I don't know thi' name, lad, but I have to tell thi' tha's got about as much life as a bloody tombstone.'

This particular spectator made a career of coming to all our home games and abusing the players. Whenever I walked to the wicket he would shout, 'Oh, good God, not him again.' He had a running feud with our skipper, Ernest Steele. When we were taking a terrible pasting in the field, and every ball seemed to fly to the boundary, he bellowed at Steele, 'Put another man there, Steely.' After thirty minutes of this, Ernest Steele turned to his tormentor and shouted, 'How many bloody fielders do tha' think I've got?' 'Obviously not sufficient,' came the reply.

When batting, Ernest liked to give the wicket a good whack with the back of his bat after every ball, to flatten out bumps, real or imagined. After one particular hefty thwack his critic yelled, 'Ay up, Steely, tha' wants to be careful, there's men working under theer.'

We played in the Yorkshire League. It was tough, hard cricket and no place for sensitive souls. For the young aspiring player it was a true test of whether or not you might make it into the world of a professional cricketer. There were old pros in the Yorkshire League capable of setting the most severe examinations.

George Henry Pope, who captained the Sheffield United team, was one of the finest all-rounders of his generation and certainly one of the best swing and seam bowlers there has ever been. Keith Miller said he learned everything from Pope about bowling in English conditions, including secreting a thick coating of Brylcreem inside his cap to keep the ball shiny. George Pope was a tall, bald man with a large nose and rubbery face. As well as being a master cricketer, he was a genius at psychological warfare. As I walked out to play against him for the first time he said in a conversational tone, but loud enough for me to hear, 'Here comes a new victim. Shouldn't take long – lbw bowled Pope.' He was right, second ball. You could say he talked me into it.

He was also a master at umpire tampering. 'Good afternoon, Mr Umpire, and how are the roses in your garden?' he would say to the official, who was flattered at how George Pope of Derbyshire and England should know he grew roses for the local show. 'And how is Elsie?' he would continue, asking by name after the umpire's wife. And there was more, after which the umpire was not simply regarding George Pope as his best friend but was also considering adopting him. It was generally known in the Yorkshire League that if George Pope appealed against you for lbw, you could start walking.

Our professional was Ellis Robinson, of Yorkshire. He was an off-spin bowler with a terrible temper if things went wrong. The Barnsley wicket at that time was a masterpiece prepared by a groundsman of genius called John Mathewman. It was a batsman's paradise. This did not suit Ellis Robinson, who was made to toil, often fruitlessly, for his wickets. The more frustrated he became, the nearer he ordered you to field at short leg, trying to psyche out the batsman. More often than not, the batsman regarded the close field as a challenge to his manhood and would attack with even greater vigour, sometimes causing considerable damage. I was given the suicide mission on several occasions. I didn't know which was worse, being hit by the ball or bollocked by Ellis, who had a fine repertoire of insults.

One day, after near decapitation by a leg-side slog that went for six, I was addressed by Ellis thus: 'And what does tha' think tha'rt playing at? Tha' stand theer as if the hairs of thy arse are tied together.'

Many years later, when I was celebrating my fiftieth birthday in Australia, a group of friends recorded a sound tape to send to me. Athol Carr, a dear friend of mine who was organising the tape, gave the microphone to Ellis. 'What's this?' he said.

'It's how you contact Mike in Australia,' said Athol, whereupon Ellis put the mike to his ear and bellowed, 'Hello, Mike, your old friend Ellis speaking.' O, rare Ellis Robinson.

Dickie Bird and I had played for a season or two when we were asked to the Yorkshire nets for a trial. In those distant days only men born in Yorkshire could play cricket for the county. It was the most exclusive cricket club in the world and, by common consent, one of the best. The dream of every Yorkshire child was to wear the White Rose of Yorkshire and we grew up believing that an England cap was second best.

I had an unhappy time. I remember it as a grey day at the county headquarters at Headingley in Leeds. I wanted to play for Yorkshire, of course I did, but deep down I knew I hadn't the confidence or belief to convince the coaches. I was further chastened by the presence of Fred Trueman and Brian Close, the new young stars of Yorkshire cricket at the time. I admired and envied their swagger. By comparison I felt a phoney. I didn't bat well and wasn't invited back, but it wasn't until much later that Dickie Bird told me what happened.

I was in a net taken by Arthur 'Ticker' Mitchell, the Yorkshire coach, and a man whose opinion counted. Mitchell was watching me bat when he turned to Dickie and said, 'Is that lad a mate of thine?'

Dickie said we played for Barnsley together.

Mitchell said, 'Does he have a job?'

Dickie told him I was a reporter on a local paper. 'A reporter, eh,' mused the coach. Then he said, 'When tha' gets a minute, tell thi' friend he'd better not give up reportin.'

That was the end for me, but not for Dickie, who went on to play for Yorkshire and Leicestershire before taking up umpiring and becoming one of cricket's most beloved and respected figures.

Shortly after the Yorkshire nets another youngster joined us in the Barnsley team. I was batting at the other end when he made his entrance at number three. He was fifteen or sixteen, slim and wearing a pair of National Health spectacles.

'They're sending in short-sighted midgets now,' the bowler

remarked to the wicket keeper, just to make the batsman feel at home.

The third ball he received the new player rocked on to the back foot and played a most perfect drive between the bowler and mid off. The ball streaked to the boundary. It was a shot of almost classical execution.

'What's his name?' the bowler asked, with grudging admiration.

'Boycott,' I said. 'Geoffrey Boycott.'

Geoffrey was different from Birdie and me. We hoped we might play for Yorkshire, he knew he would play for both the county and for England. From the earliest days he worked at the business of being a professional cricketer. He wasn't the most greatly gifted player in our team – we had a player called Hubert Padgett who made the business of playing cricket seem the easiest and most enjoyable pastime in the world – but no one in my experience worked harder at a game or analysed what was needed with more diligence and intelligence than Geoffrey.

There were times when the three of us would sit on the balcony at Barnsley and look over the sweep of the ground to the town in the distance, and wonder what the future held. None of us could have imagined the future, except perhaps Geoffrey. He became what he set out to be, one of our great openers, for Yorkshire and England. Dickie went on to become one of cricket's most trusted umpires and treasured characters and I ended up being attacked by Emu. I often sit and wonder where it all went wrong.

12

THE GIRL ON THE UPPER DECK

The moment I finally decided I would rather be Neville Cardus than Len Hutton came when I moved from Barnsley to Doncaster. The two towns were only twelve miles apart but moving away from home, getting a flat of my own for the first time in my life, was a declaration of how serious I was to climb the beanstalk of my ambition. In the mobile world of today, where young people take it for granted that they will cross continents and get to know far-flung places as well as their own backyards, a move of twelve miles would not be seen as a significant journey. But in the fifties, where I came from, it was regarded as a radical departure.

My mother gave me an eiderdown and Fair Isle pullovers. She obviously thought Doncaster was near the North Pole. My father muttered something about it being a long way for him to come to watch me play cricket. I couldn't convince him I was changing jobs, not cricket clubs. And I dare not tell him I had more or less decided to stop playing Yorkshire League cricket. It would have broken his heart.

I chose Doncaster because, in those days, it was a journalists' town. Two evening and three local papers were printed there, which meant that, along with the one or two vigorously competing freelance agencies, there was a press corps of more than forty. It was also a well-known stepping stone to Manchester and the national dailies, and even at that stage I had my sights on Fleet Street. Doncaster was a pleasant place to live and work. It straddled the main north–south highway, the A1, the Great North Road. It was the centre of the South Yorkshire coalfield, and steam engines were made there for a railway system of which it was a key junction. It had a racecourse, a decent football team, one or two agreeable pubs and a few good-looking girls.

I met one on a bus and married her.

I remember the very moment I first saw Mary Heneghan. I was on the upper deck of a double decker travelling from Doncaster to the mining village of Tickhill. I was with a colleague, Denis Cassidy, who went on to run a very successful freelance agency. We were on our way to a meeting of Tickhill council, when this tall and slender girl with reddish gold hair and a red duffel coat sat behind us. Denis, who was good at chatting up, introduced us. When I turned to look at her I remember thinking I could gaze upon that face for a long time without tiring.

She said she was a teacher on her way to earn some extra money with a keep-fit class in Tickhill, which was taking place where our council meeting would be held. After the meeting we wandered into her class of exercising women and she shamed us into joining in.

I told Denis Cassidy I might be in love. He said I should call her. I said I didn't have her number. He said she told us which school she worked at so what more information did a trained journalist require? I said I was too shy to ring the school. He said, 'Don't be so bloody stupid, I'll ring for you.' And he did, pretending to be me, which is how I came to date Mary for the first time. Pathetic really, and yet the start of a partnership lasting fifty years.

At that time I was fantasising I might break into the big time as a theatre critic. I was much influenced by American critics Dorothy Parker, Wolcott Gibbs and Alexander Woollcott. I imagined myself employed by *The New Yorker* magazine, swapping epigrams with James Thurber, S.J. Perelman and Ogden Nash at the Algonquin Round Table. This is what I confessed to Mary in order to justify taking her on our first date to the Elmfield House Players production of *Thark* at the Doncaster Arts Centre.

She forgave me and, even more admirably, in the ensuing fifty years, has never mentioned my review, written to impress her. It started: 'Struggling for an introduction I resort to a pun with the thought that at least Ben Travers would appreciate it if I say the success of his play rests on the two bawd shoulders of Sir Hector Benbow and Ronald Gamble.'

I was working for the *Yorkshire Evening Post*, edited by Jack Dibb, a large and furious man who gave the impression of constantly being on the brink of exploding. One lunchtime, after one of my theatre reviews had upset an amateur actor who ran an antiques shop in town, the hapless man turned up in the street outside our office brandishing a cutlass and challenging me to a duel. I thought we might ring the police. My editor suggested I hire a sword and accept the challenge, which would certainly make a front-page story. He wasn't joking.

For someone who neither drank nor smoked and appeared to be a well brought up middle-class girl, Mary fitted easily into the boozy, cursing, seditious group of journalists with whom I shared my life. Often she subsidised us. When we had drunk away our pay, she would fill the glass. She was alive with exuberance and energy, and laughed and danced her way through life. She was unlike any girl I had ever met and I was enchanted by her. So were my friends. At that time none of us realised the amount of deprivation and tragedy she had dealt with in her short life.

The radiant girl at the centre of our merry-making had lost both her parents before she was eighteen. Her father, from an Irish farming family, had come to work in the South Yorkshire coalfield. During the lockouts and strikes of the late twenties and early thirties, he went to America and became a cop in Chicago. When he returned, Mary was the result of the reunion with his wife. He was injured in an accident at the pit, after which he was plagued with illness and died when Mary was eight. Shortly before his death, Mary was escorting her three-year-old brother across the A1 when he was struck by a car and killed. The driver was drunk. Mary gave evidence at his trial. Even today she is fearful crossing a road. Her mother slaved to get Mary and her younger sister into teachers' training college. She died when Mary was seventeen. Mary says she died from hard work.

Once, many years after we had met and were married with three young children of our own, we were on our way in the family car to Scarborough when the children started whingeing about wanting this and that and moaning about being bored. I was passing through Doncaster at the time and took a short detour. I pulled up outside a row of scruffy houses, two-up, two-down, bathtub hanging on a nail in the wall, outside toilets. The boys asked why we had stopped. I told them I wanted them to look at a particular house in the row and tell me what they saw. They said the house looked horrible but so what?

'That's where your mother was born and spent her childhood,' I said. They didn't whinge for a long time after that. I tell that story not simply because I love and admire her but because I am also very proud of her.

It was while working for the *Post* in Doncaster that I did my first celebrity interview. I was walking down the high street for a morning coffee when I saw Jack Teagarden and Earl 'Fatha' Hines walking towards me. In sporting terms it was like meeting Don Bradman and Len Hutton, and about as likely as bumping into Ernest Hemingway and Graham Greene in Doncaster High Street. Both men had played with Louis Armstrong; both had a reserved place in the pantheon. Teagarden was one of the great jazz trombonists and a singer of unmistakable style. Earl Hines was arguably the first modern jazz pianist, inventing a style of playing that influenced succeeding generations of piano players. To a jazz lover like me, this was the greatest moment of my life.

I introduced myself. They were pleased to be recognised but unhappy because the bus they were travelling in to Bradford had broken down and they were stuck in this alien town.

'Where the hell are we?' asked Mr Teagarden. He was none the wiser when I told him.

I took them to a café for a coffee. I talked to them for half an hour about their memories of the golden age of jazz. Finally, I asked them what they thought of Doncaster.

Earl Hines said, 'All we need to know is the road out of this goddam awful place.'

I thought I would leave that quote out of my story, which I was certain was a scoop of immense significance. When I told them in the office what had happened their reaction was far from enthusiastic. Not for the first time I was confronted by the fact that my love of jazz was not shared by everyone else. As someone in the office said, it wasn't like meeting Guy Mitchell or Elvis Presley, was it?

Jack Dibb agreed. He had never heard of them. It made about six pars in that night's paper. It was time to move on. The chance came sooner than I imagined.

The last steam engine to be made in Doncaster was a story that attracted interest from the national press. The *Manchester Guardian*, home of one of my great heroes, Neville Cardus, sent a young reporter called Richard West. He said they saw Cardus in the office in Manchester only on the odd occasion when he would venture north to report a Hallé concert at the Free Trade Hall. Dick West was a slim, boyish-looking man with bright blue eyes and the most engaging smile.

When the ceremony of unveiling the last steam engine was over we were taken to the Danum Hotel for a celebratory lunch. I had to file my copy for the early edition, so by the time I took my place at the table my new friend Mr West had sampled the wine and was talking to a PR man from the rail industry. It was a time of much debate and controversy about British Rail and the more wine he consumed the more Dick West's questioning appeared to discomfort the PR man. I watched with admiration as he stalked his prey. I was even more awestruck when, with his opponent now floundering, he closed his eyes and appeared to take a nap.

When he awoke I took him to a quiet spot in our office where he wrote a funny article before opening time, after which we toured several pubs and became lifelong friends. During the pub crawl he mentioned there might be a vacancy at the *Manchester Guardian* and would I fancy a job there. For all my ambition, I had never even dared contemplate a job on one of the posh quality papers. Not for the likes of me, I had thought. On the other hand, if the *Guardian* reporters' room was staffed by people like Dick West, it might be an amusing place to work. So I said I would love to work there. He said he would have a word with the news editor, Harry Whewell, and, with any amount of luck, I might be hearing from him. A couple of weeks later, Harry Whewell asked me to go for an interview.

A short time after the interview Harry Whewell wrote offering me a job on the *Manchester Guardian*. The salary was a thousand guineas a year. Jack Dibb was not pleased when I told him. It ended up in a shouting match, with me flouncing out of his office and banging the door so hard the glass window fell out and shattered on the floor. My last view of my editor was of him leaning through the broken window bellowing, 'And you'll pay for that out of your bloody wages.'

13

WATCHING
NEVILLE CARDUS

I joined the *Manchester Guardian* in 1958. In those days, it occupied a unique place in British journalism – a daily newspaper printed in Manchester with a nationwide circulation and international reputation. It paid lousy wages but was a joy to work for if you were a reporter who wanted to be a features writer and vice versa.

The journalist who joined the paper was expected to be as adept at covering a pit disaster as a sheepdog trial. The *Manchester Guardian* took sheepdog trials very seriously. My friend and mentor Dick West once had the idea of brightening up his report by writing it from the point of view of a sheep. When he returned in triumph to the office he was called in, accused of trivialising sheepdog trials and given the sack. He took no notice of the dismissal because he knew nobody ever got sacked on the *Manchester Guardian*. Two years later, he was still working there.

In many ways the most relevant characteristic of the paper was that it belonged to Manchester, along with the Hallé Orchestra, the Free Trade Hall, and Manchester United Football Club. It was a declaration of excellence, a statement of independence, and a contradiction of the notion, more common then than now, that

Britain ceased to exist north of Hampstead. The people of Manchester, indeed Lancashire, were proud of their paper and for the first, and maybe only, time in his life the journalist found himself both admired and accepted when folk were told for whom he worked.

All this, and more, made me proud to have been given a job on this prestigious paper. My fear was that the great majority of my colleagues had been to university and I had not. I tried to console myself with the thought that while they might make a better job of explaining unilateral disarmament – a hot topic at the time – they wouldn't have a clue about reporting a chip-pan fire in Oldham.

Two things I remember about my job interview: when I was being escorted into the reporters' room I saw, leaning against the wall, an old cycle with a pigeon basket strapped on the back. Were they still sending copy by carrier pigeon, I wondered? Then, the first person I met in the reporters' room was a tall, gangly, smiling young man who introduced himself as Michael Frayn. He said he too was a newcomer, having joined straight from Cambridge. He was friendly but incredibly posh. At first he terrified me, later we became lasting friends.

Harry Whewell was more identifiably one of us. He was a small, energetic, impulsive man who wore ties with the largest Windsor knots I had ever seen, which often ended up situated beneath his left ear. It would be unfair to say that Harry's dress sense, or lack of it, set the standards for the office. In fact, as I came to know my colleagues over the coming months, I was forced to the conclusion that Harry was one of the better dressed journalists on the staff.

Roy Perrott, a fine writer who later worked with distinction for the *Observer*, favoured donkey jackets, polo-necked sweaters and large working boots. Once, when he came to the office wearing waders, Harry said to him, 'Roy, how on earth can I send you to the Town Hall looking like that?' At the time Harry was sporting a tie with a knot the size of a grapefruit and a jacket that gave away the fact he'd had an egg for breakfast.

An old Etonian, David Bruxner, wore pin-striped suits, blue striped shirts with plain white collars, braces and cracked patent leather shoes. I was never quite sure what he did, except he had perfected the art of drifting in and out of the office.

Norman Shrapnel was the chief reporter. He later went on to be the parliamentary correspondent. I can't remember exchanging more than a couple of words with Norman because he was pathologically shy. We never worked out how he managed to be a journalist, and a good one, while being unable to communicate with people. The famous story about Norman was of him running away from a public-relations man who was trying to give him a story and locking himself in the toilet until the man departed.

Another colleague, Anthony Howard, was an Oxford graduate, who went on to become a perceptive and principled observer of the political scene, as well as a key figure in my professional life. Sensing my initial discomfort at the presence of so many highly educated colleagues and sick, no doubt, at my gruff disdain for 'bloody graduates', he dubbed me 'the Barnsley Clodpole'. It was rude and cruel but not without an element of truth in summing up how I sometimes felt.

I stopped feeling sorry for myself when Harry Whewell called me into his office to discuss an article I had written. He said, 'I am not going to accept this article.' I asked why. 'Because you're trying to write like the mythical Guardian Man. Just be yourself. That's who I hired,' he said. Harry gave me the confidence to do as he advised and it seemed to work.

After my first year I had more articles in *The Bedside Guardian*, the annual publication of what was deemed the best of *Guardian* writing, than Anthony Howard, an achievement I still remind him of. One of the sure-fire ways of making *The Bedside Guardian* was to write what was called the Miscellany Page lead. This was, in effect, the top-left corner of the features page, which was reserved for offbeat stories and quirky writing. If Harry assigned you a certain miscellany page lead, it meant an extra five bob in the wage packet. I remember Michael Frayn (or it may have been Roy Perrott) rejoicing at the news Harry had assigned him to cover a mouse show in Bradford. 'Lucky bugger,' we said. My triumph was a man in Doncaster who made boots for elephants.

There was hard news as well and, because I had shorthand and knew which foot to place in the door, I had my fair share, along with another journalist who had made his way through the ranks, Joe Minogue. We were particularly in demand at party conference time when we were expected to fill a couple of pages with verbatim reports on debates. We were regarded with curious affection by journalists from other papers who had never before met a *Guardian* reporter who had shorthand.

I have never been more happy and fulfilled in all my long career in newspapers as I was at the *Manchester Guardian*. The work was challenging, the company stimulating and humorous. It was my university. The newsroom itself was a scruffy, dark place with sepia prints of past *Guardian* men on the walls and sloping desks with inkwells from a time when journalists wrote their articles with quill pens. There were three or four ancient and armour-plated typewriters stacked around the room, each weighing about the same as a small car, which, when placed on the sloping desk, slipped inexorably into our laps. Michael Frayn used to joke that the damage done to our reproductive organs by sliding typewriters made it highly unlikely we would ever have children. There were two telephones hidden away in a corner of the room.

I was in one of the booths late at night, ringing round the emergency services, trying to find a story, when a white-haired man wearing a black cloak swept into the room. I realised it was my hero Neville Cardus. He discarded the cloak with a flourish and began battering away at a typewriter. I watched him closely, convinced I might discover the secret to his flowing style. In fact he typed one word, and then discarded the sheet in a crumpled ball, before loading another and repeating the process. This went on for about ten or fifteen minutes by which time he was ankle deep in crumpled paper. Then, for no apparent reason and with no perceptible change of gear, he typed without stopping a review of a Hallé concert at the Free Trade Hall, his beloved Barbirolli conducting. When he left I picked up the discarded sheets, looking for clues. On each page was just one word: 'Cardus'.

It wasn't until sometime later that I actually met my hero and was able to approach another mystery surrounding Neville Cardus, namely how he managed to extract such marvellous quotes from cricketers. I was writing an article about the great Yorkshire and England cricketer Wilfred Rhodes, and was particularly intrigued by one of my favourite anecdotes featuring Rhodes and written by Sir Neville. The story concerned Charles McGahey, an old Essex player, going out to bat on a sunny day at Bramall Lane, Sheffield. As he walked out to face Yorkshire, the sun darkened with black clouds moving across its face. Fearing rain and the possibility of batting against Rhodes on a sticky wicket, McGahey said, 'Ullo. McGahey caught Tunnicliffe bowled Rhodes . . . no score.' And it came to pass – in both innings.

When I checked this line with Sir Neville, he said, 'Oh, I made that up.' He went on to explain that his job was to write scripts for cricketers who, in the main, were incapable of saying what they would say if they possessed his skill with words. I must have looked disappointed at his revelation. 'Don't be concerned, young man. What mattered was it came true.'

I wasn't to know it but the most significant assignment I was given at the *Guardian* was a teachers' conference at Scarborough. I thought it might be a good idea to invite Mary, who was still working and living in Doncaster. The first night of our trip we walked along the cliff edge into a chill wind fresh off the North Sea. I told her I loved her and asked her to marry me. She said she would and we went to a coffee bar to celebrate.

On the jukebox the Everly Brothers were singing their number one hit, 'All I have to do is dream'. It wasn't 'As time goes by', but that didn't stop me.

'We'll always have Scarborough, kid,' I said.

14
THE BLACK PALACE
IN FLEET STREET

We were married in Doncaster. Mary made her own wedding dress; I looked as if I had made my own suit. My best man spent the night in a police cell after being caught being pushed down the Great North Road in a large refuse bin. We borrowed Anthony Howard's car and set off for a honeymoon in Devon. We were poor but overjoyed. We rented a flat on the second floor of an old Victorian house in Didsbury and Mary found a job teaching at a local school.

My father celebrated our union by bringing over a ton of coal in sacks, which we dumped in the basement. This arrangement lasted until I grew tired of going up and down three flights of stairs for a scuttle of coal and had the bright idea of transferring the load to the landing outside our bathroom. This wasn't exactly the coal in the bath of my youth but certainly a nod in the right direction. Guests going for a pee would return looking like they had done a shift at Grimethorpe Colliery.

The highlight of our social life was an invitation to dine at the editor's home. Alistair Hetherington was a chubby and rosy cheeked man who looked like he spent a deal of time walking the moors, which indeed he did. His dinner parties were strange affairs because the guests were journalists who, in the main, drank to excess, unlike the host and hostess who drank not at all. On the particular night we were invited I noticed that a bottle of sherry, for some reason, had been placed on the hearth near an open fire. Not only was it warm but the bottle contained a fly, which had probably been boiled to death even as it drowned. The evening came to an embarrassing conclusion when one of the reporters was discovered peeing in the sink. We put it down to drinking warm and contaminated sherry. They were happy and secure days. Newspapers were profitable and, it seemed at the time, impregnable.

Granada Television had just arrived in Manchester but there was a general view among journalists that it wouldn't make much difference to our way of life. In those days, when it didn't know how best to employ outside broadcast units, and when daytime broadcasting belonged to educational programming, Granada sent an OB unit to the *Guardian* to demonstrate the workings of a great newspaper. There was a memorable moment when the cameras in the subs room focused on the chief subeditor as he read a story and prepared to give it a headline to fit on the front page. The commentator set up the occasion in tones of breathless anticipation. The chief sub, a learned and dignified man who didn't much care for the intrusion of cameras in his lair, studied the article for what seemed like a lunchtime and then, picking up a pair of scissors, cut the page in two. It somehow summed up what we felt about television; an insignificant and feckless intruder in our world, and, indeed, in our town.

A year after our marriage Mary told me she was pregnant. Our general delight was somewhat tempered by my father's observation that if it was a boy child and born in Lancashire, it would not be able to play for Yorkshire. Even I dismissed this thought as irrelevant, but I should have known my father better, as subsequent events were to prove.

About the same time Tony Howard was approached by Brian Tesler, then Programme Controller at ABC Television, to produce a local current affairs programme called *ABC of the North*. He asked me if I would take a screen test. They gave the studio interviewers jobs to me and a reporter from the *Sunday Pictorial*, Desmond Wilcox.

We recorded in an ABC cinema in Didsbury and it seemed to me an easier way of making money than writing for a living. My new friend Desmond Wilcox agreed. The programme went out on Sunday evenings. After the first show I took Mary for a drink to a pub in Manchester just to test reaction. Nothing happened except the landlord, as he pulled my pint, did a double take.

He gave me my drink and said, 'There's been a bloke on telly just now who is the spitting image of you.'

I nodded in anticipation.

'It wasn't you, was it?' he said.

I smiled modestly, awaiting the acclaim.

'Hope it wasn't because yon bloke on the telly were bloody terrible,' he said.

My first review.

My stint as a presenter didn't last long. It was interrupted by a phone call from London from the editor of the *Daily Express*, Edward Pickering. He said he wondered if I'd like to visit him in Fleet Street to talk about a job.

I told Harry Whewell and he said I should think carefully about it. He warned it wouldn't be like working for the *Guardian*. And then he said, 'But I sense you are already on your way. Good luck.'

Tony Howard cautioned against the move. He believed I would

be unhappy. I said I didn't know what they were worrying about because it would take an awful lot to make me leave Manchester and the *Guardian*. In fact it took about two minutes. Ted Pickering said, 'How much does the *Guardian* pay you?' I told him one thousand guineas. 'I'll give you two thousand,' he said. I didn't even say I'd think about it. 'Done,' I said.

It wasn't quite like that. I had arrived the day before the interview and stood outside the shiny black building in Fleet Street, watching the people coming and going. I'd followed one or two hacks into Poppins, the *Express* pub in Poppins Court, sniffed the atmosphere and liked what I sampled. I had even dared to enter El Vino's for a look around. I was standing at the bar, thinking it unlike any pub I had visited, when the barman, dressed as if he was an usher at a royal wedding, and without looking at me, asked what I'd like to drink. I requested a half of bitter.

'Wines or spirits only, I'm afraid,' he said in a manner that suggested I should take my custom elsewhere.

'I think my friend would like a glass of champagne,' said a voice behind me. It belonged to Cyril Aynsley, a man who was to have a lasting effect on my career as a journalist. Cyril was the chief reporter on the *Daily Express* and when I told him the reason I was in London he ordered a bottle of champagne in celebration. Giddy with booze, I looked around El Vino's and what a moment ago had seemed a hostile environment now began to feel like home.

In those days the *Daily Express* sold more than four million newspapers every day. It was the most successful and glamorous organisation in all of Fleet Street. It billed itself as 'The World's Greatest Paper'. The building was a declaration of its confidence and success. Every day it was polished and pampered until it shone like a guardsman's boot. Inside there were uniformed commissionaires and a lobby straight out of a Hollywood movie. You half expected to see Fred Astaire dancing down the stairs into the foyer. The women all looked like Vera Hruba Ralston or Veronica Lake. Or was I still drunk?

The editor's office had sunshine slanting through venetian blinds. Ted Pickering was a tall, slim, elegantly dressed Yorkshireman who played a major part in taking the paper's circulation to heights never before achieved and never since equalled. He had on the desk in front of him a folder containing many of the articles I had written for the *Manchester Guardian*. He said he thought I would be best employed as a features writer.

I said I liked the idea and he said I ought to visit the features department before I made up my mind. He took me through the reporters' room into the office that was to become my home for the next two years or so.

The first person I saw was Osbert Lancaster, bewhiskered, rheumy eyed and immaculately attired in pin-striped suit with buttonhole. Cyril Aynsley was there, along with several of the Vera Hrubas and Veronicas I had seen in the lobby.

Ted Pickering invited me to sit in at that morning's editorial conference to meet senior members of the staff and to see how the paper was planned. No sooner were we seated than the phone went. Ted Pickering picked it up, raised his eyebrows at the assembly and we all rose and left the office.

'What happened?' I asked. 'Lord Beaverbrook on the phone,' I was told. The Canadian proprietor of the paper was never seen in the office but his presence haunted the building, terrified the staff.

Mary shared my excitement at a move to London. But we decided she would stay in Manchester to have the baby and we made a perfectly reasonable agreement with the National Health Service for this to happen.

I took a room in Bayswater and drove to London in my Mini to start my new career. During the first night at my new address I discovered my neighbours were two 'working girls' with a regular flow of clients, many of whom noisily acclaimed the fact they were either approaching or achieving sexual fulfilment. Next morning, when I checked on my car, I discovered all four wheels had been stolen.

Then my father called. 'Job's done,' he said.

'What job is this?' I enquired.

'Mary,' he said.

'What about her?' I said.

'She's been moved,' he said.

'Where to?' I asked.

'Our house,' he said.

'Why?' I asked.

'Because we live in Yorkshire,' he said.

'I know that, but why have you kidnapped my wife?' I asked.

'I've already told you but you won't listen. If the boy is born in Lancashire it can't play for Yorkshire,' he said, as if explaining something to an imbecile.

'I know that but have you thought about the chance it might be a girl?' I said.

'Don't talk bloody daft,' he said.

A month later, at a nursing home in Wakefield, Mary gave birth to a boy. We called him Andrew John and he didn't play for Yorkshire. It didn't matter because he loved his granddad and was adored in return.

15
BRENDAN BEHAN'S
FALSE TEETH

Brian Inglis, a journalist and author who knew what he was talking about, once observed that to have worked in Fleet Street and not been employed by Lord Beaverbrook was like having gone through the First World War without hearing a shot fired. Lord Beaverbrook's chosen lieutenants in the glass palace lived in a constant state of paranoia, fuelled by long lunches and large amounts of booze. They were like mannequins in one of Harrods' windows, constantly being moved around, or in some cases, disappearing forever.

In the two years I worked on the *Express* I had three editors and four features editors. There was a general extravagance of manpower, based on the assumption that Fleet Street would last forever. I was one of the thirty odd feature writers basically employed to fill the one gap left on the features page after the obligatory political piece, the blessed Beachcomber column, Rupert Bear, and the cartoon by the greatest of them all, Carl Giles.

Down below in the engine room, the print unions ran a system so blatantly corrupt it allowed employees to use pseudonyms, such as Donald Duck and Mickey Mouse, to pick up another wage packet. The man employed bundling papers on the weekend shift for onward distribution in lorries, was paid more than a feature writer.

But why worry? We were on a luxury liner without a care in the world. If a motor manufacturer was throwing a shindig in a foreign land to launch a new vehicle and was taking the media on a freebie, the *Express* man would pay his own way, and travel first class. Television was dismissed as a trite and boring intruder to be rejected at all costs. As an *Express* man you were forbidden to appear on the box.

I risked all by auditioning as a newsreader for Geoffrey Cox, the boss at ITN. I was given a script, autocue and a camera and, after a run through, required to present what was that night's news. There was a Kenyan politician at the time called Oginga Odinga. As I performed my audition I could see this name coming towards me like Becher's Brook. When it arrived I tried everything from Odinga Ogonga, to Oginga Odonga before ending the confusion with 'Oh, fuck it.'

Geoffrey Cox was solicitous. He took me to a quiet corner of the studio and said he thought I looked OK on camera but found my performance unconvincing.

'You are a very good writer,' he said, 'but if you take my advice you'll forget about television.'

I was not at all downcast. After all, I was employed by one of the world's most successful and glamorous newspapers. I was the new boy in the features department and, as such, given the build-up, which meant my name appeared on the features page at least once a week. This might not seem a lot but there were feature writers who thought themselves lucky to get a couple of articles a year in the paper, and one or two who had not been in the paper, or, indeed the office, for two or three years.

It was on the *Express* I first started interviewing celebrities. Bernard Miles had founded the Mermaid Theatre and I was sent to interview him after he offered a job to a controversial Communist trade union leader called Frank Haxell. Sir Bernard was a clever self-publicist so my report was a sidelong, slightly cynical, glance at him and his beloved theatre. The next day a telegram was delivered to me at the *Express*. It read: 'After reading your article I have come to the conclusion you should go far. Can I suggest Australia . . . Bernard Miles.'

I went to the first night of John Osborne's *Luther* in Manchester, prior to its London opening. The young Salford actor who played the lead was Albert Finney. On opening night he took a ten-minute standing ovation and we witnessed the burgeoning of a great new talent. The day after Albert Finney's triumph I interviewed his mother. I asked her what emotions she felt as her son received the rapture of that first-night audience. She said, 'I was very proud of our Albert. On the other hand, I kept looking at him on stage and thinking, "Oh Albert lad, I don't like your haircut."'

I covered the Lady Chatterley trial and profiled the prosecuting QC, Gerald Gardiner. I reported the last night of the Crazy Gang – my everlasting memory is of a row of surgical trusses hanging in a dressing room at the Victoria Palace. I accompanied Princess Grace of Monaco on her trip to Ireland to visit her ancestral home. I covered Aneurin Bevan's funeral and remembered a night in Doncaster when he spoke and I was so spellbound I stopped taking shorthand notes and watched this great orator and mesmerising performer at work. I had a page to write but when I went back to the office I didn't need notes. I remembered everything he had said and rejoiced in the remembrance.

While editors came and went, the one constant presence in the life of the feature writer was a small man with a limp, and a love of good wines and fine restaurants, who was an alchemist at laying out a page and transforming a plain story into a seductive one. Harold Keble was the associate editor and admired by his bosses, if not liked. Bob Edwards, who succeeded Pickering as editor, described him as 'utterly malevolent'.

He was fond of calling a feature writer into his office and displaying a page layout on an easel. It would consist, in the main, of a headline. It could be something like: 'The Glory of Love?' He'd ask you what you thought. Very interesting, you'd answer, but what's the story? That's for you to find out he would say. Let's say about a thousand words by tea time and, by the way, pay particular attention to the question mark in the headline.

Keith Howard, the news editor, was a more straightforward newspaper man and a very fine one. He was also of good humour, a funny man with a keen eye for offbeat stories and the eccentrics who made them. It was Keith who suggested I go to Dublin to interview Brendan Behan.

At the time Behan was a successful but controversial playwright. Two of his plays, *The Quare Fellow* and *The Hostage*, had gained him an international reputation. He was a former house painter who had served a term in a British jail for his membership of the IRA. He was also an alcoholic – worse, a celebrity alcoholic more famous for his boozy behaviour than for his undoubted talent as a writer.

I had, in fact, met Behan before Keith Howard sent me to Dublin. I had been in an Irish pub in Fleet Street when Brendan came in attached at the waist to a rope which was in turn attached to a blind man he had found begging in the streets of London. Brendan announced to the landlord, a friend of his, 'This is a case of the blind leading the blind drunk.'

Shortly after this episode he had collapsed and was taken to hospital, where he was told that if he didn't stop drinking he would die. He was also advised that his teeth needed urgent attention and that they were poisoning his system. Whereupon, or so I was told, the *Express* arranged for him to have a set of false teeth, at considerable cost.

The story now was that he had stayed off the booze and was back home in Dublin prior to leaving for New York to launch a production of *The Hostage*. So write a positive piece about Brendan's battle with the booze, they said, and, by the way, check on our false teeth.

The man who met me at Dublin Airport looked energetic and clear-eyed but clearly was missing at least a dozen teeth. I thought I would broach the subject straightaway, so the question was: 'Nice to meet you, Brendan. The *Express* would like to know what happened to your false teeth?' He said he couldn't get on with them but they had been transferred to a friend of his who sold linen handkerchiefs in O'Connell Street and we should pay him a visit. The man was easily recognisable because Brendan's teeth were too large for his mouth, which was stretched into a permanent rictus grin. Moreover he had to take them out to speak and tell us how generous Brendan had been. It was an appropriate start to what turned out to be a remarkable few days.

Behan insisted I stay at his home, where I met his attractive wife Beatrice. She was friendly but in that reserved way people acquire when any acquaintance of their alcoholic partner may be used as an excuse for a bender. She need not have worried. In the next few days he took me to so many pubs I lost count. I was perpetually sozzled on Guinness and he touched not a drop.

'Eminence nearly killed me,' Brendan would say. Wherever we went he was greeted like a hero. He would dance on tables and sing his latest song, 'I met my love in a graveyard', which had the line: 'Oh my old Irish tomb, I'll be in there soon.' When the telephone rang at home he would pick it up and in a high voice say, 'Noel Coward speaking.'

On my last night I took Brendan and Beatrice to a posh Dublin restaurant to thank them for their hospitality. As we entered the dining room the head waiter approached, hand outstretched in greeting. Brendan removed his jacket and hung it on the man's index finger. The evening ended in the kitchens with a choir of chefs and Brendan leading the singing. I never saw him again. He went back on the bottle and died three years later, aged forty-one.

When I heard the news I thought of something he said to me in Dublin. We were talking about the time he collapsed in London and he said he used to lie in hospital during his recovery 'thinking about croaking and who would miss me'. He said, 'I thought of all those reporters who bought me booze and made a small bet with meself they wouldn't mind me croaking, providing I did it in time for the first editions.'

He didn't let them down.

16
OUR MAN
IN THE CONGO

The day after I interviewed Miss Great Britain I was told to get my jabs and fly off to cover the war in the Congo. I was to be based in Elizabethville, the capital of the breakaway province of Katanga. The Congo was a mess. After seventy odd years of colonial rule, the Belgians had pulled out and left behind an inadequate infrastructure for efficient governance. Old tribal differences surfaced and the province of Katanga, rich in mineral resources, declared independence under President Moise Tshombe. United Nations troops intervened but only added to the confusion, and the entire nation was heading toward the catastrophe that has lasted to this very day.

I was told to meet Cyril Aynsley, who was ending his stint in Katanga, at Ndola Airport, in what was then Rhodesia. We would report the arrival of the United Nations Secretary General Dag Hammarskjöld, who was on his way to meet President Tshombe for peace talks. On the face of it, a routine task, this assignment was to prove both tragic and instructive. We stood at the perimeter fence to watch the Secretary General's plane arriving, and a little ahead of schedule a plane touched down and people alighted. The watching media disappeared to write their stories.

Cyril stayed put. I asked him why he wasn't moving.

'Nothing to report,' he said.

'But we saw the plane and Hammarskjöld arrive,' I said.

'You saw a plane arrive and a man who might be Hammarskjöld get off. But can you be certain?' he asked.

Even when he was being bullied by the newsdesk into confirming the story of the Secretary General's arrival because it was appearing in the opposition papers, Cyril refused to compromise, maintaining what they were printing was a rumour and not a fact. He was proved triumphantly right when it was discovered that the plane had crashed six miles from Ndola Airport and all on board had been killed.

Cyril Aynsley was one of the finest journalists of his generation and I count myself lucky to have worked with him. He was tough but courteous, punctilious in the way he researched and wrote his stories, a marvellous example to an imposter such as myself, which is how I felt when in his company.

Cyril went home and I travelled to Elizabethville where I found a room in the Leo Deux Hotel and met up with Dan McGeachie, a colleague on the *Daily Express*, and a *Daily Herald* journalist who was to become a lifelong friend, Jon Akass. McGeachie was a blond, rugged and fearless reporter who had already demonstrated the kind of man he was in a hotel bar in Ndola. We were sitting at a table having a drink when a black man and his family came tentatively into the room. It was a time when people were challenging the unofficial and unspoken apartheid of the era. As the white manager moved to throw them out, McGeachie stood and said, 'My dear friends. Thank you for coming. Please join us.' We sat and drank with people we had never met before, with McGeachie's direct stare challenging the manager to do something about it.

Jon Akass was also a good man, handsome with brooding good looks. One of the best all-rounders in Fleet Street, he was a marvellous writer.

Our hotel was the meeting place for Tshombe's mercenaries, about a hundred of them, almost exclusively European, who were employed to sit and await a war that might not happen. There were a few professional soldiers among them but the majority appeared to be social misfits who had seen too many war movies. One used to sit in the hotel bar juggling with two hand grenades. 'My presents for the United Nations,' he would say if anyone asked. At night the bar resembled the Last Chance Saloon in Dodge City.

Now and again one of the mercenaries would feel the need to fire his pistol into the ceiling. As the bar was situated beneath my bedroom I used to sleep in the cast-iron bath as a precaution. I was terrified of being shot in the arse. As I settled down at night in my armour-plated bunker, I felt sure Cyril Aynsley never did this, not to mention my other great hero, Ernest Hemingway. Moreover, it seemed to me that my diet in those days consisted mainly of United Nations accreditation passes.

Travelling outside Elizabethville meant being stopped at roadblocks set up by renegade soldiers, who were often whacked on drugs and would demand identification. They were mostly illiterate but able to recognise the United Nations passes because of their bold blue lettering. Possession was an excuse for a beating, so coming upon a roadblock I would eat my press card. My record was three in a day.

I swiftly came to the conclusion that, while I might have dreamed of a life as a war correspondent, I wasn't up to the job. It seemed to me I spent most of my time in a state of disorientation. I couldn't settle in the new surroundings. It was difficult to make sense of the situation I found myself in, and I was unable to focus on the job in hand. I filed just a couple of stories in three or four weeks and the office became restless. I decided to restore my reputation with a bold exclusive.

The chance came when I was talking to a pilot in the bar of the Leo Deux who said he could fly me up country to the border town of Kaniama where a state of emergency had been declared after skirmishes between Congolese troops and Katangese gendarmerie. This might be the end to all the posturing between the two sides and the start of the war. He would provide the necessary passes guaranteeing cooperation from the troops in the area and there would be two or three others in the plane but no other British journalists.

There was shooting as we landed about twenty kilometres from Kaniama, but it was sporadic and distant. It was a typical African airstrip – a skid mark in the bush with a few tin huts at one end. About a dozen gendarmerie sat around in the afternoon sun. They wore the standard combat jacket, camouflaged trousers and a variety of footwear ranging from plimsolls to climbing boots. They were all lance-corporals. There were no privates in Tshombe's army.

They watched us without much interest as we walked towards them across the tarmac. We said hello. No one stirred. In the distance there was the faint chatter of small arms fire. One of the soldiers reflectively picked his nose, another pushed his helmet farther back on his head with the business end of his automatic rifle. More silence. We didn't really worry. This was the old Katanga routine. The photographer in our party produced a box of cigarettes and proffered it to the nearest soldier who grabbed it, extracted a cigarette and put the box in his pocket. 'Passes?' he asked.

We produced them. The finest there were. Signed by General Moke, Commander-in-chief of the Katangese army. And in Swahili too. They described us as 'Friends of Katanga' and instructed all troops to give us every assistance. The smoking soldier looked at them dispassionately and handed them around his colleagues. Most of the soldiers held them upside down when reading them. They were handed back.

A soldier asked me for a cigarette. I handed him the packet. He put it in his pocket and grinned. I grinned back and said, 'We want to go to town to see what the fighting is like.' He kept grinning. The first soldier said, 'You will have to wait for the major.' We asked how long the major would be. He shrugged. It depended, he said. The major was bringing in some deserters and might take a long time about it. All the soldiers laughed at this, but it seemed a pretty obscure joke to us. We pointed out that our passes were signed by General Moke. And wasn't he the big boss, never mind the major?

'Big boss in Elizabethville, maybe. But here . . . ?' The soldier shrugged his shoulders.

There was nothing to do but wait, so we wandered around the airstrip. At the entrance there were two native policemen in their blue uniforms and white helmets. One of them was wearing suede winklepickers. But they seemed friendly and both spoke English. They told us they were Rhodesians who had joined the Katangese police force after independence.

One of them explained, 'Rhodesia no good for us. Katanga good. We bosses here. Katanga Number One.' He said the major would not be long. The deserters he was collecting had been arrested after they had done a bunk during the border fighting and tried to make it back to their villages. They were to be taken to the nearby army camp for punishment but the major had promised that he would first bring them to the airstrip so that his men could have a look at them.

It took the major another hour to arrive, but when he did it was in style. He sat in the front of a jeep, one leg negligently hanging over the side. He wore sunglasses and a neatly cut light-brown uniform. The back of the jeep seemed to contain a platoon of gendarmerie. The jeep stopped opposite us and we saw for the first time that the soldiers were guarding three very bruised and frightened-looking fellow soldiers who were hatless and had their arms bound behind them. The major watched, hand on hip, as the three deserters were hauled from the vehicle and thrown, face downwards, on the road. Their guards then started to beat them. Rifle butts were crashed into their necks, boots were planted again and again in their groins, they were hauled to their feet and smashed and clubbed to the floor by rifles and clenched fists. The major watched it all without emotion.

Our party stood by, rooted, helpless, except the photographer who slipped into the middle of the mob taking pictures.

And then the two policemen moved in. One of them drove his heel into the mouth of one of the prisoners and slowly and deliberately turned it through a full circle. The other contented himself by kicking all three prisoners about the head with his winklepickers. By this time the dozen gendarmerie we had met on the airstrip had joined in. I suppose that the beating lasted about five minutes. It seemed much longer. And the unreal terrifying thing about it was that throughout their ordeal the prisoners did not utter a sound of any sort. They just lay there in a dreadful awful silence.

The beating was stopped by kind permission of the major. He gave the command to put the prisoners in the jeep. They seemed unconscious. More likely they were dead. They were tossed on to the floor of the jeep and their guards piled in on top of them. The major slid into the front seat, arranged one leg nonchalantly over the side and drove away. There were spots of blood on his suede boots.

The two policemen rejoined us. Well, not all of us. The photographer was a little way away being sick against a tree. The policemen looked wild-eyed, flushed and excited. I asked what would happen to the prisoners. Winklepickers said, 'They will be taken to the camp for punishment.' What punishment? He grinned and drew a finger across his throat.

We left. There was nothing else to do.

Our pilot, who had been allowed into town, returned about this time. He later admitted he had a girlfriend in Kaniama. We began to suspect we had been conned, that we had paid for our pilot to have an afternoon in bed with his mistress. But we were all too traumatised and depressed by what we had witnessed to take him to task. We were late flying into Elizabethville and, as we approached the airport, I saw tracer curving out of the bush and over our plane. The locals were enjoying a bit of target practice.

About a week later I was at a party in Elizabethville and met a high-ranking officer in the Katangese police force. He was saying how well-behaved his men were and I couldn't resist telling him what I had seen.

He was unperturbed. 'They were deserters. They deserved their punishment,' he said.

I pointed out that no one deserved that kind of beating.

The officer, who was a little drunk, became angry. 'You are trying to tell us how to behave. I know how to behave as well as any of you people. I can prove it. Have you been in the Boy Scouts?'

I said no.

'Well I have. I was a Boy Scout and I know how to behave. Once I even went to a Scouts' jamboree in Birmingham,' he shouted.

It was a fitting epitaph to my time in the Congo, surreal and discomfiting. It had the virtue of convincing me that I would be happier in future interviewing beauty queens than reporting men being kicked to death. The problem was it would take a couple or so more wars for the people who employed me to cotton on.

17

DISENCHANTMENT

I wrote my 'exclusive' but it didn't appear. I wasn't told why. A week or two later I returned to London and went for a drink with Richard West, now working for an excellent magazine called *Time and Tide*. I recounted my adventure and he said I should write it for his periodical. I said the *Express* wouldn't allow it, he said the *Express* wouldn't know about it if I wrote under an assumed name. He said 'Warren Brady' sounded suitably hairy-chested and convincing for a war correspondent.

Mr Brady wrote a couple of articles for *Time and Tide*, as did Jack Braithwaite, another West invention, who wrote about life up north in Yorkshire. One day Jack Braithwaite received an offer from Brian Glanville, the journalist and author, then scouting for Secker & Warburg, to write a book about life in Yorkshire. We met in a suitably discreet bar away from Fleet Street where I confessed my duplicity. Later we became colleagues on *The Sunday Times* where I wrote a sports column about the heroes of my youth in a style first invented by Jack Braithwaite.

In the meantime things at the *Express* gave every indication I had been shunted into the feature writers' knacker's yard where you either used your spare time writing a novel or drank yourself silly. I chose the latter course. Every day I would turn up at the office, draw a fiver from petty cash, and head for El Vino's. There I would sit and await the call to duty. More often than not it never came, in which case I would wait for Poppins to open. Here I would cash a cheque and then give it all back in a boozy session.

I would catch a late train from Waterloo Station and hope to get off at Surbiton. The certainty of reaching my destination was somewhat diminished by my habit of falling into a deep sleep as soon as the train set in motion. More often than not I would awake in Portsmouth and have to catch the next train back. Once I fell asleep on the return journey and ended up back at Waterloo five hours after I had left it. On another occasion I awoke to the sound of seagulls and lapping waves. I thought I had been kidnapped and taken to a Russian submarine. In fact, the train had been shunted into a seaside siding at the end of its journey.

Worst of all, awakening as the train pulled into a station, I wiped the steamed window to find out where I was and all I saw was '—on'. I thought 'Surbiton'. In any event I opened the carriage door and fell onto the express line at Wimbledon. I was hauled to safety by a couple of railway employees and then visited by the railway police who, quite rightly, told me what a chump I had been before seeing me home.

Mary said if I was drinking because I was unhappy at the *Express* then I must leave and get another job. I said we were broke and that we had a small child and a large mortgage and that I didn't have a job to go to. But I knew she was right. I stayed a while longer. I volunteered for work in Manchester with the northern edition of the *Daily Express* and realised, every time I journeyed north, how much I missed that town.

Also it was the cricket season and I was pampered by the news desk, Keith Howard particularly, because I was needed to play in the needle match against the *Daily Mail*. The rivalry between the two newspapers was bitter and profound and the annual cricket match was as much a circulation war as a game. It was while playing for the *Daily Express* I met my great hero Keith Miller.

I had first seen him when I was ten and he came to England with the Australian Services team. He was tall, broad-shouldered, dark-haired and Hollywood handsome. He hit sixes, bowled like the wind and caught swallows. I was smitten. When I met him at the *Express* he had retired from cricket and was employed to write about the game. He was a reluctant member of our team.

He didn't like playing what he defined as 'comic cricket', nor did he like taking candy from children, a fact he had amply demonstrated in times past. Playing for Bradman's team against Essex in 1948, he walked to the wicket with Australia well on the way to a final total of 721, let the first ball he received hit his stumps and departed the field with the parting shot, 'Thank God that's over.' His captain, Bradman, was not pleased. Bradman and Miller didn't get on. It could have been the rumour that Bradman, lately signed by the *Daily Mail*, might turn out for them that enticed Miller to play for the *Express*.

The game allowed me the chance to stand next to my hero as we fielded against the *Mail*. He was at first slip and I was at second. I noticed a man near the sightscreen semaphoring Keith. This went on for an over or two before I asked my hero what was going on.

'He's a mate. He's signalling the winners at Wincanton,' he explained. Keith Miller liked a bet.

Ten minutes later, with the semaphore man still active, the *Mail* batsman snicked a fast ball, which flew towards my right hand. I wasn't a bad fielder in those days, before the reflexes became dulled, and as I started to move, there was a flash across my body as Miller threw himself full length and took an extraordinary catch, ending up in front of the third slip. As he caught the ball, he rolled over, handed it to me and said, 'I wonder what won the two thirty.'

We beat the *Mail* and our next game was against the *Daily Mirror*. Miller was excluded from the team on the grounds that no one cared if we won or lost against the *Mirror*. We won, and I scored a century. I calculated I could stay until retirement at the *Express*, providing Keith Howard didn't move and I didn't lose form. In fact, my final game for the *Express* was played in Manchester against the *Daily Mail* XI, which, I seem to remember, contained several Lancashire players plus a very aggressive quick bowler with a nasty temper called Don Mosey. Don later became a cricket commentator for the BBC and was affectionately known by Brian Johnston as 'The Alderman'.

Back in the office I began to feel more and more like a spectator than a participant. In the features department there was much to occupy my attention, including our latest acquisition, John Braine. The author of *Room at the Top* had become one of the most famous literary figures in Britain. The *Express* employed him to write film reviews and gave him a seat next to me.

John Braine seemed to me like the Mad Hatter in *Alice in Wonderland*, living in a state of perpetual panic. He wrote his reviews in longhand in a school exercise book and endeavoured to eliminate the noise of a busy office by stuffing his ears with long strips of cotton wool that dangled on to his shoulder pads like fluffy icicles. His writing was laboured and slow and he paid little heed to deadlines. I remember an exasperated Harold Keble admonishing him with the line, 'You are writing a review of a bloody film not *Room at the Top* volume two.'

On the other side of the desk Bernard Levin wrote about the theatre, Nancy Spain about television, Herbert Kretzmer, who later gained international fame as a lyricist, wrote elegantly and wittily about anything, and in the midst of it all sat Osbert Lancaster, painstakingly recording the doings of Maudie Littlehampton and her tribe, in between visits to his club. In the entire two years or so I spent at the *Express* I never spoke a word to Osbert. He never even acknowledged I was there. Some time later I bought a drawing of a costume design he created for a production of *Lucia di Lammermoor*, as a reminder of the silence between us.

The end came when I was sent to cover a train crash in which several people had been killed. When I reached the scene I called the office and asked them how much they wanted. There was a long silence and then I was told that actually, old boy, what we would like you to do is set up a couple of the victims' relatives to be interviewed by Godfrey Winn. This instruction was not an uncommon one to *Express* journalists.

Godfrey Winn wrote excruciating sob articles popular with women readers. He was hated by everyone who worked at the *Express*. Bob Edwards, in his book *Goodbye Fleet Street*, wrote: 'The news desk, from the news editor to the lowliest reporter, loathed it when Godfrey Winn was sent on a big story.' I told the newsdesk I was not employed to be his gofer and refused the job.

The next day I went into the office and told them I was leaving. It neither surprised nor bothered them. The editor was demonstrating how to drink from a *porron*, a Spanish wine decanter from which you pour wine from a height into your mouth. The wine had spilled on to his hair and down his shirt front. It was my last image of the *Daily Express* and Fleet Street.

I went home and told Mary.

'Where now?' she said in her wonderful unflappable way.

'No idea,' I said, and I hadn't.

Tony Howard heard the news and called me. He was friendly with an up and coming entrepreneur called Michael Heseltine who, along with his partner, Clive Labovitch, had bought a magazine called *Man About Town*. They were about to give it a makeover. Nick Tomalin, a journalist I had briefly met in a Fleet Street pub, was to be the editor. Why didn't I give him a call?

Which is how I came to work for Michael Heseltine. The office was above a supermarket on the Edgware Road. I was the features editor and gave myself all the best jobs. I interviewed Ursula Andress in bed. She was in bed, I wasn't. It was the sixties. We were young and daft and carefree and out of that volatile mix we created a magazine that became recognised as one of the most influential style magazines of them all.

Much of the success was due to the diminutive, seemingly perpetually grumpy art director, Tom Wolsey, who gave the magazine an appearance so beguiling it made you want to stroke it. Next, Michael and Clive bought *Topic* magazine, which was described as Britain's answer to *Newsweek* and *Time*. Oh yeah! They brought in Clive Irving (with whom I had worked on the *Daily Express*) as editor. I was his deputy. Clive was a brilliant editor. He did the hard and often inspired editorial grind with two other splendid journalists, Jeremy Wallington and Ron Hall. I looked after the columnists and soon rounded up a talented and convivial bunch, among them Ronnie Scott, which gave me entry to his club and the music I adored.

Ronnie became a friend but an elusive columnist. I had to organise search parties to find him on the day he was meant to deliver his column. More often than not he'd be found at some card game and his eight hundred words would be written, during a game of poker, on paper napkins, beer mats, backs of envelopes. On one famous occasion he rang me from a game, asking me to give him an advance on his wages to fund 'a winning streak'. I did so and some time later sent a messenger to collect his copy, bearing a note from me saying: 'How goes the winning streak?' The messenger returned, minus the article but with a note from Ronnie saying: 'Winning streak going well. Send more money.'

Topic didn't last long. It went bust. It didn't spell disaster for Michael Heseltine because it wasn't his money. He went on to a life in politics and a career as a very successful businessman.

Nick Tomalin joined *The Sunday Times* and proved himself a journalist of great courage and distinction. He was killed by a sniper on the Golan Heights on the border of Israel and Syria in the Yom Kippur war of 1973. I still see his lopsided grin. I miss him to this very day. Clive Irving took Jeremy and Ron to *The Sunday Times* where, under that brave crusading editor Harold Evans, they set up an investigative unit called 'Insight' and revolutionised the manner in which newspapers unearthed the big stories.

Perhaps its greatest triumph was in unmasking the thalidomide scandal, one of the few times it made you proud of being a journalist. Clive asked me to join him but I'd been hearing the Hovis tune again and fancied going back up north. I imagined editing an old-fashioned weekly, the kind with small ads on the front page. I would join the Rotary Club, buy a Labrador and take lung-filling walks across Ilkley Moor.

In fact what happened was I received a call from Barrie Heads, then an executive producer at Granada Television. We had met when I was covering a Labour Party Conference during my time on the *Manchester Guardian*. He was looking for a producer to work on local programmes and rang to see if I was interested.

'But I don't know anything about producing television,' I said.

'Nor do we,' he said, with a laugh.

I was hooked and on my way.

18

GRANADALAND

When you walked through the door into Granada Television in Cross Street, Manchester you felt the place was special, certainly different from the other media temples I had worked in. The main reception area was dominated by a large compelling painting by Francis Bacon, the canteen illuminated with a challenging mural by John Bratby. In every office hung a portrait of P.J. Barnum, the American circus-owner, as a reminder that we might be journalists, but never forget the razzle-dazzle.

Everything bore the stamp of Sidney Bernstein, the socialist millionaire who founded the company with his brother Cecil. It is said that when deciding to apply for an ITV franchise, Sidney studied a map of Britain, checked the rainfall figures and chose the area that came to be known as Granadaland because it had a large population in a part of the kingdom where it rained most of the time. It was still in its infancy when I arrived but already had a reputation as a troublesome child.

The late David Plowright, with whom I was to work and who later became head of Granada, once described the company as 'the most innovative, self-opinionated, insufferably arrogant television company of the lot'.

Another colleague, Brian Armstrong, who spent thirty-seven

years at Granada, summed it up best of all. Brian said Granada was like a 'large, sprawling, vexatious family always biffing each other on the nose, but if anyone comes from outside and says anything about them they get a whack'. It was quite unlike any organisation I had worked for before, or since.

In the early days only ten per cent of the programme-makers at Granada had any previous experience of telly. The rest of us, mainly recruited from newspapers, learned as we went along. The pervading atmosphere was one of creative anarchy. We didn't have long and boring meetings talking about the meaning of programmes. We started with a running order, wrote a script, hired a front man, pointed a camera at him and hoped for the best.

Barrie Heads, who had hired me and had worked for the *Yorkshire Post*, said he wanted me to produce a five nights a week live show called *Scene at 6.30*. It came under the auspices of local programming but he asked us to pretend we had never heard the word. He wanted a programme to match the changing mood of the time, to be irreverent and funny and seditious.

We hired good writers, including Peter Eckersley, who went on to become Granada's Head of Drama, and Arthur Hopcraft, who first displayed his talents as a playwright at Granada.

Leslie Woodhead, who pioneered television drama documentaries, revealed his formidable talent as writer, producer and director on the show. Young men fresh from university, including Michael Apted and Mike Newell, cut their teeth on *Scene at 6.30*. They both went to Hollywood, Apted directing *The Coalminer's Daughter*, *Gorillas in the Mist*, *Enigma* and the Bond movie, *The World is not Enough*. Newell directed *Four Weddings and a Funeral*, *Donnie Brasco*, *Pushing Tin* and *Harry Potter and the Goblet of Fire*.

Fronting the programme were Mike Scott, who went on to become Granada's Programme Controller, Gaye Byrne, who hosted the best talk show I have ever been a guest on, *The Late, Late Show*, which ran in Ireland for thirty-seven years, and the formidable Bill Grundy.

Bill, who sadly is best remembered as the man who presided over a notorious television occasion when the Sex Pistols reacted to his lack of enthusiasm for their music with four-letter words, was a difficult man to keep sober but not to produce. He was one of the best front men I ever worked with and I always believed that when Richard Dimbleby died Grundy was the one who should have taken his place on *Panorama*. At his best he was a superb forensic interviewer. He was intelligent, formidably well read, always well briefed and fearless. Sadly, as his career drifted, he let drink overwhelm his personality. But he taught me much about appearing in front of camera.

As the show progressed and became a very successful part, not just of Granada's programming, but of its persona, we took the decision to let those of the production team who could write and produce material and who fancied their chances in front of camera have a go – which is how I made my debut as a front man. Not being stupid, and being the producer, I fixed it so I went on air with Bill Grundy. He took me to one side and told me to look at the camera and pretend I was telling a story to Mary. He advised me to lean into camera as if engaging it in conversation, and to slow everything down because the inevitable adrenalin surge brought about by a debut and live television would certainly make me gabble.

Then he said, 'But most of all remember, if there is a cock-up, just look pleadingly in my direction.'

I got away with it. I reached the end of the show without fainting or making a fool of myself and, as the end credits rolled, I started to leave my seat heading for a large drink. Grundy stopped me. 'You have forgotten something,' he said.

'What's that?' I asked.

'Say thank you to the studio,' he said.

It was probably the most important lesson I ever learned in all my years of television. It is easy to ignore the guys behind the cameras, in lighting, or sound, the whole army of people responsible for getting you on air. If you do, they simply shrug and think there goes another performer with his head stuck up his bum. But if you thank them for making the show run smoothly, they become part of your team. We needed all the cooperation we could muster in those distant and daft days.

The notion of the television all-rounder reached its apotheosis with the creation of Granada in the North. This was a device to further Sidney Bernstein's idea of Granadaland as a separate kingdom whose inhabitants tuned in to only one television channel, watched movies at Granada cinemas and, when they ate out, did so at Granada motorway cafés. At one time there was a rumour that Sidney intended issuing passports to be shown at motorway checkpoints to allow access to his domain.

The idea of Granada in the North was that each night, when early evening broadcasting began, one of us would pop up on screen with a headline of news and then a summation of the evening's programming. We were like on-air station announcers, except every appearance was preceded by the Granada symbol, so even if a programme came from ATV it looked as though it belonged to Granada. At the end of the evening, round about eleven o'clock, we finished the day with a ten-minute late-night magazine programme. This was done from an unmanned studio, which is to say one with a locked-off camera but no cameraman.

On duty, the trick was to avoid too many visits to the New Theatre Inn, the local Granada pub, better known as Studio 3. (If anyone phoned your secretary, she would say, 'He's busy in Studio 3.') This particular night Bill was on Granada in the North duty and I was drinking in the pub with Johnnie Hamp, who produced the nightly music spot on *Scene at 6.30*. Bill kept bobbing in and out of the pub and, as the night progressed, became more and more drunk. We tried to dissuade him from making the last appearance for the late-night sign-off.

I offered to do the show, so did John, but with that unshakeable belief drunks have in their own sobriety, Bill insisted on going back to the studio. We went upstairs in the pub to watch the programme.

When it came on air all the camera showed was an empty desk with a hand on top as if its owner was looking underneath for something that had fallen onto the floor, like a script. The language coming from beneath the desk indicated the search was not going well and that the searcher was getting increasingly fed up with looking. Eventually, after two or three minutes of worsening language, a sign came up saying: 'Normal Transmission Will Resume As Soon As Possible. We Apologise For The Fault.'

An even more spectacular cock-up was produced by another old friend of mine from Fleet Street days, Denis Pitts. Denis was an accomplished journalist we hired to look after our London bookings. He proved to be a crafty operator whose Fleet Street habits sometimes did not meet with the approval of the Granada accounts department. He was once challenged on a mileage claim for a car trip from London to Brighton and return. The accountant said that after the most careful scrutiny he could prove that the claim was at least eighteen miles too much.

'Ah,' said Denis, 'but did you take into account reversing.'

He had done some interviewing in our London studio and now felt it was time to take on Granada in the North. I sat him down and told him to keep it simple. This was his debut, so eliminate all those ideas that might get him into trouble, such as overcrowding the studio or relying on film and tape inserts, which could break down leaving the worst of all scenarios, time to fill and nothing to fill it with.

That night I switched on to see if Denis had taken my advice. He had not. He announced his studio guests including a hairdresser from Rochdale, who had won a national award, and two of his models, a man who collected toy soldiers along with the pride and joy of his collection, a film about Spitfires, and, best of all, a lion-tamer from a local circus with his lion.

From the start things did not go well. The model girls were frightened by the animal and knocked over the display of model soldiers, causing their owner to have a row with the lion-tamer. With this happening over his shoulder, Denis tried to move into the studio behind him, forgetting he was attached to the desk by a neck mike. As he tried to move smoothly towards the engulfing chaos he was jerked backwards by the cord like a man who had been shot. He ended up draped over the back of his chair. From this position, and while attempting to unwrap the microphone cord, which was threatening to garrotte him, he decided to introduce the film about Spitfires. The film came up but without sound. As the Spitfires won the Battle of Britain, the only noises we could hear were model girls shrieking, a lion rumbling and its keeper arguing with a hairdresser.

When we returned to the studio it had been cleared of everyone except Denis who by now had a weal around his neck and looked like a failed suicide. He signed off with the epic line: 'We hope you enjoyed the show. Goodnight.' It marked the end of Denis's career on camera and almost the end of Granada in the North.

Scene at 6.30 was, however, unstoppable. The greater part of its success was due to the nightly music spot booked by Johnnie Hamp. Johnnie had already found the Beatles and given them their first chance on television. Ever after, as hit followed hit, they appeared on the show. They became our resident group. Along with an inspired director, Phil Casson, Johnnie produced the first Beatles solo television show. The Animals, then unknown, did the studio warm-up. We followed the Beatles from their modest start, when Paul McCartney asked me for my autograph for his mum, to the frenzied beginnings of Beatlemania.

Johnnie had a shrewd eye for new talent. One day he called from London and said he had seen a great band that was going to be massive – the Rolling Stones. They arrived at the studio and rehearsed. Barrie Heads, our executive producer was a Bing Crosby kind of man and sometimes curmudgeonly. He called me and said he didn't like their music or the cut of their jibs. Pay them off. Johnnie pointed out we had nothing to put in their place. In those days we didn't hang on to video tapes, we simply recorded over them. Reluctantly, Barrie relented, and only because we had nothing to replace them, and the Stones made their television debut.

Many years later Bill Wyman gave me a copy of the contract I had signed. On their very first appearance I also interviewed Mick Jagger. It was a wonderful piece of stilted chat. I asked how long he thought the band might last and he said maybe a couple of years. He sounded quite posh at the time. I looked constipated. It became a tiny segment in Martin Scorsese's documentary about the Stones, so when people ask me what else I did apart from telly, I always say I was in a movie made by the director of *Taxi Driver*.

19

A SPOT OF TROUBLE IN ZANZIBAR

In between the laughter and the cock-ups and the visits to Studio 3 we worked hard and produced a variety of programmes. We created a weekly jazz programme hosted by Benny Green, a show about art with Harold Riley, and a medical programme with Michael (later Lord) Winstanley, a natural television performer who could talk the leg off an iron pot.

We were all expected from time to time to produce *What the Papers Say*, a nightmare in those days of live television because it was fifteen minutes of script tightly linked to captions. The autocue of the sixties was not the sophisticated machine of today. It looked like a roll of bog paper and, to continue the comparison, often tore as if perforated. Then all the producer could do was hope the performer was up to it, which is why we all wanted to work with Brian Inglis or Bernard Levin.

Bernard had a photographic memory, as he proved one night when, three minutes into his script, the autocue failed and with only the faintest of pauses he continued from memory. He performed the script well enough for it to match nearly all the cues. He was a prickly, combative man who always seemed to be hurrying between confrontations without time or inclination for pleasantries. That said, I liked him a lot and we muddled along in a style pleasant enough for me to imagine a friendly response when I asked him to contribute to a charity book I was compiling.

The idea was to replicate an old Victorian visitors' book, which had a list of innocuous questions – Favourite Flower, Favourite Book, Favourite Quotation etc – for the guest to fill in. I wrote to Bernard asking him to be one of my celebrity guests. He replied, by return: 'Dear Michael. Thank you for your kind invitation. Upon mature reflection I think I would rather be dead. Yours, Bernard.'

Brian Inglis was a most beguiling man. He had an enviable grace of manner and a quiet humour that made him an irresistible companion to both men and women.

He was deputy editor of *The Spectator* in 1956 when he wrote and presented the very first edition of *What the Papers Say*. He went on to appear in another 160 editions over the next twenty years, and he became a television celebrity – a description he would have scorned – by presenting *All Our Yesterdays* for eleven years. Brian was both the complement and the antidote to the brash and aggressive side of the Granada personality, which the younger journalists like to think they invented.

In fact, they took their lead from an audacious Australian called Tim Hewat. Tim had been northern editor of the *Daily Express* before moving to Granada, and he quickly established a reputation as an innovative and imaginative creator of current-affairs programmes. He had the idea of following the Aldermaston March with multi-camera crews, editing the film overnight and producing within twenty-four hours a fascinating filmed account of the event. It had never been done before. He formed *World In*

Action, a revolutionary concept in that he eliminated the on-camera reporter and relied instead on good pictures and a vigorous script.

He was big and brash, a man who asked you a question and then looked away as if he already knew the answer. Derek Grainger, who worked at Granada in these early days and who was a perceptive chronicler of people and events, describes him as 'the ultimate hairy ape'. If Brian Inglis was the charming, diplomatic face of Granada, Tim Hewat was the battering ram.

Many years after I had left Granada I went to Australia to work for the Australian Broadcasting Commission. I called Tim, who by this time had retired to a farm near Melbourne. We had not met for ten years or more and he came to my hotel for a drink. In my room he spied the list of questions for the talk show I was to record the next day. Without being invited he picked it up and began reading. He threw it down and said, 'Crap.' He wasn't being unpleasant and I wasn't upset. I knew that in Tim Hewat's world the only way to tell a story was his way. In other words he wasn't being unpleasant, merely himself.

It was Tim who revived my career as a war correspondent. I was called in one day and told that, as a reward for all my hard work on *Scene at 6.30* and the rest, I was to be given a working holiday in Turkey.

This entailed filming in Istanbul and Ankara to get the Turkish side of the civil war in Cyprus. Shouldn't take long, Tim said, then I could spend a few days relaxing in Istanbul, looking at the Bosphorus. He introduced me to my cameraman, a twenty-two-year-old newcomer to *World In Action*, Chris Menges. Chris was a quiet, seemingly shy young man with an almost diffident manner, yet a fearless operator who went on to become one of the great

Hollywood cinematographers. He made his name with *Kes* and won Oscars for *The Killing Fields* and *The Mission*.

We soon concluded our filming in Turkey and I was contemplating my holiday when Tim Hewat rang. 'Bit of trouble in Cyprus. Get over there as quickly as you can,' he said. We filmed for a few days and I went to the airport to send our report back to the office. In those days you couldn't bounce the report in by satellite. You had to doorstep BA pilots and crew and ask if they would take the film back to England.

Having completed this transaction, I was plotting ways of recommencing my holiday when I received another phone call from Tim Hewat. Trouble in Zanzibar. An uprising. Get there immediately.

I said, 'Do you have any idea how far Cyprus is from Zanzibar?'

Tim Hewat replied, without pause, 'I have just measured it on a map and it's only a couple of inches.'

We eventually arrived in Dar es Salaam, in what was then Tanganyika, to be told that the island of Zanzibar had been closed to the world. We went to what we were assured was the local press club and there encountered a young and worryingly bleary eyed Australian pilot who said he would fly us into Zanzibar but wouldn't stop. This meant he would taxi on the runway long enough for us to hop off and then he would make his getaway. Which explains how we came to be standing on the tarmac at Zanzibar Airport, surrounded by soldiers in combat uniform and blue peaked hats who were not pleased to see us.

We were arrested, taken to a hotel and incarcerated in the bar, along with one or two other journalists who had sneaked into the country, including one who had hired a dhow and had swum the last mile or two through shark-infested waters.

They kept us locked up for a day or two until I managed to negotiate permission to film the aftermath of the revolution, which meant being closely escorted by a military guard. The soldiers were sullen and suspicious with us, hostile and brutal to the prisoners we tried to film in a barbed-wire compound.

After twenty-four hours we were put in the back of a jeep and driven through a cemetery, past freshly dug graves, before being taken down to the port where a Royal Navy ship had arrived to take away British nationals caught up in the revolution. We sailed to the mainland under a magnificent African sky illuminated by the biggest, brightest stars I have ever seen. We slept on deck and, as we dipped deep to Mombasa, watched a Doris Day movie on a white sheet the crew had rigged over a clothes line. We hired a plane, flew down the Rift Valley to Nairobi, and caught a flight to London where I was interviewed by ITN News as the first journalist out of Zanzibar.

When I got back to Granada I was met by Tim Hewat who asked if I had enjoyed my holiday.

The managing director, Sir Denis Forman, said he had seen me on the ITN News and maybe I should think about a career in front of camera. The idea was I should front Hewat's new programme *The World Tonight*. Correspondents from all over the world would broadcast live into a studio set-up where the presenter would be found in front of a collection of clocks each depicting a different time zone. With the satellite technology of today, it might have been a good idea. In the sixties, with the industry in the Stone Age, I looked like a man standing in front of a lot of clocks doing a radio programme. The programme was never made, which in those days wasn't regarded as a disaster. It simply meant we invented a replacement.

What made Granada such an exciting company to work for was

that it didn't dwell on failure. Moreover it discouraged analysis as to why a programme didn't work and regarded looking back as a waste of time. It ploughed on, like the pioneer it was, constantly exploring the limits of the new and exhilarating business of television. Barrie Heads and David Plowright were encouraging facilitators but there is no doubt the gentle but firm hand steering the company belonged to Sir Denis Forman.

He carried with him an unruffled authority. He had been a major in the Royal Kents and fought in one of the bloodiest battles of World War Two at Monte Cassino. His lower left leg was shattered and amputated below the knee. He was part of a remarkable generation that survived a bloody war, had witnessed its horrors and knew something we didn't. What that generation experienced shaped their lives ever after and gave them a sense of priority, a balance, which made them rounded and fully fledged human beings.

As a newcomer, I had been invited to dinner with the bosses in the Penthouse, on the top floor of the Manchester studios. I was given a place at Sir Denis's side. At the end of the first course I felt a foot on mine and the application of gentle pressure. Was this some kind of Granada ritual, a test perhaps? This was, after all, the company created by Sidney Bernstein, a man whose list of people banned from appearing on his television station included men with beards and those wearing pocket handkerchieves or bow ties.

The pressure continued, applied more heavily until I was in such pain I wrenched my foot clear. I looked at my host who seemed totally unaware. I sought guidance from David Plowright who was sitting next to me. I whispered what had happened.

'I think the boss is playing footsie with me,' I said.

'You daft bugger, he's trying to find the bell press on the floor to tell the butler to bring the next course,' he said.

I decided I would stay at Granada.

A couple of years later I celebrated my thirtieth birthday with a hangover. I can't remember the event but according to Leslie Woodhead I arrived in the office wearing dark glasses and looking unwell.

'For God's sake what's up?' Leslie said.

'It's my thirtieth birthday. Life is over,' I said.

If we eliminate the depressing effect of alcohol on the human personality, there was substance to my statement. I was beginning to feel restless. It started when I took a call one day from Donald Baverstock, who was producing the BBC's *Tonight* programme. This was the one BBC programme we all admired. Everyone who worked on *Scene at 6.30* looked with admiration and envy at its sleek style, particularly at its stable of wonderful reporters, including the incomparable Alan Whicker, Kenneth Allsop, Trevor Philpot and the blessed Fyfe Robertson.

Baverstock came straight to the point. This was a courtesy call to inform me he intended to approach Peter Eckersley and invite him to join *Tonight* as a reporter. I told him I couldn't stop him but we would be reluctant to lose Peter. When I informed Peter of the impending offer, he asked me what he should do. 'Bite their bloody hand off,' I said.

I had no doubt he would have been brilliant on the programme. He gave the world an irreverent sidelong glance, wrote beautifully and had an attractive studio manner. In the end he decided against going and went on to become head of drama before dying from cancer in 1981 aged forty-six. He was one of those human beings who, as you remember him, you find yourself smiling at the memory. His friend Jack Rosenthal told a story at Peter's funeral, which summed him up. Jack said he visited Peter in hospital when he was dying and, at the end of the visit, asked his friend if there was anything he could get him. Peter beckoned him close and whispered, 'There's a lovely blue handbag in Kendal Milnes I've had my eye on.'

After Baverstock's call, delighted though I was for Peter and happy my judgment had been confirmed, because I had persuaded him to join Granada, I also felt envious and angry at the BBC. I asked myself why they hadn't chosen me, why I wasn't invited to join *Tonight*. I make no excuse for this selfish reaction except to say ambition often tramples on decent manners.

On the face of it I had everything I ever needed at Granada. The work was fascinating; I had never worked with such a talented and agreeable collection of people. We had just bought our first house in Cheshire. Nicholas, our second son, had been born in a hospital in Knutsford, much to the annoyance of my father, who had failed this time in his attempt to kidnap Mary and take her to Yorkshire. He was only slightly comforted by the thought that at least the baby had been born in Cheshire and not Lancashire. Had that happened, I would have considered keeping the birth a secret from him. Moreover I had just been asked by Harold Evans, a journalist I had known on the *Manchester Evening News*, now newly arrived at *The Sunday Times*, if I would write a regular column about sport. It was the start of an entirely new career, which sustained and delighted me for the next forty years.

It gave me an excuse, as if I needed it, to spend more time at Old Trafford and develop a blossoming relationship with Sir Matt Busby and a young footballer who was to prove one of the greatest there has ever been, George Best. My relationship with Manchester United started when Tommy Taylor, a gifted centre forward whom I watched at Barnsley, was transferred there. Busby knew what he was doing. The young raw talent was transformed into an international player of real quality. Then came the Munich air crash and Tommy was one who perished.

I reported the first game Manchester United played after Munich. It was against Sheffield Wednesday and the makeshift team, held together by a veteran maestro called Ernie Taylor, began a revival that formed an imperishable bond between the club and anyone fortunate enough to witness it. The *Guardian* reporter said, 'Tonight a Phoenix took flight.'

Then I saw George Best's first game for Manchester United. Matt had told us to watch out for something special but none of us was prepared for what we saw. West Bromwich Albion was the opposition, Graham Williams, a nuggety Welsh international full back, marking George. I wrote at the time that Best had the physique of a toothpick, but the heart of a bull terrier. He beat Williams every way up and celebrated his domination by pushing the ball through the full back's legs, nutmegging him. Because of this display of showboating, Graham Williams was in a mood seriously to foreshorten Best's career. Sir Matt wisely removed him at half-time.

Many years later I was with George when Mr Williams approached. 'Do me a favour George and stand still so I can see your face,' he said.

George asked why.

'Because all I ever saw of you when we played against you was your arse disappearing down the touchline,' he replied.

We filmed a story about George, telling of a young soccer player living in digs, with ten sackloads of unopened fan mail threatening to damage the floor of his bedroom. It was the birth of the 'Fifth Beatle', star of that well-known musical *Orgy and Best*, the 'First Rock 'n' Roll Footballer' and, even as we celebrated his arrival with cheesy headlines, we had no idea where it would lead. We simply rejoiced, without a thought of the sadness to come. It was not a time to be solemn about anything. Didn't I have the best job in the world?

My television fame gave me the recognition that opens doors. I soon learned the trick was to enjoy the moment but never be seduced by it. It helped having been a producer in that I knew the disparaging things people said in the control room about performers. When you know that, you tend not to get too big-headed. I was also just one of a glut of famous faces. Granada in the North had given all my colleagues an experience of that moment when you are recognised, so no one was allowed to feel special or singled out.

Where else could I eat in a canteen with Annie Walker and Ena Sharples and then move to my studio to hear a young Dionne Warwick sing songs by a brace of promising new composers – Burt Bacharach and Hal David – or meet Nina Simone, Sarah Vaughan, The Hollies, Dizzy Gillespie, Dusty Springfield and Kenny Lynch, then, as now, our most swinging singer.

At that time, Pat Phoenix, who played Elsie Tanner in *Coronation Street*, was the most famous and desired woman in Britain. Elsie was the fantasy figure for any man who ever fell in love with a barmaid. Nearly twenty million people watched *Coronation Street* in those days but the salaries paid to the cast bore no relation to the show's commercial worth to Granada. Still don't. I remember Mary and I having dinner with Pat in her cottage as she bellyached about Granada's stinginess. She said the cast was expected to open Granada TV shops, a task she found particularly irksome, especially since the actors didn't receive a fee for so doing.

'They must give you something,' I said.

'Come upstairs and I'll show you,' she said.

Dame Edith Evans, another example of growing old fearlessly.

Sir Ralph Richardson was unpredictable and unmanageable. He was also magical and irreplaceable.

Catherine Bramwell-Booth was ninety-six when I interviewed her. She had just won the Speaker of the Year award. An inspiration and a joy.

Trying to look like a hard-nosed hack in the 1960s.

Early days at Granada. I was a producer – presenter Mike Scott thinks that's pretty funny.

The start of *Tea Break* at Thames TV. The cast included (*back row, left to right*) Rita Dando and Mary Parkinson, and (*front row*) Mavis Nicholson, Sylvia Duncan and Jill Tweedie.

The first ever *Parkinson* show. Terry-Thomas was the star guest.

John and Yoko in the very first series of *Parkinson*.

Mary was a fearless interviewer. Watching her in action and not knowing she was my wife, one guest said to me, 'I'd hate to be married to her.' Actually, it hasn't been so bad.

Taken shortly after I was voted Best Dressed Man on Radio 2.

Happy families in the days when young men wore neckwear to match the curtains.

Fashion model Mary P.

Back from holiday in America. The hat reveals why I almost never wear them.

At the time, we thought we looked fab!

The 'Famous Five' celebrating before the roof fell in.

Paul Newman in racing mode for a documentary made for Australian TV. Producer David Lyle (on Newman's left) was one of the reasons I enjoyed Australia as much as I did.

Tom and Annie Yeardye and Adam Faith, relaxing poolside at the Beverley Hills Hotel.

Left: A meeting with the Iron Lady at No. 10.

Below: The interview with Tony Blair made the headlines.

In the attic she revealed a stack of TV sets. It looked like the storeroom of a Granada shop.

'Another bloody telly, that's what we get,' she said.

It was the best of times, but I was edgy.

Then, in the course of one week, I received two phone calls that changed the course of my career. The first was from Desmond Wilcox, the reporter I had worked with on *ABC of the North*.

He had been making a name for himself as a current-affairs producer at the BBC in Manchester and was about to produce a new programme, *Man Alive*. Would I be interested?

Next I was called by Paul Fox, then head of current affairs at the BBC. He wondered if I would like to meet with Derrick Amoore, producer of another new show, *24 Hours*, to discuss maybe joining as a reporter. The front men were Cliff Michelmore and Kenneth Allsopp. The team included Fyfe Robertson, Julian Pettifer and Trevor Philpot.

I thanked Desmond Wilcox and agreed to meet the *24 Hours* people. At Lime Grove I had a long and boozy lunch with Paul and Derrick and they offered me a job. I was excited but terrified. This was a different league and I wondered if I might be inadequate to the demands. As it turned out my fears were well founded, but it took a while to find out.

In the meantime, I was exhilarated at the thought of working with my heroes. It meant moving to London. Mary, with her customary patient acceptance of disruption and change, made things easy for me.

My bosses at Granada were not happy. Sir Denis Forman talked me through my decision to leave with his customary easy charm until I told him that, much as I loved Granada, nothing they could offer would make me stay. Such was the family feel at Granada in those days I genuinely felt a bit of a heel, as if telling my parents I wanted to leave home. I was therefore not surprised when Sir Denis told me that people who left the company were, generally speaking, not welcomed back.

On the other hand, Cecil Bernstein took me into his office and said he would keep a light burning in the window for me. That's exactly what he said. Sentimental, maybe, but I have never forgotten his kindness.

So I was off, but I would return.

20

THE SIX DAY WAR

When asked to sum up my stint on *24 Hours*, Sir Paul Fox, the man who gave me the job, said he thought I was 'a lazy bugger'. It was one way of explaining my output for the programme, which, in the eighteen months I was there, was as meagre as it was unremarkable. I was never comfortable on the programme. I didn't feel I belonged. All the old insecurities about not being able to step up to the level set by the reporters on *24 Hours* induced a kind of nervous paralysis. It didn't help most of them were heroes of mine. I felt fraudulent.

My colleagues could not have been kinder or more supportive. Working with Cliff Michelmore and Kenneth Allsop in the studio was to watch two supreme stylists at work. It was obvious, however, they were not bosom buddies. There was a strained atmosphere in the office created by their mutual antipathy. Ken was a fastidious man who chose his company carefully. He could appear remote and indifferent, snobbish even. A journalist and author of great intellectual clarity, he enjoyed television but only, I suspect, because it gave him the means to be an independent author. By comparison Cliff was jolly in a blustery kind of way, savouring his reputation as the programme's front man, delighting in his renown as a consummate broadcaster. Cliff is still alive, still vigorous at the age of eighty-seven, one of the great broadcasters of our time.

151

Kenneth died of an accidental overdose, aged fifty-four, in 1974. He took powerful painkillers to reduce the constant and severe pain caused by having a leg amputated because of tuberculosis during the war. Or did he lose the leg in a plane crash? The mystery of how Ken lost his limb added to what can only be described as his enigmatic magnetism. Men admired him, women were captivated by him. Mary thought him one of the sexiest men she had ever met. We met for dinner and he turned up in a black cloak, causing a pause in conversational babble when he entered the restaurant. The limp became part of the allure.

At the inquest into his death it was reported that a book of Dorothy Parker's collected works was found beside the body. Two passages were underlined: 'There is nothing good in life that will not be taken away' and 'Mrs Parker can find no other means of dealing with the pain of being.'

It was fascinating observing Cliff and Kenneth at work preparing for a programme. Kenneth would take the research and the suggested link and worry it to death. He would work and rework the material until he had the interview clear in his mind. Cliff, on the other hand, skimmed the research, and concentrated on writing notes in the margin of the running order. One day I asked him what it was he was writing.

'I'm looking at the running order to spot where there might be a breakdown, and when I find it I write my ad libs,' he said, which is why he was unflappable when things went wrong, as they often did.

The crucial difference between working at Granada and the BBC was that, whereas at Granada it seemed we were all too busy working and learning on the hoof to worry about office politics and pecking orders, Lime Grove was full of discontented people manoeuvring for position, scheming their way through the labyrinthine back streets of the largest and most powerful broadcasting network on the planet.

24 Hours had taken over from *Tonight* and included many people who had worked on the early evening programme. Not all of them approved of the change. Moreover those who had experienced *Tonight* in its heyday were of a particular tribe memorably described by Grace Wyndham Goldie as 'people who strutted about Lime Grove in a body respecting the audience but despising other broadcasters'.

At Granada we had direct access to the people who mattered most, at the BBC we were not sure who they were, never mind where they lived. Paul Fox was our boss. Indisputably so. After a poor studio performance we would flinch at his approach, certain of an uncompromising reprimand. On the other hand, the next day the slate was wiped clean and we started afresh. I think I exasperated him. He backed me to do the job and he never lost the belief he was right. So did Derrick Amoore. He gave me every opportunity to prove myself, became a friend and a sturdy drinking companion, but I was never able to do my best work for him, or indeed work him out. He was a man of eccentric habit. He would spend the morning shooting an air pistol at a dart board in his office. In the middle of a conversation about football he would say something like, 'Tunisia. Why don't we hear about Tunisia?' and a film crew would be duly despatched. He handled his staff with a light touch, treating rumours of discontent and possible mutiny with amused disdain.

After my studio stint they sent me on the road with a film unit. In December of 1966 I flew to Jordan to interview King Hussein about an Israeli raid on a Jordanian village. We visited the village, talked to the survivors and looked across the border into Israel, little realising we would be back in six months covering what became known as the Six Day War.

I covered the war with one of the most remarkable men I ever met in journalism, Slim Hewitt. He was one of an influential group of journalists who had moved to the BBC from *Picture Post* in the early days of television. He was a tall, stooped, lugubrious-looking man with a long nose and soulful blue eyes. He was at the end of his career when I worked with him but his reputation was such that whenever I had to do a piece to camera with Slim behind the lens, it seemed to me I was speaking to a monument. He had been everywhere, seen everything and was generally unimpressed. The only reward he sought at the end of a day's work was 'egg and chips and a cuppa tea'. He ordered the treat wherever he went, whether it be in a Bedouin tent in the Sahara or at the traditional blow-out after filming, in the best hotel in town.

We arrived in Tel Aviv with the war rumbling in the distance. It was a waiting game; would it, wouldn't it happen? At the time I was writing for *The Sunday Times* and, having composed an article about Barnsley Football Club and their legendary hard man, Skinner Normanton, took it to the Israeli censor for onward transmission. He was a scholarly man who taught English at the university. He looked bemused as he read my article. At the end he said there were certain words he had not come across before such as 'ayup' and 'tha' what' and 'siree'. Might these be coded messages for Israel's enemies, he enquired?

He was teasing me but clearly thought I was wasting his time with such frivolous and incomprehensible nonsense. He handed my copy back to me unaltered.

'I suppose some might find humour in it,' he said, and then, as an aside, 'By the way, the grammar leaves a lot to be desired.'

I did, however, have some more appreciative readers in Tel Aviv. I was telephoned by a young South African medical student who asked if I was the Michael Parkinson who wrote about sport for *The Sunday Times*. I said I was and he said, 'I know you love cricket. Would you like to play for the university at the weekend?' My caller was captain of the team, a tall red-headed pace bowler. I took a catch at third slip off his bowling and spent the game wondering about the seeming absurdity of playing cricket in Jerusalem with a war brewing.

Then the office asked us to fix an interview with Abba Eban, the Israeli Foreign Minster. We were told to set up in his study at the official residence and the first thing I noticed was a bookcase with a complete set of *Wisden*. Mr Eban was an enthusiastic and knowledgeable talker about the game and we needed reminding by Slim Hewitt that our conversation was supposed to be about more serious matters. The interview took place on Saturday and as we were leaving we were told it was embargoed until Monday.

Monday morning I awoke to the sound of air-raid sirens in Tel Aviv. *Panorama* called me in my room and asked for an update on the war. I didn't know it had started. Nobody told me. I waffled on to no great purpose. No one should be awakened by a call from Robin Day – particularly when he hasn't a clue what is going on.

The Israelis enforced a news blackout throughout the day while their planes and tanks effectively destroyed the opposition. Cairo Radio told us Tel Aviv was in flames. At least we knew that wasn't true, and we bitched and threatened to no great effect to be let off the leash. We were told there would be a press conference at 9 p.m. It eventually took place at 2 a.m. when a half colonel in the

Israeli army, Moshe Pearlman, announced that Israeli armoury was approaching the Suez Canal and the Israeli air force had destroyed 374 Egyptian planes.

At the end of his announcement, with the media straining to get to the fighting, Colonel Pearlman asked, 'Any questions?' I was sitting next to one of the great journalists of our time, James Cameron.

'I have a question, Moshe,' he said.

'What is it, James?' asked Colonel Pearlman, recognising an old Middle East hand.

'Are you telling us the truth?' Cameron asked.

The basic trade of the reporter summed up in one question.

We set off in a car into the desert towards the Canal. Everywhere was devastation, evidence of the lightning savagery of the Israelis' pre-emptive strike. Our car broke down and we hitched a ride on a bus taking journalists to the action. We saw a squadron of tanks parked off the road, the crew brewing up, and went to meet them. The squadron commander's face was blackened with the desert sun. He removed his helmet to reveal his red hair, grinned and said, 'We meet in strange places.' It was the young student I had played cricket with.

On the way back the bus was forced to leave the road to make way for a convoy, five miles or more long, carrying supplies to the front. When we tried to get back on the road we were stuck. We also discovered we were in a minefield. This information was given to us by a jolly accompanying officer who suggested we get out and give a communal push while praying we didn't step on a mine.

'By the way,' he said as we laboured together at the rear of the vehicle, 'did I hear you talking about playing cricket back there?'

I nodded.

'Good. Then maybe you can explain to me something I have always wanted to know about that game. What is a googly?'

At least it took my mind off the possibility of blowing myself up.

When I returned home I knew I had gone on my last assignment. I simply wasn't designed to be one of that special breed who lived with a packed case by their beds and couldn't wait to be sent to a foreign land. I was a feature writer trying to be a hard-nosed foreign correspondent and it didn't work. I had tried but was found wanting. If I had a future on television, it would be elsewhere.

Fyfe Robertson, that exemplar of television journalism, took me for lunch and offered me advice I have never forgotten.

'Get into the studio as soon as you can,' he said. 'No one ever became rich standing in a ploughed field in Peterborough talking about the price of potatoes. The money is in the studio. And besides, it's warmer.'

The BBC was understanding and accommodating in dealing with my discomfort. It was decided I would take a six-month break from my remaining year of contract to write a biography of Fred Trueman. We had bought a lovely old Victorian terraced house in Windsor, Mary was pregnant and I looked forward to spending time at home with our growing family.

I was eager to write about Fred Trueman. He had been an inspirational figure in my life, and not just as a sporting hero. In the fifties, when my generation began to articulate the need for change, it looked for leaders to march at the head of the column. Fred Trueman seemed ideal. He was the son of a Yorkshire miner and a fast bowler with attitude. He didn't know his place. An opponent with a striped blazer and a fancy hat added a yard or two to his pace.

Of all the popular games of the time, cricket most represented the status quo. The amateur was captain and lived in a separate dressing room. The pro did most of the donkey work and was not expected to complain. From the very beginning Fred displayed a mind of his own. He could be both crude and objectionable to anyone who stood in his path but reserved his special contempt for those he believed disliked him because of where he came from or the way he spoke, or both. He became a hero to my generation, particularly in Yorkshire, because we imagined ourselves striding into battle behind his broad shoulders.

Fred didn't quite see it like that. His crusade was a one-man war, F.S. Trueman versus the Establishment, and he went his own way until, after his retirement, he announced his admiration for Mrs Thatcher and left a lot of people ruminative, not to say baffled.

I set about the task of exploring his life and it seemed to me the first job was to strip the myth from the reality to discover which of the thousands of anecdotes about him were true and which were false. One I knew to be true was when I played against him while he was on leave from the RAF and on the fringe of the Yorkshire team. I opened with Dickie Bird and watched in trembling fear from the other end as he bowled like the wind at my friend. The third or fourth ball struck Dickie in the chest and, amid great palaver, he went down. I joined the opposition players in a sympathetic circle around Dickie who was giving every indication of being mortally stricken. Eventually we had him on his feet and ready to proceed.

As I walked back down the wicket I saw the only person who had not commiserated with my pal was Trueman, who was settled in a miner's squat, chewing a blade of grass.

As I passed he asked, 'How's thi' mate?'

I attempted to be jocular. 'He'll live, Mr Trueman,' I said, using the prefix as a pathetic show of respect.

'That's all right then,' he said. 'But think on, you're next.'

I asked Fred how many such stories about him were true. Not many, he said, but, on the other hand, strange things happened to him.

I asked him for an example and he told me a bizarre story of making a cricket tour to India when, during a seemingly never-ending journey by rail, the train made an unscheduled stop in the middle of nowhere. Fred alighted to be greeted by the station master. In need of a pee, Fred asked him for directions to the toilet, whereupon the station master escorted Fred to a room where he drew back a red velvet curtain to reveal a Victorian chamber pot mounted on a plinth. What is more, the pot had the legend 'F. S. Trueman' painted on it. Fred could offer no explanation as to why it was there or how on earth the station master knew that one day his hero would arrive in need of such a facility. All Fred would say by way of explanation was, 'It's one of life's great mysteries. I seem to attract them.'

I thought a great title for the book would be *A Pisspot in India*, but Fred had other ideas. I advised him the title should be snappy and, if possible, have Fred in the title. He told me he had just the thing: *Fred: T'Definitive Volume On T'Best Fast Bowler That Ever Drew Breath* he said, in triumph.

I said it wasn't so much a title, more the first chapter of the book. We had a couple more meetings but it became obvious that he was too busy to concentrate fully, so we agreed to part.

John Arlott wrote the book instead and called it *Fred: Portrait of a Great Fast Bowler*. It was excellent and I called John to tell him so. I was also intrigued how he managed to get Fred to sit down long enough to tell his story.

'Oh, I didn't bother speaking to him,' said John.

The difference between a poet and a hack.

Shortly before Fred died I went to a dinner where he was selling off some of his memorabilia. I bought his last touring blazer, but with a heavy heart. Gods shouldn't trade their laurels, but maybe they have to because we are careless with our heroes.

When Fred Trueman died he had earned his place in the pantheon. He was one of the greatest fast bowlers of them all, in my view in the top six of all time. He had instructed Veronica, his wife, not to hold a memorial service. When she asked why he said he didn't want those people who criticised him when he was alive saying nice things over his grave. He departed displaying two fingers to his detractors, and those of us who thought he had lost his appetite for the fight were shamed by our doubt.

Having lost the book, I had time to spare. I was wondering what I might do next when John Bromley, a journalist I had met in my Fleet Street days, and now head of sport at the newly franchised London Weekend Television, asked me if I fancied a job producing a programme about sport that looked at serious issues, such as drugs and corruption. It seemed to me this was the perfect opportunity to blend my work at *The Sunday Times* with a job in television. I didn't stay long, but it was fun while it lasted.

21

PAID TO WATCH MOVIES, FOOTBALL AND CRICKET

London Weekend Television came into being with a shedload of stars and a solemn affirmation of particular emphasis on 'quality programming'. Where had we heard that before, and how many times have we heard it since? My own title was executive producer in charge of sporting documentaries, which sounded grand. In fact, I was like a captain in Fred Karno's Army – bags of orders but no one to give them to. Not quite true. I was able to work with one of my favourite sportswriters, Ian Wooldridge, and together we endeavoured to produce an antidote to the public-relations promotion of sport, which was as prevalent then as now.

We did one of the first exposés of the effects of anabolic steroids on athletes, interviewing a Scandinavian shot-putter who had developed secondary female characteristics, including breasts approaching those of my beloved Jane Russell. We tried to challenge the orthodoxy of television sports journalism, but without too much enthusiasm from the management. We were promised a prominent spot in the schedules, which turned out to be Sunday afternoon.

What the department lacked in opportunity it made up for in

jollity. Jimmy Hill and John Bromley were hospitable bosses, former Olympic athlete Adrian Metcalfe an enthusiastic and talented lieutenant, and another Olympian, Liz Ferris, was also a doctor whose supply of emergency oxygen in her office proved an indispensable aid for curing hangovers. We chugged along, going nowhere really; nor was the company as a whole. Ratings overall were not special. The bosses, mainly BBC men, thought they were still working for a public service broadcaster, and there were outbreaks of skirmishing in the corridors. We avoided most of it and simply kept sniffing the oxygen.

Then came another one of those phone calls. This time it was Sir Denis Forman and he came straight to the point. He asked me if I recalled his parting words about not being welcome back at Granada. I said I did.

'Well I want you to forget you heard them,' he said. 'I want you to return to do *Cinema* for us.'

This was the programme I had lusted after more than any other. The idea of being paid to see every film ever made and to interview my heroes (not to mention my fantasy figures) seemed to me a definition of the perfect job, particularly when my other job at *The Sunday Times* allowed me a free ringside seat at all the great sporting events. I was being paid to watch movies and football and cricket. The job the hobby, the hobby the job. Paradise.

And so it turned out. My producer on *Cinema* was my old Granada colleague Johnnie Hamp, who not only shared my love of movies and the stars who appeared in them, but allowed me to take a humorous and irreverent approach to what had hitherto been a straightforward presentation.

We had to submit the clips we intended to use to a censor. In those days the IBA was very strait-laced about what could be shown at 8 p.m., after *Coronation Street*, which was our spot. After having several clips rejected on the grounds they were titillating and might cause fundamental disruption to the British way of life, Johnnie and I came up with what proved to be a cunning plan. If we had a scene that we knew would upset the censor – and it could be something as inoffensive as a shot of a woman's bare back – we would precede it on the show reel with a clip from a hardcore porn movie. By the time the censor had recovered from the shock, our questionable scene had flashed by unnoticed. The porn clips became a feature of our shows to the censor and proved very popular.

The scripts only occasionally caused adverse comment. Sidney Bernstein once called Johnnie after reading my script to ask what the word 'puddled' meant. Johnnie said it was a north country slang word describing a confused state of mind.

Sidney said, 'Take it out. They won't understand in Tooting.' We left it in.

Sidney loved Tooting. It was the home of one of his most profitable cinemas and therefore had a spiritual significance in the Bernstein empire. Ever after, I tried to work Tooting into the script. Recalling a movie called *Land of the Pharaohs*, a biblical epic, I featured a clip of Jack Hawkins playing a pharaoh unveiling his latest masterpiece. He drew back a curtain to reveal a glorious panorama of glistening palaces and gleaming domes.

'Behold, Tooting,' I said, whereupon the camera I was addressing started shaking as the cameraman was convulsed with laughter. Take 2. The same result. Ditto with takes 3, 4, 5 and 6. By this time the studio was overwhelmed by the condition known as corpsing hysteria. There is no known cure except a break in proceedings, which we took.

During the delay I decided I couldn't say Tooting again without corpsing myself, so when it came to take 7, and Jack Hawkins drew back the curtain, I said 'Behold, Stevenage.' This set off an even greater hysterical outburst than Tooting had done. We settled for Stevenage in the end, but only after many more takes.

With an audience of ten million or so we didn't find it too difficult to persuade the great Hollywood names to be interviewed for the show. The frustration was talking to someone as substantial as Alfred Hitchcock and using just a few minutes of the interview. On the other hand, a few minutes were far too many for some I interviewed. Sam Peckinpah appeared in front of me looking like he would rather be elsewhere. He was supposed to be promoting his masterpiece, *The Wild Bunch*.

'You started life as a scriptwriter,' I said.

'No, a director,' he said.

Take 2.

'You started life as a director,' I said.

'No, a scriptwriter,' he said. We ploughed on to no great purpose.

Jack Nicholson appeared in what could best be described as a mellow condition and obviously feeling no pain. He appeared not to remember too much about the movie he was plugging, nor to be quite sure which country he was in. But he smiled a lot in winsome fashion.

The interview took place at Granada's London offices in Golden Square. At the back of the building, in a cul de sac called Kingly Court, was the Tatty Bogle Club. This was run by Joan, a formidable woman who loved movies and was constantly encouraging us to introduce our interviewees to the joys of her establishment. Lee Marvin had such a good time he asked Joan which was her favourite movie of those he had starred in. She said *Cat Ballou* and she particularly loved the scene where, as the drunken gunfighter, he went to draw his guns and his pants fell down.

'Let me show you how I did it,' he said, and proceeded to re-enact the scene to the point where a great Hollywood star was to be found standing in a drinking club in London with his trousers round his ankles.

Jack Lemmon also took to Joan and spent a while chatting and drinking. We were both smoking cigars and I noticed he trimmed his with a lovely filigree silver cutter. I admired it and he said it had been given to him by Billy Wilder after they finished making *Some Like It Hot*. I thought no more of it. I saw him back to his hotel and we parted in the manner of brothers in drink. The next day I checked my jacket before sending it to the dry cleaner's and discovered the cigar-cutter. He had slipped it in my pocket. I called the hotel but he had left.

About a week later I had a note from him that started: 'Dear Michael, this is the first time I have been allowed by my doctor to put pen to paper since we met.' He was a funny, warm man and I remember hoping at the time I would meet him again, and I did, sooner than I imagined, but in another part of town.

When I look back at the interviews I did for *Cinema*, it's clear that many of those people came to be regulars on the talk show. Ralph Richardson was one. He was plugging *The Battle of Britain* and arrived in motor-cycle leathers astride a high-powered bike, which he wheeled through the doors at Golden Square and parked in the foyer.

One guest I had on *Cinema* whom I could never persuade on to the talk show was Sir Laurence Olivier. I interviewed him in the office of the building site that became the National Theatre. He started the interview in formal suit and ended up with loosened tie and jacket removed, revealing red braces. He was promoting a film of Chekhov's *The Three Sisters* but I wanted to talk to him about working with Marilyn Monroe on *The Prince and the Showgirl*.

I had once employed a driver who took Marilyn to and from the studios when she was making the film and he told me that every night when he picked her up she sobbed all the way home. I mentioned this to Sir Laurence. He said she was unhappy and that made her difficult to work with. He wondered what made her happy and the answer came when together they travelled to America to promote the film. As they left the plane they were faced with a phalanx of photographers and immediately Marilyn came alive. As he watched her posing, flirting with, and teasing the stills cameras, Olivier suddenly realised she was a model, as in command in this situation as she was discomforted and forlorn in front of a movie camera.

Cinema worked so well I starting getting offers of other jobs. A BBC producer, Cecil Korer, offered me a quiz show, *Where In the World*, based on a knowledge of geography. Travelling to Manchester by train to record the show, I sat in the same compartment as a stunning young woman, Shella Baksh, runner-up in the recent Miss World contest. Cecil had booked her as a guest on the show. She was as vivacious as she was beautiful and he brought her back several times. As he remembers it, he was sitting in his office one day when he received a call from Michael Caine, asking how he could contact the beautiful girl he had seen on the show. Shella became Shakira, then Lady Caine.

I also received a call from the famous American agent, Mark McCormack. He said he would like to represent me, particularly when I told him my salary from Granada for writing and performing a programme that regularly made the top ten in the ratings was

£200 per show. He explained that with some of his clients he took up to forty per cent or more of the monies he negotiated, but the deal he would offer me was ten per cent of my earnings if I delivered Geoffrey Boycott and George Best as clients.

It took me five minutes to arrange and not much longer for the two of them to fall out with Mark's organisation. Geoffrey liked the thought of having a high-powered agent but could never come to terms with the fees. George simply chose to ignore Mark's advice.

McCormack's plan for George was to negotiate a deal in America that would set him up for life. I sat in while Mark told George that a move to America could earn him enough money to guarantee a comfortable future. He would make him a dollar millionaire. All George had to do was sit tight and await a call from Mark telling him the deal was done. Whatever he did, he must not get into conversation with other people who might tempt him with deals for America.

A month or two later Mark rang me at about midnight to tell me he had heard that Best had signed for an American club and not the one Mark had been negotiating with. Could I find out? I rang George's nightclub in Manchester. He wasn't difficult to find in those days. I told him about Mark's phone call and he confirmed he had an agreement with someone else.

'But what could this guy offer you that Mark didn't?' I asked.

'He gave me twenty grand in readies,' said George.

I reported back to Mark, who asked how on earth anyone could think a handful of readies was as good as a lifetime of financial security. I told him George lived for the moment and not the future. It was part of his charm as well as a reason for his downfall.

Granada liked the success of *Cinema* but was less sure about the attention I was attracting from other television companies. There were whispers in the media I might be given my own talk show and I met Stella Richman, the Programme Controller at London Weekend, who revealed her plans for a weekend talk show, which I would host. To underline her enthusiasm for the idea, she said the company would buy me an interviewing suit from a tailor I had never heard of called Doug Hayward – which is how I came to visit Mr Hayward's salon in Mount Street and became not simply a customer but a lifelong friend.

I never heard from Ms Richman again.

It didn't matter too much because, in the meantime, Jeremy Isaacs, who was now Programme Controller at Thames Television, and with whom I had worked at Granada in the early days, asked if I would consider doing an afternoon talk show, the first of its kind. I didn't leave Granada so much as drift away. I loved *Cinema* and enjoyed a happy working relationship with Johnnie Hamp, but they didn't like me working for other companies and, besides, I could see something larger looming. I wanted that talk show. Stella Richman had fired my ambition. A move to Thames for an interview-based programme would be the ideal preparation.

I joined Thames and began work on the show, *Tea Break*. It started with a close-up of a plate of arrowroot biscuits and panned up to reveal the host. It wasn't much but it was my own. It was aimed predominantly at women and the production team, apart from a couple of men, was entirely female. The programme eventually morphed into *Good Afternoon* and there were co-presenters, good journalists including Elaine Grand, Mavis Nicholson and Jill Tweedie.

Mary would come to London on a shopping expedition and visit the studio to meet me after the show. One day Jeremy Isaacs asked me if I would object to his asking her to take a screen test. He said every time he saw her at Thames he was certain she would make a marvellous performer. I said it sounded a good idea, and so it proved. Mary developed into a top-class presenter. She looked fabulous on camera – it truly loved her – and with her stylish fashion sense, she provoked a rapid and sustained response from the audience.

She also developed into a tenacious interviewer, with a particular interest in issues affecting her as a mother and a teacher. It was the time Maggie Thatcher, then Education Secretary, decided to stop free milk in schools. A junior minister was sent along to explain the decision. My guest on the programme was another politician, Timothy Raison. He was sitting next to me when we went on air; I introduced the programme and then set up Mary's interview. She was brilliant. She had obviously researched the item well, she knew what she wanted and she questioned the junior minister so thoroughly and skilfully he was reduced to a gibbering wreck.

I watched the performance with growing pride along with Timothy Raison who, as Mary reduced his colleague to rubble, whispered to me, 'By God, I'd hate to be married to her.'

Tony Preston was head of variety at the BBC. One day in the spring of 1971 he called and said he wanted to suggest me as the host for a new late-night talk show the BBC was contemplating. Would I be interested?

'What a good idea,' I replied. 'I'd like to meet and talk about the possibility.' I didn't tell him that in my wardrobe I already had the suit I'd be wearing for the first show.

22
TALK SHOW HOST

I was thirty-six when I walked into the Television Centre in 1971 and never imagined the show I was about to do would define my working life for the next thirty-six years. In the seventies the BBC was a much different organisation from nowadays. For one thing there were a lot of Indians about but not too many chiefs, and the people who ran the organisation – Paul Fox was Controller One, David Attenborough, head of programmes, Bill Cotton, head of light entertainment, Brian Cowgill, head of sport – have their own special place in the television Hall of Fame. They presided over the biggest television factory on earth and the most prestigious. When I was in Israel for the Six Day War, I discovered my official accreditation came a poor second to my BBC Club card in the matter of impressing people and opening doors. It was the time of massive audiences, only three channels and an industry created by a remarkable generation of men and women. Much of what they see and hear on television now must make them cringe.

Walking into the BBC in 1971 was, to my fanciful imagination, like walking into MGM in its heyday. I was soon to discover that then, unlike now, the BBC did not pay Hollywood rates.

Bill Cotton had seen the Jack Paar show in America and liked what he saw. Before Paar, the late-night slot had accommodated a range of variety shows. He refined it into the talk show as we know it today. He was a volatile talent who once walked off halfway through a show because of a dispute with NBC. He told his audience, 'There must be a better way of earning a living than this.' Three weeks later he returned with the line, 'As I was saying before I was so rudely interrupted.' Cotton liked his interviewing style and commissioned a series of shows to find an equivalent in Britain.

At the same time, Richard Drewett, a young producer on BBC2's *Late Night Line Up*, had seen the Dick Cavett Show in America and admired the way the host mixed current affairs and light entertainment interviews. He badgered Bill Cotton with his idea for a similar kind of late-night talk show. There was a vacancy. Simon Dee had disappeared; Derek Nimmo wasn't doing great business. Bill took the idea to Paul Fox suggesting I was the man to fill the gap. Paul told him I was an idle fellow. Nonetheless he thought it worth a punt, providing they found the right producer. Bill teamed me with Richard Drewett and we were given eleven shows in the graveyard slot of summer broadcasting to show what we could do.

I felt comfortable with Richard from the first moment we met. He was tall and thin with blue eyes and a droll take on life. We had much in common. We loved red-nosed comics, the Goons and Woody Allen, movies, sport and music. Richard played trumpet and piano and shared my love of Sinatra, the Great American Songbook and jazz.

When we met, even before we discussed editorial policy, we indulged our love of music by commissioning a signature tune. Richard wanted a big band in the studio and asked the musical director, Ken Jones, to provide it and write a signature tune. Ken said working Saturdays would interfere with watching West Ham

United play so turned it down. I wanted Laurie Holloway as musical director. He was a neighbour and I greatly admired his wife, the singer Marion Montgomery. Sadly, Laurie had been offered a job working in America as Englebert Humperdinck's MD. We couldn't compete with the money on offer, never mind the Vegas lifestyle.

Then Ken Jones recommended Harry Stoneham and when we met we liked what we saw. We asked Harry to write something upbeat and jazzy, a tune that would sound good played by a big band. We sat in a basement at the BBC and Harry doodled on the piano. Too slow, we said. He changed the tempo. After about an hour we agreed on the theme and Harry – although we didn't know it at the time – had a nice little earner.

I said I wanted to walk on to the set down a staircase that lit up individually with every step I took, like Georges Guétary in *An American in Paris*. What kind of chairs? What colour for the set? How many guests? Do I do a piece to camera at the top of the show, like Johnny Carson?

All this was chewed over before any general discussion about the show's editorial content because, frankly, Richard and I didn't want any debate about the kind of guests we should book. Between us we had made up our minds that we could blend serious interviews with showbiz; that we would seek unusual combinations and, moreover, keep the guests on throughout the programme so that the interview might become a conversation. We decided that the music should encompass everything from jazz to classics and much in between except the pap designed specifically for the hit parade. When I tell you the year we went to air the big hits included 'Grandpa' by Clive Dunn, and 'Chirpy, chirpy, cheep, cheep', you will see we were not being élitist or even particularly finicky.

We excluded others from our discussion because from the very beginning Richard had misgivings about the show coming under the aegis of light entertainment. He suspected, correctly as it turned out, that enthusiasm for our idea of a new kind of talk show might quickly disappear at the thought of Pierre Salinger, President John Kennedy's former spin doctor, sitting next to the glamorous and sexy film star Shelley Winters, which was likely to be our second show.

We had a second show but not an opener. The problem booking a high-profile talk show is that, until it becomes high-profile, potential guests are reluctant to appear. We needed a big showbiz name for the opener.

Richard's parents had a place in Ibiza next door to Terry-Thomas. Thomas was the gap-toothed comedian and actor whose ultra posh upper-class accent had brought him great renown. As a favour for the friend and neighbour, Terry-Thomas said yes. It was Wimbledon week and the most intriguing of all the tennis stars at the time was Arthur Ashe, the first male black tennis pro to win at Wimbledon. Seeking a possible headline, we booked Ray Bellisario who was one of the first paparazzi. He specialised in snatching pictures of the royal family and, in those innocent times, the nation was divided between those who would have him flogged and those who would prefer to see his head on a pike on Tower Bridge.

In the hope of creating a row in the studio, we arranged to have the leader of the League of Empire Loyalists in the audience. With this motley crew, we set sail.

No evidence remains of that first series of eleven. At the time, the BBC employed a committee to decide which shows were to be kept for posterity and which should be scrapped. It decided ours were expendable and wiped the lot, which included interviews with John Lennon and Yoko Ono, Orson Welles, Peter Ustinov and Spike

Milligan and a double act featuring Fred Trueman and Harold Pinter, not to mention Shirley MacLaine and the splendidly eccentric Sylvia Brooke, the Dowager Ranee of Sarawak.

When John Lennon was murdered, Bill Cotton called me and said he wanted to replay our interview. I explained what had happened. Bill said it was a fair bet that someone at the BBC, in the VTR department most likely, would have made a bootleg copy. He put the word round the BBC but without any response. Twenty or more years later I was called by an American film producer making a film about Lennon's life called *Imagine*. He asked if he could use part of the interview. I told him it no longer existed. He said, 'What do you mean? It's sitting on my desk.' What he had was a telecine recording. He wouldn't say how he acquired it.

The line-up for that show was John and Yoko, George Melly, Humphrey Lyttelton and Benny Goodman. Lennon said he would only talk about the Beatles if I sat in a sack. Don't ask why. I think it was one of Yoko's potty ideas. For a greater part of our conversation, I played the part of a talking sack while John reminisced about the Fab Four.

The Pierre Salinger/Shelley Winters interview slipped by without too much twittering from on high. I had particularly looked forward to meeting Ms Winters. When I was a kid I had a pin-up of her in my wardrobe. She was in there with Jane, Veronica and Vera Hruba.

I met her in make-up and wished I hadn't. She didn't much resemble the girl in my wardrobe. It didn't help that she appeared to be bald. In fact, her make-up artist had flattened her hair under a tight skullcap, prior to transforming her in a manner I could only observe with open-mouthed incredulity. The make-up girl had a series of what looked like laces with strips of adhesive attached to the ends. She affixed them to Ms Winter's face under her chin, the side of her head alongside her eyes and above her eyebrows. Next, she gathered the ends together and tugged them upwards, creating an instant facelift. She then tied them in a knot on the top of her head and covered it with a blonde wig. After the application of several layers of thick make-up, the woman in the chair was transformed into a fair approximation of the object of my teenage lust.

While this was taking place, Ms Winters chatted on about this and that completely unaware of the traumatic experience I was undergoing. When it came time to interview her, I dare not make her laugh in case it loosened the knot under her wig and the whole edifice collapsed.

We booked Spike Milligan – the first of many shows he did for us – and cast him alongside Robert Shaw. When he discovered who he was on with he threw a tantrum – again one of many – saying Shaw held extreme right-wing views and he wouldn't appear with him. He fled to the car park and it seemed likely we might do his interview sitting in a Ford until he relented. He was, of course, brilliant. He just had to create a little drama to get the juices flowing. Over the years we were to discover that Spike's idea of an ideal show was the one-man variety, featuring Spike Milligan.

George Best appeared with Michael Caine. For the next ten years or more we were to chronicle George's sad decline into alcoholism and despair, and similarly we charted Michael Caine's rise from promising young actor to movie legend and a knighthood.

We validated our decision to book shows featuring guests from different backgrounds but sharing similar, and unexpected, interests when we brought together Trevor Howard, Fred Trueman and Harold Pinter. What the screen actor, sportsman and playwright had in common was cricket. In this case, it was not simply an interest in the game, more an obsession with it. Harold Pinter formed his own cricket team. Trevor Howard stipulated that any script conferences relating to a new film take place in the pavilion at Lord's.

'Now then, Harold lad, what's tha' been up to?' was Fred Trueman's classic line to Pinter when they were introduced.

The combination worked beautifully and we realised we were on to something. Our secret plans were working. Booking the show grew easier as word got around but we were still searching for the big solo star to impress the agents. Our ideal was Orson Welles, then a man of towering reputation in the world of movies and theatre. We were certain he would deliver a performance that would impress the critics, delight the audience and, most of all, convince our bosses to give us another series. Richard, a clever and tenacious booker, finally managed to persuade him to come on the show and I spent a week or more worrying and fretting over the structure of the interview. It was our first one-man show and it had to work.

Come the day, I was still fussing over the interview when there was a knock on my dressing-room door. I opened it and came face to face with Orson Welles, an enormous figure, blocking out the daylight.

'Mr Parkinson?' he said, as he swept past me into the room. He was dressed entirely in black – including a black shirt, black bow tie and a large black fedora.

He looked around the room and saw my questions on the dressing table. 'May I?' he asked, and gave them the brief sweep of his gaze. Then he looked at me and said, 'How many talk shows have you done?'

I told him this was the eighth.

'I've done rather more than that,' he said. 'That being the case, would you mind a little suggestion?'

I nodded.

He indicated the questions. 'Throw those away and let's just talk.'

And we did. Everything from the making of *Citizen Kane* to the innate good manners of peasants in a remote part of Spain. He was exceptional, not just in the scope of his intellect and knowledge, but in his use of language. If anyone guaranteed the future of the show, it was Orson Welles.

The first series had been a success. One critic said it showed such certainty of becoming a long-running show he wished he could purchase shares in me. The same writer, five years later, said he was glad he hadn't.

The last show of the first series brought together Shirley MacLaine and an extraordinary old woman called Sylvia Brooke, the Ranee of Sarawak. In any list of English eccentrics she would have pride of place. She was consort and, by custom, slave to Sir Vyner Brooke, an Englishman who ruled the jungle kingdom of Sarawak, on Borneo, during the last decades of the British Empire. In her time she shocked polite society by her behaviour. She did the conga with prostitutes in Sarawak, causing a visiting MP to observe, 'A more undignified woman it would be hard to find.' She proposed marriage to J.M. Barrie; George Bernard Shaw was in love with her; the press called her 'the most charming of despots' and her own brother called her 'a female Iago'. Now, aged eighty-six, she had put it all down in an account of her life and played to perfection the part of the loveable oddity.

When I called on Shirley MacLaine in her dressing room and

told her I would like to interview the Ranee first and have her stay on during MacLaine's own interview, she shook her head. She said, 'The deal is I go on first, then I disappear.'

I asked why she wanted it this way. 'Because I have read the book. Do you think anyone can follow that?' she said.

She was right. The Ranee was a gilt-edged gift for a talk show, funny and indiscreet.

Talking about her husband's bad habits, including his incontinence, she recalled the time when, while entertaining guests on the verandah of her Sarawak palace, there appeared to be a sudden downfall of rain. 'Not the rainy season, is it?' asked a guest. 'No, it's the Rajah peeing over the balcony,' said the Ranee.

She was sensational. As we came off, Shirley MacLaine was waiting in the wings.

'Was I right?' she asked. She was.

Shirley MacLaine became a regular on the show over the years and one of my favourite guests. She was talented, smart, funny and an outrageous flirt. One time, in the middle of answering a question about President Nixon and the meaning of life, she stopped and began staring at my navel. Most disconcerting. 'What?' I said. Then she poked her finger into my belly button and said I had a button missing. 'We pop 'em off, wives sew 'em on,' she said.

Some time later when I interviewed her brother, Warren Beatty, he came on set, shook hands and said, 'So you're the guy who's trying to make out with my sister.'

I couldn't deny it.

Paul Fox wanted a second series and he wanted it more or less straightaway. He suggested that we might start it with a replay of the Orson Welles interview. When we told him it had been wiped he said he would willingly find the money for a rematch.

Richard Drewett had become friendly with Welles and was discussing making a film with him to elaborate on their fascination with the art forger Elmyr de Hory. Out of their collaboration Welles made *F for Fake*. Richard told me that one morning Welles asked him to visit him in a warehouse on an industrial estate in North London to discuss the movie. Welles was filming a sequence in the dimly lit warehouse. Richard asked him what the sequence was.

'We are standing in Chartres Cathedral,' said Welles, demonstrating his well-known theory that all film directors are illusionists.

He was editing *Don Quixote* in Madrid when Richard asked him for a return match. Welles demanded a fee of £2,000 to do another one-man show. The standard fee in those days was £500 but we wanted him badly and he knew it.

On the day of the interview we received a call from Spain saying Mr Welles was at Madrid airport and not boarding his plane to London until we made two guarantees. First, his fee of £2,000 must be paid to him in cash upon arrival at London airport. The second demand was that, because of his large size, three seats must be removed from the first-class cabin so he might be accommodated in style and comfort.

Given all we did to get him to the Television Centre, Mr Welles did not let us down. He made a grand entrance carrying a staff and looking like Moses about to part the Red Sea. Once more I encountered his powerful personality, his overwhelming presence. It wasn't just about his size – although he was so big we had to find a special chair for him to sit on – there was something else that emanated from his personality. I have experienced it since but only with a handful of people. Muhammad Ali had it, so did Richard Burton, Billy Connolly and Nelson Mandela. I have pondered for a long time what makes them remarkable without coming to a satisfactory conclusion except to say that much of what they exude is willpower.

With Orson Welles in our sights, we needed another big name to start the second series. Someone suggested Muhammad Ali.

Not bad, we said.

23

ALI, THE GREATEST

The first boxer I ever saw was an old stumblebum, a local pugilist who had his brains scrambled in the ring and shuffled down the street as if wearing snow shoes. We used to call after him, 'Jackie Pace, Jackie Pace; all ears and no face'. He would turn and assume the fighting pose and draw his thumb across his snotty nose.

My father took me to a boxing booth when I was a teenager and the spieler convinced us the young lad with the skin like milk chocolate and the rippling physique was worth a look. We were told he was a world champion in the making. They asked for volunteers to take him on and a big navvy about three stone heavier took his shirt off and stepped into the ring. The young lad circled him once, avoided a haymaker and hit him in the centre of his forehead with a left hook that knocked him out. Later, the loser came round with his cap, hoping for money from the spectators. He had a large lump where he had been slugged. He looked like a unicorn.

The fighter's name was Randolph Turpin and it would take a while before he beat Sugar Ray Robinson, the best all-round fighter I ever saw, and became world champion. Not long after that, I went to interview him. He was on the skids, grunting instead of talking, reading *The Beano*. Shortly after, he put a gun in his mouth and killed himself.

I am not dewy eyed about the so-called Noble Art. Quite the opposite. You cannot make one sensible argument in favour of boxing as a sporting spectacle. As Muhammad Ali once put it, addressing a press conference: 'Do you ever ask yourself what all you white boys are doing watching two black men try to kill each other?'

If you remove Ali's racial propaganda from the quote, it is the question every person who ever watched a fight must ask himself.

That said, in a lifetime of observing sporting contests, I have to admit that none matches the visceral joy and excitement of a great boxing match. And if required to offer examples of what I mean, I would say that the two fights I witnessed between Ali and Joe Frazier at Madison Square Garden displayed a balance of skill, bravery and sheer bloody willpower, as well as grace and endurance, that was as aesthetically pleasing as it was profoundly moving.

Long before I met Muhammad Ali, I admired him as much for his political convictions as his fighting ability. He refused to join the draft because of his belief the war in Vietnam was a mistake.

'No Viet Cong ever called me nigger' might not be seen by military historians as a reason for not fighting the war, but it was a conviction Ali upheld through three years when he was refused a licence to fight. During that time he was offered all manner of deals, but he was steadfast in his decision. There was much more to this pugilist than a good punch. All else apart, he was a master showman. No one promoted a fight, or himself, with greater skill and enthusiasm. Best of all for me, he was God's gift to the talk-show host.

Whenever I am asked the inevitable question to choose the best from the thousands of people I have interviewed, then I don't have a single answer. I loved interviewing old people: Dame Edith Evans, Catherine Bramwell-Booth, Ben Travers, Artur Rubinstein. Comedians were among my favourites: Les Dawson, Jack Benny, George Burns, Jimmy Tarbuck, Tommy Cooper, Billy Connolly, Spike Milligan and many more. What about the great Hollywood stars: Jack Lemmon, James Stewart, Fred Astaire, Henry Fonda, Bette Davis, James Cagney. Then the great talkers: Orson Welles, Jonathan Miller, Peter Ustinov, Professor Jacob Bronowski, Stephen Fry. And don't get me started on musicians, beautiful women and my sporting heroes.

But if I am asked who was the most remarkable human being I ever encountered, it would have to be Ali. I interviewed him four times and lost on points on just about every occasion. If you put the four interviews together they span a decade in which he not only became the most famous man on our planet, but went from being world champion to Jackie Pace. How that happened, more pertinently how it was allowed to happen, will be debated so long as Ali casts his shadow over boxing, but anyone seeking the story of his decline need only contrast our first meeting in 1971 and our last ten years later.

The first encounter came about mainly because of Richard Drewett's genius as a booker. Ali was in London promoting a soft drink and had planned a visit to a bottling plant in the Home Counties. The entrepreneur behind the scheme agreed Ali should appear on the show, but advised that the drinks people be kept in the dark because they might raise objections. They would be told that, while on his way to the factory, Ali would make a short detour to the TV Centre to record a five-minute news item. Meanwhile, we had a studio ready and waiting for the great man.

He was smuggled into the studio where we discovered his chair was too small. We sent for the Orson Welles furniture. Ali was the sort of man you didn't so much look at as inspect. In those days, he was a beautiful human being. He had a bonny face (no other word will do) with perfect teeth and merry, amused eyes. His hands were narrow with long tapering fingers, hands that should be holding a paint brush or a bow instead of being used to batter people. He was tall and slender but didn't look unusually big until, having sat down, he then stood up and we found the chair clinging to his back like a carapace.

This was the time of the capricious Ali, explaining how he watched a wrestler called Gorgeous George selling tickets and decided he would promote himself in the same way. 'So I talked and talked and told them, "If you talk and jive, you'll fall in five." And I told them I was the best in the world and the best of all time. Better than any Americans or Russians or Chinese or anyone else. I could whup any man on earth. And I kept telling them I am beautiful, I am the greatest until they said, "The nigger talks too much," and bought a ticket just to see me beat.'

He told how he came back from the Olympic Games with a gold medal and was given another medal stating he was a freeman of his home town. Wearing the medal, he went into a diner and the owner said, 'We don't serve nigras.' Ali replied, 'That's OK. I don't eat 'em,' and threw his medal in the river.

In that moment were sown the seeds of disaffection that would lead to the politicising of Muhammad Ali. It was then he became a Muslim.

The hour or more we talked flashed by, except for the minders in the car park, who kept looking at their watches and thinking it must be the longest news interview ever. The viewing figures were enormous. Indeed over the years we were to discover that the only guests who would guarantee adding an extra two million or more were Ali and Billy Connolly.

Two years passed and Richard had another brainwave. Ali was

to fight Joe Frazier in Madison Square Garden – a rematch of their classic encounter when Frazier beat him.

'Wouldn't it be fun,' Richard mused, 'if we could persuade the two fighters to appear together on our talk show on the eve of the fight?'

I thought it a great idea but unlikely to happen.

The BBC also thought it was a great idea until it was pointed out it would have to be done in the United States. Too expensive, they said. Richard suggested we try a joint production with an American TV company.

We called Dick Cavett in America. Cavett hosted a talk show for ABC and we had already shared a production with him when we tried out the new-fangled Atlantic satellite in an attempt to do the first transatlantic talk show. Cavett had Bette Davis and Mort Sahl in New York; I had Jonathan Miller and Jackie Stewart in London. It was a good idea, but the technology of the time did nothing to enhance our ambition. The delay was such that Jonathan Miller worked out if he died in our London studio, it would take another four or five seconds before the event was registered in New York.

During our collaboration with Cavett's company, Richard and I had visited New York to scout the set-up. Dick Cavett was a small handsome man who worked as a writer for Jack Paar before getting his own talk show. I admired him but didn't much like him. He was too poised and self-contained to be approachable. He was an adroit performer, different from Johnny Carson, Merv Griffin and the rest who were around at the time, in that generally he saw the interview as a means of extracting information rather than a scripted contrivance for cheap laughs. He also managed to plug products without sounding as if he was being paid a fortune to do so. Indeed, he would rattle through the adverts like a man renouncing his religion at gunpoint.

We watched him record a show featuring John Lindsay, then the young and sexy mayor of New York. Cavett's show was in trouble. The network had told him to improve the viewing figures or suffer the chop. Mayor Lindsay was also having problems running the Big Apple.

Cavett asked, 'Tell me, Mayor Lindsay, what is it like to be a failure?'

Lindsay grinned and said, 'Let's wait until the autumn and have a joint press conference.'

Interviewing Philippe Cousteau, son of underwater explorer Jacques, Cavett picked up a length of bone, polished like ivory, from the table and, commenting on its mysterious beauty, handed it to an ardent member of the women's lib movement who was also on the show. She handled it lovingly and commented on its smooth texture.

'Do you know what it is?' Cavett asked.

She shook her head.

'A walrus's penis,' he said.

It was worth the trip to New York for that one moment.

Cavett and the network jumped at the idea of an Ali and Frazier confrontation. It would be done from Cavett's studio and go out on the eve of the fight both in the States and Britain. Both fighters agreed to the deal and Richard and I booked in for a week's preparation before the event. That was when I began to feel that my misgivings about Cavett were justified. I felt he wanted to take over the show, to make it appear not so much a joint production, more a Dick Cavett event with the country cousin from England making a fleeting appearance. We relied on Cavett's organisation for our basic research because, in those days before the internet, access to research was a tedious and time-consuming business. Moreover we needed to get together with Cavett and his production team to plot the interview, to work out who talked to whom and when.

With a couple of days to go and having been continually stalled by the Cavett office, we were finally convinced that the so-called collaboration had, in fact, become a contest. What we were experiencing, of course, was the ultra competitive cut-throat business of American television. By contrast, British television was a benign industry, mollycoddled by the knowledge that any share of a three-channel market was substantial enough to keep everyone happy.

I managed to get Cavett on the phone and asked him how we would manage dividing the interview. He said he thought we might wing it. I said we had both been in the business long enough to know that winging it was not the way to make a successful show. We left it at that.

On the day of the recording I was angry, disgruntled and not at all happy with the prospect of doing a show that was our idea but which had been effectively hijacked. I was made to feel even farther from home when, while sitting in make-up, I was approached by one of Cavett's staff who said, 'Dick wanted you to have this.' He handed me a document which contained a plan of how the show would go and included smart replies and gags to the responses his questions might provoke.

Looking back at a recording of the show, you might come to the conclusion I was superfluous to requirements and I wouldn't argue with you. Such was the solo nature of Cavett's performance that, during a commercial break, Ali turned to me and asked, 'What are you doing here, man?'

'That is a very good question. I don't seem able to get a word in,' I said.

I didn't mention the fact I was too busy thinking of ways of killing Cavett after the show to worry about a silly thing like being made to look a spare part in front of fifty million people.

Coming back from the commercial break, Ali announced to our host that he wasn't going to bother answering his questions for a while because he was going to speak to his friend from London, who was not only a better interviewer than Mr Cavett, but also much better looking. That let me in and it was a generous gesture, which contrasted vividly with his cruel taunting of Frazier.

I had grown to like Joe Frazier. In the run-up to our interview I visited his training camp in Philadelphia and persuaded him to let me spar with him. Philadelphia became Frazier's home once he left South Carolina. Angelo Dundee, Ali's trainer, once said, 'Philadelphia is not a town. It's a jungle. They don't have gyms here, they have zoos. They don't have sparring sessions, they have wars.'

I have never felt as alien as I did when I entered the ring in Frazier's gym. I was kitted out in a white T-shirt with 'Smokin' Joe' across the front. It should have said 'Piteous Parky', which is what I looked like, or 'Petrified Parky', which is how I felt. The wise guys at ringside who had come to see Frazier work out regarded me with amused contempt.

Smokin' Joe inspected my stance and suggested a round or two with me throwing rights, which he would duck inside and pretend to hit me around the body while making all the right grunting noises but pulling the punches so as not to put me in hospital.

Choreographed thus I began to feel comfortable in my new surroundings, dancing with my new-found best friend. I thought

I would liven things up a bit by trying a different routine, which involved me feinting with my right and trying a left jab that found its target. I shall forever remember what happened next. Frazier looked at me, smiled and then cuffed me on the head guard. It was no more than a gentle reprimand but the fact is for the next few seconds I heard bells and thought I had walked into a door. Smokin' Joe's manager called time and told him to get some serious work done on the heavy bag.

I watched with a mixture of fear and admiration as he launched a two-handed assault on the equipment, each blow making a noise like a door slamming.

Frazier and Ali were made for each other in more ways than one. As boxers, they could not have been more different. Norman Mailer called Frazier 'a war machine'. He was the battering ram, Ali the rapier. Frazier came at his opponent in a low crouch, taking three shots to get two in, remorseless, indomitable and savage. His punches were fearsome and damaging and he could fell a man with either hand. Ali was upright, beautifully balanced, jabbing and weaving with a clear disdain for the cruder aspects of boxing. He fought with his head pulled back as if being hit on the face was the ultimate insult. He didn't so much beat an opponent as teach them a lesson.

In the shadowy world of heavyweight boxing there are some encounters you can witness and come to the conclusion that one or the other fighter, for whatever reason, is not giving of his best. No one, not even the looniest conspiracy theorist, could watch the three Ali–Frazier fights without understanding that both fighters regarded each other with something approaching complete loathing.

Ali hated Frazier because of what he saw as his disrespect for his religion. He chided him because the white population supported

Frazier more than Ali. He characterised Frazier as an Uncle Tom, called him ugly and stupid.

What incensed Frazier was Ali posturing as a representative of the downtrodden black man. Frazier was the twelfth son of a South Carolina field worker who peddled bootleg liquor on the side, Ali middle-class by comparison. Joe Frazier was shiny black, Muhammad Ali milk chocolate because of an Irish great-great grandfather. Ali, with his looks and his showmanship, had danced his way through life; Frazier had slugged it out in working boots.

It was *Guess Who's Coming to Dinner*. If Sidney Poitier or Ali walks through the door, that's one thing. If Joe Frazier turns up, then it's going to be a different ending.

The studio confrontation we devised was certainly an event but little else. All we learned was what we already knew, that each man shared an implacable hatred of the other. Nor had the show done anything to cement Anglo-American relations, Mr Cavett being swept away in a limo before I had the chance of a word in his ear.

In many ways the fight was like the interview, the anticipation being of a higher order than the actual result. Ali won on points and went on to defeat George Foreman and fight Frazier for a third and final time in what became known as the Thrilla in Manila.

Our trip to New York hadn't worked out quite as we had planned, but we had pulled it off, even if it involved a loss of innocence on our part. A couple of other things made it all worthwhile.

We saw in a listings magazine that a pianist called Ellis Larkins was appearing at a club after a long illness. Larkins was a jazz pianist with a gentle filigree style of playing. He had also recorded a session with Ella Fitzgerald that, to this day, remains the apogee of the accompanist's art. As Richard and I sat and admired Larkins' set, a large handsome man, in a fedora and camel-hair, belted overcoat, came into the club and tipped his hat to Ellis. The pianist smiled and nodded a welcome. He then segued seamlessly into 'Every day I have the blues' and the stranger, settling into the curve of the piano, began singing in a rich, smooth voice. It was the legendary Joe Williams and we sat enraptured until an hour later he tipped his hat to Ellis and walked off into the night.

Then I had a phone call from a friend who asked if I would like to meet Hugh Hefner. Certainly, I said. One of Mr Hefner's assistants rang me. She sounded like she was wearing the uniform. Mr Hefner would like to invite us to California to join him in his latest play pen. The visions of sun and talk and gorgeous girls seemed irresistible, but I had to turn it down.

'Sorry,' I said, 'but this coming weekend I have to be home.'

Obviously not accustomed to being knocked back, the woman said, with a bit of edge in her voice, 'It must be important.'

And I said, 'Yes it is, you see I'm playing cricket for Datchet on Saturday.'

There was a pause. Then she said, 'You're doin' what?'

It would have taken too long to explain and, in any event, she would never have understood.

Twelve months later I interviewed Muhammad Ali again, a one-man show in which I was on the receiving end of the kind of angry disdain he had shown my sparring partner in New York. In a lifetime of interviewing people, this was the most unforgettable encounter of them all.

24

ALI IN AUTUMN

'Now God is involved, now you are fighting a spiritual, holy war when you face me now.'

Muhammad Ali, Parkinson Show, December 1974

I met Muhammad Ali and his entourage at the Mayfair Theatre where we were to record a one-man show. He was accompanied by a line of bodyguards wearing dark suits and shades. Ali nodded towards them and said, 'This is Brother . . .' and went along the line. I moved forward with hand outstretched. They looked away.

Ali was celebrating his resurrection. He had beaten George Foreman in what was known as the Rumble in the Jungle and was now world champion. It wasn't simply that he had beaten big old ugly George but had humiliated him. As the best of our sportswriters, Hugh McIlvanney, wrote: 'We should have known that Muhammad Ali would not settle for any ordinary old resurrection. He had to have an additional flourish. So, having rolled away the rock, he hit George Foreman on the head with it.'

We had decided this would be the interview when we sidestepped the showboating and tried to concentrate on the nature of the man. The problem with interviewing Muhammad Ali was you could never be sure who was going to turn up. This was a man who reinvented himself every morning when he woke up.

What we needed was a quiet studio for a serious one to one; instead we were in a West End theatre crammed with worshipping admirers and an atmosphere ripe for ballyhoo. It all went more or less to plan until I produced a book written by Budd Schulberg, a friend of Ali's. I said it was a fascinating book, pointing out one or two contradictions in his personality made all the more pertinent because Schulberg knew him well and was a friend.

Ali bridled and said Schulberg was an 'associate' not a friend.

I put to him a quote from the book: 'He [Ali] is devoted to a religious movement that looks on the white race as devils, whose time of deserved destruction is at hand and yet he's got more genuine white friends than any black fighter I have known.' Again, Ali insisted they were not friends but 'associates'. I pushed him further and asked him how he regarded Angelo Dundee, his trainer for many years. He said he was an 'associate'.

He then launched into a diatribe about how whites hated blacks, which included the observation that I was too small mentally and physically to 'trap' him on my TV show, which, in any case, was a joke. This was the first time I had seen Ali become really angry. The eyes were bright with rage. I had witnessed the play acting when he was fooling around or selling tickets, but this was different.

The audience sensed it, too. This was a side of Ali they hadn't seen before. In America Ali divided the nation; in Britain he was generally admired both as a prize-fighter and an amusing talk-show turn. The Ali on stage at the Mayfair Theatre was someone else, angry, racist and confrontational.

I sat listening to his rant, wondering how to deal with it, and decided all I could sensibly do was sit tight until the eruption of anger abated. I tried to analyse what had caused it and came to the conclusion it might have been a fear of being asked to read the offending passage from the Schulberg book, which he would have found a problem because the most extraordinary fact about this remarkable man is that he is semi-literate.

I asked him about his reading difficulties; he said, 'I study life, I study people and I'm educated on this, but when it comes to reading and writing I'm not. I may be illiterate in that but when it comes to common sense . . . I'm rich.'

The interview lurched to an end with both of us sitting back in our seats displaying the kind of body language that left no doubt about what one was thinking of the other. After the show there was no kissy-kissy, you-were-marvellous-darling farewells. He left with his entourage without a goodbye and I remember feeling, regretfully, that it would be unlikely if we met again.

I went to my dressing room where I sat wondering just what had happened and why. I felt I had been clumsy in my approach to the question about his white friends and further concerned that the outburst it had provoked might alienate a part of the audience who had hitherto adored him. My concern was based on the belief I have that, while Ali's faith is genuine, he was exploited as a propaganda outlet by people whose extreme views he might have echoed but never espoused.

I was thinking all these things when there was a knock on my dressing-room door. It was my father, who had been in the audience. As usual he came to the point.

'What do you reckon then?' he asked.

'Not much, Dad,' I said.

'Nor do I.' Then he said, 'Can I ask you a question?'

I nodded.

'What was up with you tonight, our Michael?'

'What do you mean? What on earth could I have done?'

'Why didn't you thump him?' said my father.

I looked at him for a full minute, at the angry determination in his face, and then I started laughing.

I did, in fact, meet Ali once more. Seven years later he came to London to promote a movie and we thought it might be a good idea to have him on the show with Freddie Starr, who, at the time, was more famous as an entertainer than someone who ate a hamster. In the years since our Mayfair encounter Ali had won and lost the world title. There were worrying reports about his health. His doctor, Ferdie Pacheco, had resigned four years earlier in 1977, having lost the argument with Ali's advisors that he should stop fighting to avoid serious neurological damage.

He fought Larry Holmes in October 1980 and was badly beaten. It was revealed after that fight that he had been examined at the Mayo Clinic some time before, when it was noted he was slurring his speech and his mobility was 'restrained'. Two months after the beating from Holmes, Ali sat down opposite me at the BBC Studios for what was to prove the final, and my favourite, encounter.

First impressions were not good. He didn't shuffle on to the set, but he was slower and bulkier. The features were bloated, the physique thickened, the voice jaded and slightly slurred.

'I'm tired, man,' he said, as he sat down, as if to explain what might follow.

What did ensue was mellow in comparison to our other encounters. The interview had an autumnal quality, a sense that we were both older and more reflective. The fact was we were both on our way out. I was leaving the BBC and moving on, and Ali, for all his talk about continuing his career, was face to face for the first time with his own mortality. He wouldn't, of course, contemplate retiring. He was talking about the rematch with Holmes.

I asked if he wasn't concerned about Ferdie Pacheco's view that he could end up with brain damage. Pacheco had told him, 'You are going to be a shambling wreck. Go to the gym and see these guys that talk funny, that's going to be you.'

Ali said, 'If I had a low IQ I'd enjoy this interview.' He went on to argue that the very nature of his profession meant he was a risk-taker. 'Look at my face. Twenty-seven years of fighting and not a mark,' he said, ignoring the fact that what we couldn't see and were concerned about was the damage done behind the mask.

We talked about alternative careers. He had just made a feature film, so what about acting?

'I've been acting ever since we first met,' he said.

He was on the show to promote a film called *Freedom Road*. In it Ali played a slave who went on to become a politician. It wasn't very good. On the other hand, its première in London was the most memorable I have ever attended. Ali was seated in the front row of the balcony, surrounded by his Black Muslim entourage, and in the row behind sat his special guests, including Daley Thompson and Freddie Starr. Ali kept up a running commentary during the movie, nudging his neighbours or turning to tell us, 'Watch this scene now, man. This is great.'

Towards the end of the film, with a white-haired Ali on his death bed, he turned to us and said, 'This is a real sad scene. So watch carefully.'

Thus instructed, we watched Ali die a death more melodramatic than poignant, and as we did so the breathless silence was broken by a loud fart, which seemed to come from the right of the balcony, then another, which came from the left, and another from directly behind the great man where sat Freddie Starr. A gifted impressionist, one of Mr Starr's unspoken talents was to make the sound of a person breaking wind and to throw it across a room, thereby avoiding detection. His efforts on this occasion caused consternation on the front row with Ali's entourage scanning the balcony for the perpetrator of such a dastardly outrage.

Starr's appearance on the show with Ali was a calculated risk, but we just about got away with it, mainly because Ali was the only man in the world whom Starr would concede was more interesting than himself. On the show Freddie started as he meant to go on. 'All my family were boxers except my father,' he said, as he sat down. I fell for it. 'What's he?' I asked. 'A cocker spaniel,' he said.

During a section imitating singers, at which he is brilliant, Freddie pulled a black stocking over his face, donned dark glasses and did a Ray Charles impression. I was horrified. There were stirrings among Ali's entourage in the audience. Ali looked at me, smiled and shook his head.

If he was angry he didn't show it but he certainly had his revenge later on when, during a break, with Freddie dancing round the studio saying he was faster and prettier than Ali and was going to whup him, Ali stood and whispered to me, 'Get behind me and grab my arms.' I did so and he pretended to struggle free as Freddie – who, by now, had convinced himself he was a real contender – was shadow boxing in Ali's face. Ali said to me, 'Let go,' and, as I did, he glided forward and flashed five left jabs around Freddie's head, each missing him by centimetres. Any punch, had it connected, would have caused serious damage to Mr Starr's smile. Freddie calmed down after that.

Starr's demise as an entertainer was particularly sad for those of us who believed he had it in him to be one of the truly great all-rounders. I saw his club act, before his valium addiction addled his talent and confused his personality, and he possessed a virtuosity equalled by only a very few entertainers.

After meeting on the show, Ali adopted Freddie as his new best friend. At one point at the party after the première of the film, Ali was to be seen working the room with Freddie tucked under his arm like a trophy.

Liam Neeson, the actor, told me of being in the line-up to meet Ali and, as the great man approached, thinking of what he might say to him, how he might distil into a few words his true admiration. When Ali finally appeared in front of him and shook his hand all he could blurt out was, 'Pleased to meet you. I think I love you.'

Ali went on to fight once more. He lost to Trevor Berbick and was punished by a fighter whose presence in the same ring as Ali was in itself the most pertinent indication of the great boxer's decline. Two year after fighting Berbick, Ali came under the care of Dr Stanley Fahn at the Columbian Presbyterian Medical Center. Dr Fahn diagnosed Ali's condition as 'Post-traumatic Parkinsonism due to injuries from fighting'.

He went on to explain Ali's condition: 'My assumption is that his physical condition resulted from repeated blows to the head over time . . . Also since Parkinsonism causes, among other things, slowness of movement, one can question whether the beating Muhammad took in his last few fights was because . . . he couldn't move as quickly and thus was more susceptible to being hit.'

Ali is not the first fighter, nor will he be the last, to have his life blighted by his occupation. We can debate until kingdom come who takes the blame but ultimately, in the case of Muhammad Ali, the real reason he fought for so long was that which made him a great champion: his indomitable courage, unyielding resolve, unquench-able willpower. To expect him to take a careful approach to his life, to work solidly and cautiously towards a pension, is to misunderstand the soul of the prize-fighter. You might as well require a racehorse to finish its days pulling an ice-cream cart as a pensionable occupation.

There are those who need to examine the part they played in observing his downfall and wonder if they could have persuaded him to quit sooner than he did. But then again, Ali told Dr Fahn that he thought the damage had started in the third fight with Frazier in Manila, some time before the first manifestations of slurred speech and a physical slowing down. Moreover anyone with even a passing acquaintance with Ali would attest to the implacable quality of his willpower.

Arguably, the athlete who was boxing's greatest figure is also the sport's biggest tragedy. The lesson for boxing is that if a fighter as great as Ali can be affected by the sport, then no one is safe. We didn't meet again after 1981. In 2000, when Ali was voted Sportsman of the Millennium, I was asked to present him with his award at the BBC TV Centre. I refused because I didn't want to encounter at close quarters that once glorious man now wrecked by a terrible illness.

I felt, wrongly perhaps, I couldn't celebrate that which had brought about his downfall. The fact is, as the years went by, I grew to admire and like him more and more, and never more than on that last occasion we met when I observed him dealing with his diminishing faculties with faultless courage and humour. I wanted to remember him as he once was and as he described himself: 'When will they ever have another fighter who writes poems, predicts rounds, beats everybody, makes people laugh, makes people cry, and is as tall and extra pretty as me? In the history of the world and from the beginning of time, there's never been another fighter like me.'

Nor, I venture, will there ever be.

25

EMU AND
MEG RYAN

When asked to define the talk show I said it was an unnatural act performed by consenting adults in public. That was at the beginning of my stint and now, looking back on more than six hundred shows and nearly two thousand guests, I see no reason to change my mind. It is an unnatural act because the basic premise is so daunting. The guest is told that the simple task is to sit opposite the interviewer and chat about themselves and, providing the interviewer showered that morning, and bothered to do the research, there is no reason why it should be anything other than an agreeable experience.

All you have to do, they tell you, is relax. What they don't tell you is how to relax when the band starts playing and you walk on in front of five hundred witnesses in the studio and millions watching at home, with a microphone stuck into every orifice and the lighting generating sufficient heat to give the sweat glands a nudge.

I always felt a great deal of sympathy for the guests as they walked on, particularly the first-timers. You could see the concern in their eyes; sense their confusion at finding themselves in a strange environment. With very few exceptions every guest would take a while to settle, to relax into a working partnership with the host. My first job was to convince them they were going to enjoy the next hour of their life and it would take me only a couple of minutes to discern whether or not the interview was going to work.

A talk show is a consensual act between host and guest and if one or the other won't play, then the result is a disaster, and I have had my fair share of those. It says something for the nature of the job that, at the end of a lengthy stint interviewing some of the most famous people of the twentieth and twenty-first centuries, you are mainly remembered for calamities rather than triumphs.

If I am to list my disasters in terms of those that provoke most street reaction, then it would be the Emu in first place, followed closely by Meg Ryan.

The Emu occurred in 1975 in a show that starred agony aunt Anna Raeburn, Billy Connolly and Rod Hull and his pet. I feared I might be attacked but was quite unprepared by the ferocity of the creature on Rod's arm. There were warning signs in the make-up room where the bird sat on Rod's knee and divided its time between snarling at me and leering at the make-up girl.

It has long been my belief that people who make a living by sticking their hands up the backsides of emus and other creatures, not to mention dolls, are not like the rest of us. Also it is strange how we, the victims, tolerate their behaviour. I remember one performer – I will not mention his name – who, with a puppet on his hand, spent his entire time in make-up touching the girls in intimate places. Had I done the same I would, quite rightly, have been locked up. In his case, all the girls did was giggle and say, 'Naughty boy,' as if it was some living mischievous pet stroking their bums and worse.

Of course, it only works if you believe in the artifice and I have been as guilty as any in falling into the trap. For instance, when I interviewed Miss Piggy I convinced myself that I was in love with the Pig and she would leave Kermit and share my dressing room at the BBC.

I even forgave her when she stared at my head and said, 'Can I ask you a deeply personal question?'

'Of course,' I said, besotted.

'Is that a toupee?' she asked.

At the end of the show I was having a drink with Frank Oz, who created Miss Piggy, and I mentioned to him the curious business of believing in the Pig. Mr Oz asked me to explain.

'Well,' I said, 'for a time out there I was having a serious conversation with a pig.'

'So?' he said.

'Well, look at it another way, for a time out there I was actually romancing a piece of cloth.'

'That's bad,' he said. 'But even worse – and I want you to think seriously about this – is that for twenty minutes out there you were making love to my right hand.'

I was never in danger of falling in love with the Emu. I didn't like the creature but we booked the act because we thought it might be an event. It was certainly that. At the end of his attack on me I was shoeless, jacketless and without a shred of dignity, scrabbling round the studio floor. Ever since I have been reminded of the catastrophe on a fairly regular basis.

Rod and the Emu were the first guests on the show and we were rid of them before bringing on Anna and Billy. However, at the end of the show, Rod and the Emu made an unscheduled return with the intent of more havoc. I told them, in no uncertain terms, to go forth and multiply. They had a look at Anna but decided not to attack her because the violence isn't funny when directed against a woman.

It was then that Rod made the biggest mistake of his professional life. He moved menacingly towards Billy Connolly. Now Mr Connolly is not a man to deal sympathetically with an assault by another man's alter ego disguised as an emu. He grabbed the bird by the neck and, talking to the beak, said, 'I tell you what, Emu, you peck me and I'll break your neck and his bloody arm.'

After Rod had died and his son revived the act, we were approached to see if the Emu could make a return to the show. We said only if it could sit next to Meg Ryan.

With some disasters, like the Emu, it is easy to analyse cause and effect. With Meg Ryan I still can't work out what exactly went wrong. She was promoting a film called *In the Cut*, which I had seen and didn't much like. However, being an erotic thriller, it raised some interesting questions, such as what had attracted 'America's sweetheart' to such a film. There were ominous signs when I visited her dressing room to say hello. We had never met before, but I had admired her films, including *When Harry Met Sally*, and was genuinely looking forward to interviewing her for the first time. She was with an entourage of publicity people but there appeared to be a certain *froideur* between them.

Ryan was on with Trinny and Susannah and sat behind the set while the girls chatted away about some new show they were doing on what clothes tell us about people, power dressing and all that. They did a good spot and certainly raised enough interesting points for a following guest, particularly a woman, to pick up on.

When we first designed the set we built a cosy sitting room at the back where waiting guests could see and hear what was happening in the studio before they went on. This was a way of furthering our ambition to let the show be as conversational as possible. When I met Meg and looked into those wonderful blue eyes I decided to settle her with a few questions about what Trinny and Susannah had been saying.

She seemed surprised, as if she had been beamed into the show from another universe. Eventually she said to the girls, 'Oh, did you just do a fashion item?'

I knew in that moment I was not going to make friends with Meg.

She later claimed I talked down to her in an aggressive manner. Her spokesman said I would not have been as robust with a male interviewee. The fact is she was uncooperative from the start. One reviewer said she 'glided from slight frostiness to naked hostility via snooty disdain'.

There comes a point in an interview where it serves no purpose to continue. The only question left is why did you bother turning up and then not trying. She had stated she had worked as a journalist for a short time. I told her she obviously didn't like being interviewed, that her demeanour and body language suggested she wanted no part of our show and, that being the case and she having been a journalist, if she was in my shoes, what would she do?

'Wrap it up,' she said, which was the only sensible quote I got from her all night.

In many ways the on-screen relationship between host and guest is one aspect of the interview you cannot account for or, more importantly, anticipate. You can prepare for someone being drunk, nervous or unwell but you cannot legislate for that moment when the guest walks on and you sense the antipathy. It doesn't happen often and it has nothing to do with personal prejudice. I have interviewed many people I imagined I didn't like but had never met and, more often than not, having interviewed them, completely changed my mind.

Simon Cowell was the paramount example. I didn't like what he stood for in the music industry. I thought he promoted mediocrity through the kind of so-called reality shows for which I have total and utter contempt. That opinion still holds firm and yet, when I interviewed him, I was impressed by his candour, his ability to laugh at himself, and his great charm. When he confessed to me he didn't like music, I felt like taking him home and adopting him.

On the other hand, you can really admire someone, and long to meet them, only to be disappointed when you do. My first meeting with Helen Mirren was like that. I enjoyed her as an actress and thought she was a beguiling woman, an intriguing blend of intelligence and sex appeal. When she first came on the show she wore a revealing dress and carried an ostrich feather. This might have accounted for a clumsy line of questioning about whether or not her physical attributes stood in the way of her being recognised as a genuine actor. Ms Mirren bridled and wondered if I was asking if breasts prevented her from being taken seriously. I was wrong-footed and blundered on to a point where I could feel her hostility. We didn't meet again until many years later, and we recalled that first meeting. Helen said she thought I behaved like a complete ass and I couldn't disagree.

Kenneth Williams was someone I didn't like before I met him, and having met him for the first time found no need to change my mind. The feeling was mutual. In his published diaries Williams records that in December 1971 he was asked to appear on a show I was doing for ITV. 'I said certainly not. North Country nit,' he wrote. In 1974, having already appeared on the show three times, he tells in his diary that he 'loathes' me. By 1981, having appeared on the show more times than anyone else apart from Spike Milligan and Billy Connolly, he thinks I am 'very likeable and patient'. When he appeared with me on *Desert Island Discs* he wrote: 'I get along fine with Michael Parkinson 'cos he's direct and honest and lets you become uninhibited.'

For my part, I went from disliking him to understanding him, or at least recognising those insecurities that bedevilled his personality. He was capable of being rude, cruel and arrogant. His saving grace was he could be incredibly funny and I treasure some of the moments he created on the show.

My favourite is his account of touring with Dame Edith Evans and fetching up in a seedy hotel in the north country where, after the show, Dame Edith asked an old and doddering waiter for a drop of sherry. As the waiter bent over to pour the drink he broke wind in spectacular fashion. Dame Edith wrinkled her nose in distaste and said in that wonderful voice, 'This place has gone off terribly.' Performed with Kenneth's wonderful imitations, the anecdote becomes a classic comedy vignette.

Our relationship was professional and distant, except for the time I was working in Australia and decided to bring him over for a couple of shows. When it was announced he was in Sydney I was called by Sir James Hardy, winemaker and yachtie, who told me Lady Hardy was Kenneth's greatest fan and would be honoured to meet him. Would I like to bring Kenneth and Marti Caine, who was also in town, on to his boat for a trip round the harbour? He asked if I would explain to my guests that his boat was not a gin palace, but a yacht that had raced in the Sydney to Hobart and therefore the guests would need to dress accordingly. I explained this to Marti and Kenneth who said they understood.

Next morning when I called to pick them up Marti was wearing killer heels and Kenneth looked like a bank manager about to board the 7.30 from Surbiton to the City. He wore a belted raincoat, sensible suit and brogues. The crew, who rowed in to collect us, were as amused at their passengers as Kenneth and Marti were confused by the sight of a racing yacht. It was not what they had imagined, particularly Kenneth who looked around for somewhere to sit and ended up perching on the side of the boat like a man who has decided he was not stopping for too long.

He was discovered thus by Lady Hardy who, as she went to greet him, started telling him how much she admired his talent and had looked forward to this meeting.

He cut across her welcome. 'It's all very well but what about my backside?' he asked.

This was not what Lady Hardy was expecting.

'You see, missus, I've got terrible piles and if I sit on damp wood like you've got here on this boat, then they play up something awful. I've always had trouble with my bum, you know. I've had the finest people in Harley Street up my bum, you know. You can't imagine the work that's been done up there.'

He was now on a comedy monologue and unstoppable.

Lady Hardy had blanched at being thus harangued and shortly disappeared down below where she no doubt took to her hammock.

Kenneth wrote in his diary that while on board the yacht he reflected on his reasons for coming to Oz. 'From the time I boarded the aircraft for this trip there has been a feeling of unreality: the continual question "what on earth am I doing?"' Kenneth Williams in Australia would have made a marvellous television documentary. I think it fair to say that at the end of his first visit neither he nor Australia quite knew what to make of each other.

The only time I ever saw Kenneth Williams lost for words was when we put him in the studio next to Jimmy Reid. Reid was a trade union leader who, in the seventies, led the sit-in at a Glasgow shipyard threatened with closure. His eloquence and intelligence made him a national figure. Previously, I had interviewed Kenneth on a show with Sir John Betjeman and Maggie Smith, but what started out as a celebration of Betjeman's talent ended in a row with Kenneth after a diatribe about the political unrest in the country. I told him that, when he started criticising working men such as miners and dockers, he didn't know what he was talking about. I accused him of talking crap. He said he had never been so insulted in all his life. A short time after, we booked Jimmy Reid on the show and asked Kenneth if he would like to debate the state of the nation with him. He agreed and we brought them together at the television centre for a very different kind of *Parkinson* show.

Before the interview we showed them the studio, the walk-on and then sat them down for a sound check. In such a situation you ask a daft question just so the sound man can get a proper level. The cliché question is: 'What did you have for breakfast?'

Kenneth said he didn't want to discuss breakfast, he would rather recite poetry. It seemed obvious to me this was a deliberate attempt to upstage Jimmy Reid, to demonstrate that he was now operating in Williams's world and might be discomfited. At the end of the poem, beautifully delivered, Kenneth looked at Jimmy in a challenging manner.

Jimmy said, 'That was Yeats, wasn't it?'

Kenneth looked surprised but nodded in agreement.

I asked Jimmy what he had for breakfast.

He said he would like to perform a poem. He did so in a clear, confident voice and looked towards Kenneth.

Williams said, 'I've never heard that before. Who wrote it?'

Jimmy Reid said, 'I did.'

After the programme Paul Fox called Richard Drewett and told him to keep the format free from the kind of political debate he had just seen. This did not please Kenneth. He wrote in his diary: 'It certainly shows the BBC in its mediocre light. Bland, bland, bland and *Blankety Blank*.'

I thought Paul's instinct was right, although it was worth a try. If we had shown the rehearsal rather than the show, it would have been much better. Not that Kenneth would have welcomed it.

Our last meeting was in June 1987, when I was hosting *Give Us A Clue*. Kenneth was a regular and welcome guest and found, in performing charades, the perfect vehicle for showing off. He wrote in his diary: 'To Teddington. My team on *Give Us A Clue* was Simon Williams and Martin Jarvis. No show could be more enjoyable 'cos all the people there are delightful to be with. Michael Parkinson asked me (as he always does) "What are you working at?" and I said, "Fuck all."'

Ten months later he died, aged sixty-two and irreplaceable.

26

LIGHTING UP FOR BETTE DAVIS

When I was sitting in the back row of the Rock Cinema in Cudworth watching my Hollywood heroes, I never imagined that one day I would say, 'Ladies and gentlemen, my next guest is Fred Astaire . . . James Cagney . . . John Wayne . . . James Stewart . . . Lauren Bacall' and see them walking down the stairs towards me.

How could I have dared believe while watching Bette Davis and Paul Henreid play that famous and romantic last scene from *Now, Voyager* that one day I would play the Henreid part opposite Davis. I was greatly affected by the movie when I first saw it, particularly the moment where the romantic theme soared in the background as the lovers parted, and Henreid pulled off his marvellous trick with the cigarettes when he put two in his mouth and lit them, handing one to Davis, creating the definitive gesture of shared intimacy for my generation.

When I interviewed Bette Davis for the first time I asked if we might replay the scene and she agreed. When the time came, Harry Stoneham played the theme and, just like Paul Henried, I put two cigarettes in my mouth and lit them before handing one to Miss Davis.

She was about to make the observation that no matter what

happened we would always have the stars when I saw her recoil in disgust. Her cigarette had stuck in my mouth and, in disengaging it, I had managed to pull off the greater part of my lower lip.

Miss Davis regarded my bloody offering and, instead of her declaration of undying love, remarked disdainfully, 'I don't think so.'

The seventies was a good time to do a talk show. The studio system, which had produced and controlled the great Hollywood stars, was changing and the men and women who created the Golden Era of movie-making were willing for the first time to talk about those days.

Unlike today, where celebrity is stripped bare and picked over by the media on a minute by minute basis, the Cagneys and the Fondas and the Stewarts had only ever been seen as thirty-foot figures on a big screen. When they walked down the studio stairs it was like gods descending from Mount Olympus.

The added bonus was that they were, in the main, interesting people who, because of the war, had experienced life outside acting. To talk to men who had flown missions over Germany as well as played Hamlet was to deal with a more fascinating creature than a mere actor. There was a hinterland, a background, a testimony to having lived a life other than that bounded by a proscenium arch.

James Stewart was not just an actor of great skill and charm, one of the most charismatic of all leading men, but he had served as a colonel in the US Air Force. He had flown in combat. He wasn't merely a celluloid hero. Not that he ever brought it up. He was the most genuinely modest man of them all with a wonderfully wry sense of humour. Talking about his famous drawling voice, he said he was advised to go to a voice coach so he might be convincing as an Austrian in a stage play. After three lessons the voice coach kicked him out in despair. She said, 'There is no way I can teach you an Austrian accent. On the other hand, if you would like to learn how to speak English, then I might be able to help.'

When I asked him if he ever analysed his screen image to try to discover what audiences found so attractive, he said, 'I'm the plodder. I'm the inarticulate man that tries. I'm a pretty good example of human frailty . . . I don't have all the answers, but for some reason somehow I make it. I get through. When I am at the head of the wagon train, for some reason we get across the water.'

His wife confirmed that in real life he was as absent-minded and dreamy as he sometimes appeared on film. She said when she was pregnant and nearing her time, her husband worked out a carefully prepared routine of how to get her to the hospital. On the day, she told him the baby was coming and he said not to panic as he was fully prepared. He drove to the hospital in record time only to find when he arrived that he had forgotten his wife. As he raced back home he passed the ambulance taking her in.

Henry Fonda was keen to talk about his talented children, particularly Jane. He told me, 'She is one of the most incredible actresses I have ever seen. When I saw *Klute*, as an example, I couldn't wait to sit and talk to her, not father to daughter, but actor to actor. I realised one scene that particularly knocked me out was improvisation, which I couldn't do if I was paid a lot of money. It just tore me apart.'

When I interviewed Jane Fonda many years later she told me how distant her father had been, how he seemed unable to communicate with his family. I remembered our interview and told her what he had said.

'He never told me,' she said, sadly.

I explained he described her as one of the most extraordinary actresses he had ever seen and her eyes filled with tears.

'Why didn't he tell me?' she said.

We gave her a copy of her father's tribute. How strange he could have so publicly and proudly praised her and yet not found it possible to tell her himself, knowing, as he surely must have, how much she craved his approval.

One day we received a letter from a man called Leslie Gaynor. He was a fitter for Hovercraft in the Isle of Wight. He said he had the biggest collection in the land of Bing Crosby memorabilia, that Bing was a personal friend of his and if we wanted him on the show he could fix it. We thought he was a nutter. But then why would he say these things if there was not an element of truth in them? So we asked him to come to London and not only did Mr Gaynor get us Bing Crosby, he was also indirectly responsible for Fred Astaire appearing on the show.

It is a mark of Crosby's unaffected good nature that he made his first appearance on *Parkinson* not because Orson Welles had been on the show or he had anything to promote, but out of friendship for Leslie Gaynor. He was the most relaxed and laid back of them all. He arrived alone at the BBC TV Centre in a black cab. We had sent a limo, which he had dismissed.

When he appeared a second time on the show he also dismissed the limo. I asked him why he preferred London cabs to limousines. He said he had been coming to London for more than forty years and had always used London cabs. I persisted. But why?

'Well, I must confess that in all the years I have been coming to London and using cabs I have never been charged a fare. The cabbie always says, "Bing, because of all the joy you have given me and the family over the years, the ride is on me."'

'That is a true definition of a superstar,' I said.

Then I thought for a moment and said, 'But come on, there must have been an occasion when the cabbie didn't recognise you?'

'True,' he said.

'What did you do then?' I asked.

'When I thought they were not sure, I would move that little glass partition, sing two or three bars of "White Christmas" and they knew who they had in the back of their cab,' he said.

When he arrived at the reception desk at the TV Centre he was carrying a hat box under his arm. He said to the receptionist, 'Hi, I'm Bing Crosby. Can you direct me towards the gal who's going to fix my toop.'

His hairpiece was in the box.

He told me his favourite song was 'White Christmas' and he never tired of singing it. When he performed it on the show I was astonished to see him reading the words from autocue. He had an effortless style and possessed the greatest gift of all, that of making everyone in the studio believe they wanted to work for him.

That said he wasn't a pushover. He had very exacting standards and expected everyone else to match them. It is true that, like Sinatra, he didn't care much for rehearsal, which is not the same as saying he didn't care about getting it right. Again like Sinatra, when he came into the studio to rehearse he was word perfect and faultless in his delivery. He expected everyone else to be the same.

He ran through his number twice, the band was happy, it sounded good. Then the director asked if he would mind doing it one more time. Crosby agreed. When he had finished, the director pleaded with Bing for another take.

Crosby asked why.

The director said, 'I think I can do it better.'

Bing smiled and said, 'I can't.'

I did a duet with Crosby, which is a bit like saying I danced with Ginger Rogers or opened the innings with W.G. Grace.

Bing said if I was any good he was going to retire and play golf. At the end of our performance, he looked at me and said, 'Guess I'm back on the road again.'

That reminded me of Jack Benny's great story about his friendship with the violinist Isaac Stern. Playing violin was part of Benny's comedy act, but he was good enough to perform with symphony orchestras in concert halls. He told me that after a concert with the Detroit Symphony Orchestra, he had dinner with Isaac Stern who said, 'You know, Jack, when you walk out in front of a big symphony orchestra in white tie and tails and violin, you look like one of the world's greatest violinists. It's just a damn shame you have to play.'

Bing Crosby returned to England a couple of years later to make a record with Fred Astaire, produced by Ken Barnes. John Fisher, who was a researcher on the show at the time and soon to become the producer, one of the very best I have ever worked with, went to the recording studio at Wembley. Astaire did not like being interviewed. He had never done a major television interview. He was persuaded by a combination of John, Crosby and his daughter Ava Astaire, who lived in Ireland and enjoyed the show.

Of all the stars to appear on *Parkinson*, Astaire was the one I was most in awe of. I love dance, admire dancers greatly and have never seen anyone who even comes close to Fred Astaire. Gene Kelly told me, 'I dance like a truck driver. He dances like an aristocrat.' When I was a kid I used to foxtrot home from the cinema, imagining I had Ginger on my arm. George Axelrod, the American writer, said he once saw Astaire walking across a Hollywood canteen, drop a cigarette on the floor, stamp it out and continue without any perceptible change of rhythm. He said in that moment he invented a new verb, 'to astaire', which meant going through life without making an awkward or ugly movement.

We asked Fred Astaire if he would dance on the show. He said his dancing days were over but he would sing a few of the songs that had been written for him. We booked the best session men in London for rehearsal. Fred Astaire arrived, like Crosby, alone and carrying a small case. He met Harry Stoneham, our MD, opened the case and said, 'I've brought the dots.' The top copy of music was 'A foggy day in London Town' and across the first page was written 'To Fred from George and Ira'.

Harry said, 'I can't use these. They belong in a museum.'

For twenty minutes or more, Astaire sang those glorious songs written for him by the most illustrious composers of the Great American Songbook. I was reminded of Oscar Peterson's statement that Astaire was the greatest interpreter of popular songs of the lot because of the way 'he danced on the note'.

When he finished, the musicians applauded. That tribute in itself would guarantee him certain entry to the pantheon.

He was nervous about the interview, not sure he was interesting enough to warrant an hour-long show. It wasn't false modesty; he simply couldn't see what all the fuss was about. Backstage, as we waited to go on, I tried to settle him by telling him how I used to dance my way home from the cinema and, if I wasn't imitating Fred Astaire, would try to walk like John Wayne.

Then the band started playing and I walked on and fell from the top stair to the bottom. Take 2. When I reappeared at the back of the set, Fred Astaire was laughing. 'Guess you got mixed up between me and the Duke,' he said.

When he walked on he seemed not to touch a step. He descended in what can only be described as a graceful glide.

When it was announced that John Wayne was to appear on the show I received a telegram from Carl Foreman, the Hollywood director and scriptwriter of *High Noon* and *The Guns of Navarone*, saying that if I didn't closely question him about cooperating with Senator Joe McCarthy in the days of the Hollywood witch-hunts, then it would be an insult to all those who had been blacklisted. Foreman himself had suffered from the testimony of people such as Wayne, who had named names in the infamous communist purges.

Wayne arrived on the show looking less rugged than he appeared in his movies, mainly because he had recently been in hospital with lung cancer. He still looked like a star and walked on in that singular style. He didn't much like being asked about the McCarthy days, and even when we left the subject and moved on to talking about movies he treated me warily and with suspicion. At the end of our interview I asked him to sign his book. It wasn't until a couple of days later I opened it to see the inscription. It read: 'To Mike Parkinson. A fellow travels a long way, John Wayne.'

I'm still not sure if he was being folksy or trying to tell me something.

Robert Mitchum was one of my great Hollywood heroes. When I was a kid I wanted to look like Mitchum. I wanted the dimple, the sleepy eyes and the quizzical lift of the eyebrow. Most of all, I wanted the back of his head, which was flat and allowed for a wonderful DA. Mine had a big rear knob, which, when I was younger and skinnier, made me look like a visitor from the Planet Mekon. I decided that, when I was rich and famous, I would have the knob surgically removed in Harley Street, but Mitchum's other attributes I could work on straightaway. Thus I went to bed at night with sticking plaster over my chin, clamping the flesh into what I hoped would turn out to be a dimple. I would raise my eyebrow with elastoplast and fix it to my forehead. I lay there looking like a road accident and none of it worked.

Mr Mitchum was renowned for his hatred of interviewers, so it came as a shock when he agreed to a one-man show. There was plenty to talk about. Except for the fact he had worked with Jane Russell, his movies were the least interesting part of a man who refused to conform, who did his own deals with Hollywood and life and who had a reputation for being what they used to call in those days a hell raiser.

He also had a reputation for smoking a lot of dope and that was what I smelled before I met him. There was what can only be described as an exotic odour coming from his dressing room at the TV Centre as I approached. Mr Mitchum was surrounded by friends, including dear old Ronnie Fraser, the actor, who told me he had been appointed Mr Mitchum's bag carrier, which meant he had the bag with the dope in it.

Robert Mitchum greeted me in convivial manner. What he said was, 'Hi, kid. Wanna smoke?'

I said I wouldn't mind a cigar.

He looked at me pityingly. 'Do you wanna smoke some shit?' he said.

As they say in the tabloids, I made my excuses and left.

It was a fascinating encounter in the studio, mainly because Mr Mitchum answered most of my carefully prepared questions with either 'Nope' or 'Yup'.

We struggled along until I came to the point where I had little else to ask him. In these situations I had planned a coded instruction with the production team. If I asked the guest: 'Has anyone ever taken a swing at you in a bar?' it meant this was possibly the penultimate question. If I followed up with: 'When did you learn how to tap dance?' it meant start the car because we are shortly heading home.

So I asked Robert Mitchum if anyone had taken a swing at him in a bar. He said 'Yup'.

This was my chance. 'What happened?' I asked, thinking you can't say yup or nope to that.

He said, 'I was in a bar having some lunch and a man came up to me and shoved a pen and paper between my fork and my mouth and said, "Sign that." I looked at him and said, "Do you mind if I finish my lunch and then I'll consider your request." So the guy says, "You think you're a tough son of a bitch, don't you?" This upset me.'

He paused. The audience was transfixed. It was the first time he had spoken more than four consecutive words.

'What happened next?' I said.

'Well, I took my fork and put it under the guy's chin, and pushed it through the roof of his mouth and out the top of his head.'

There was an awed silence in the studio as he looked at me begging the next question.

'Are you pulling my leg?' I said.

'Yup,' he said.

He finished his performance by singing 'Little old wine drinker, me,' before heading upstairs to his cronies and a celebration.

As we left the studio, he said, 'How was it, kid?'

I said something like maybe it could have been better. He said, 'Let's go back and do it again.' I thanked him but said you couldn't repeat an interview. He might have said, 'What interview?' but he was heading for a bar.

Our hospitality room at the time was run by a wonderful Cockney woman called Lil who had seen them all come and go and whose loyalty was such that her opinion of the guests was entirely based on how kind they had been to me.

Mr Mitchum was not in her good books.

'Would you like a drink, sir?' she enquired.

'Vodka,' said Mitchum.

She reached behind for the optic measure.

'Lady, the bottle, please,' said Mitchum.

She handed him the bottle.

'Would you like ice, sir?' she asked.

Mitchum nodded.

'I suppose you would like the bleedin' bucket,' she said, and gave it to him.

Completely unfazed, he put two or three ice cubes in his mouth and drank from the bottle. Shortly after, he turned to me and said, 'OK, kid, let's go party.'

The last I saw of him he was leading his entourage into the night with that shoulder-led swagger I am still trying to copy.

I liked him a lot. He had a majestic quality and yet there was also a sense he was one of a disappearing breed. As he ambled into the night he reminded me of a melting iceberg.

27

THAT'S SHOWBIZ

Richard Burton was a hero of mine long before I ever saw him act. In the sixties I bought a recording of *Under Milk Wood* with Burton playing the narrator. I knew it almost line by line. It was the definitive reading by the most wonderful voice of them all. I liked the man before I even met him, not because of his acting but rather his kindness to a friend.

Cliff Morgan was taken ill and I went to see him in hospital. Cliff was one of the greatest rugby players of them all, and he followed this with a distinguished career in television. He is a man beloved by all who know him. The illness incapacitated him and meant he would have to spend some time recuperating. I was impressed by the size of his room at the hospital and started teasing him about paying for it.

He said, 'Look in that drawer.' There was a telegram. The message read: 'This illness is on me. Richard.'

At the time of our interview Richard Burton was a recovering alcoholic who had just returned from a stay in a clinic in Switzerland. His companion was Princess Elizabeth of Yugoslavia. The interview was to take place late morning and we decided not to have any booze on show in the Green Room. Burton seemed edgy while waiting and, as soon as his girlfriend left the room, asked for a drink. His hands were shaking. One of his entourage produced a whisky, which he brought unsteadily to his lips. It seemed to settle him, the trembling calmed, and he said he was ready for the studio.

Because it was taking place in the morning we had been unable to round up the usual audience. Instead, we tannoyed around the BBC that Richard Burton was to be interviewed and asked anyone who was interested to come along. The majority of people free at that time were chefs and kitchen staff so, when I introduced Richard Burton, he was faced with an audience of people in white coats. 'Christ, I thought I was back at the bloody clinic,' he said.

It was a memorable interview. He told of playing Hamlet with Winston Churchill in the audience speaking the lines with him.

'I couldn't shake him off, whatever I did, wherever I went. "To be or not to be", he was with me to the very end. Afterwards I thought he might come backstage. We waited but he didn't come, so I thought I might as well have a drink, get sloshed. I was just about to start when the door opened and there was Sir Winston. He bowed very graciously and, very courteously, said, "My Lord Hamlet, may I use your lavatory?"'

Burton told me that when the drinking was at its worst he was consuming up to three bottles of hard liquor a day. He said, 'Trying to get some food into my mouth was an extraordinary business. I was in a Roman Catholic hospital in Santa Monica and I insisted that I fed myself. I held the spoon but my hands would not obey me. They flew all over the place. A friend of mine who was there said, "I know you're in a Roman Catholic hospital, but there is no need for you to make the sign of the cross every time you eat."'

He said he had been on the edge of a 'terrible precipice' but had survived and had decided to regain control of his life. He didn't. He died of a brain haemorrhage in 1984 aged fifty-nine. He was one of that tiny handful of men I met who possessed an indefinable power of personality.

Looking at him was to understand how much drink had ruined his looks, diminished his physique and reduced the range of that great voice. And yet his charisma remained powerful and compelling.

James Cagney was also a real star, one of the truly legendary figures of Hollywood. He was the man who defined the gangster movies of the twenties and thirties, the street dancer who never had a lesson in his life and who Fred Astaire said was the greatest of the lot, and the actor whose strutting walk and cocky, optimistic persona epitomised America surviving the Depression and becoming the most powerful nation on the planet.

Billy Wilder, the director, also told me he thought Cagney the greatest star of them all, and fulfilled an ambition to work with him when they made *One Two Three*. He said that Cagney, renowned for the speed at which he learned his lines – 'one take Cagney' – and for professionalism on set, found it difficult to master a long speech that Wilder had saved for the end of the shoot. He struggled so much that instead of one take, Wilder devised a means of breaking it into three sections.

When filming was finished Cagney told Wilder he was retiring. When Wilder asked why he said he was no longer 'one take Cagney' and didn't want to be second best. He left Hollywood and bought a farm where he remained for twenty years or more before he was persuaded out of retirement by Milos Forman, who cast him in *Ragtime*, a movie he was making in England.

Pat O'Brien, who played opposite Cagney in the Hollywood

glory days, accompanied him, and the two of them agreed to do our show together. For the first twenty minutes or so, Cagney was wonderful, recalling the gangster movies that made his name, telling me the origin of his famous shoulder-shrugging, arm-jabbing trademark gesture, denying he ever said 'you dirty rat'. Then he became agitated, wriggling in his seat, giving every indication he would rather be elsewhere. His friend O'Brien stepped in and we hobbled to the end of the show.

'Are you OK?' I asked Cagney as the music played.

'Fine, but I'm dying for a pee,' he said.

When I met Milos Forman, I asked him what it was like working with Cagney and he said just to have been in his presence was sufficient reward.

I felt the same way.

Forman said he became friendly enough with Cagney to persuade the great man to attend a prestigious television show where he would be introduced at the end of the evening as a very special, surprise guest. This would be one of the first times Cagney had ever made such an appearance. Even in his heyday he avoided the spotlight, ducked publicity. Forman said by this time Cagney was so frail he was in a wheelchair. As the show approached its climax they wheeled Cagney into position, awaiting a cue that never came. The show had overrun and, with the closing credits being shown and Cagney sitting in the wings, Forman said he felt anger, despair and frustration that one of the truly great motion picture stars was being treated in such a careless manner.

He looked in desperation at Cagney, who smiled, shrugged his shoulders and said, 'That's showbiz.'

I first met Kirk Douglas when being measured for a suit. We shared the same tailor, Doug Hayward, whose shop in Mount

Street was a salon for actors, writers, photographers, landed gentry, soccer players, racing drivers, models, royalty and associated layabouts, all of them chosen and approved by a remarkable lad from Acton who left school at fifteen and became one of the great stylists of the sixties and onwards. John le Carré based his character in *The Tailor of Panama* on Doug. He became not simply one of my best friends but part of our family. He was a loveable man with the most engaging manner and became an invaluable source of information about who was visiting town. Doug knew all the people who visited London and who didn't announce their arrival in *Celebrity Bulletin*.

He introduced me to Kirk Douglas, who said he would agree to an interview next time he was in town, which turned out to be for a tribute retrospective of his work at the British Film Institute. To celebrate, I went to Hayward for a new suit. He persuaded me to buy a black blazer with light grey pants and a black and white striped tie.

I didn't meet Kirk Douglas before the interview (although Hayward said he had popped in the shop) but I did meet one of his PR people, who asked me not to stand up when Mr Douglas walked on stage. When I asked why he explained that because I was taller than Kirk it might upset the star.

As I came to know Kirk Douglas over the years I understood that this request was most likely made without his knowledge because I met few stars more certain of their stature and standing than Mr Douglas.

I arrived at the South Bank, where the interview was to be held, in my new Hayward get-up and, as I did so, a large black limousine disgorged Kirk Douglas dressed in black blazer, light grey pants and black and white striped tie. Hayward's idea of a little joke.

I appeared on stage wearing my driver's jacket, which had a pleated back and large brass buttons, and his tie, which had a green palm tree on it. I was glad not to stand up. I would like to have been invisible.

Some time later, when I was a house guest of the lyricist Sammy Cahn and his wife Tita, we were invited to Kirk Douglas's new home. It was to be a housewarming party and the guests included Gregory Peck, James Stewart, Billy Wilder, Sidney Poitier and Johnny Carson. I was seated between Wilder and Carson.

At the end of the meal, Kirk Douglas stood up and welcomed everyone to his new home, stressing how much smaller and cosier it was compared to the one they had left. It seemed big enough to me. Put a moat round it and you had Dover Castle.

Anyway, Kirk banged on about downsizing and then, to my horror, invited his guests to stand up and say a few words. He started the speeches clockwise around the table, which at least gave me a few moments to try to think of something appropriate, or even witty, to say. It immediately became obvious this was a well-known ritual among the group because the guests had clearly prepared material beforehand and were in competition with each other for making the wittiest speech.

I thought of fainting as a way out of what I was now certain would be a terrible disaster. When Johnny Carson stood up it meant I was next. By now I was almost paralysed with fear.

Carson stood and said, 'Kirk, I think your new downsized small home is wonderful. That is all I am prepared to say because, as you know, I never play small halls.'

In the ensuing laughter I was forgotten.

ITV had bought the Carson show and was about to run it against *Parkinson* in Britain. I thought I'd pop along and see Carson at work. I had never sat in the audience of a talk show and didn't want VIP treatment, so I turned up with Mary and the kids at the studios and stood in line. We were shepherded by blazered young men with the wholesome good looks you used to see in those Mickey Rooney/Judy Garland college movies.

Our shepherd heard us talking and asked, 'You guys from England?'

We told him we were and he said, 'Johnny's show is going to be seen in England.'

We said we had heard the rumour.

'Have you ever seen Johnny's show?' he asked.

'No,' I lied. 'What's it like?'

He said, 'There's a guy in Britain called Parkinson who does a talk show.'

We said we had heard the name.

'Well Johnny's show is like that but with more laughs,' he said.

Sammy and Tita Cahn became special friends. Sammy was a significant contributor to the Great American Songbook. He won four Academy Awards and, in collaboration with Jimmy Van Heusen in particular, helped sustain the second half of Frank Sinatra's recording career. It was through Sammy I hoped to get to Sinatra.

We tried, Lord knows how we tried.

Sammy took me to a cocktail party Sinatra was hosting. He introduced me as his best friend from England who did the greatest chat show in the history of television.

Frank said, 'Good to meet you, Mike.'

Sammy said, 'Now he knows your name you're halfway to getting him on the show.'

As I was leaving I said goodbye and thank you to my host.

'Goodbye, David,' said Frank.

Above: This is how to swing a golf club.

Right: This is how not to swing a golf club.

Below: Vic Lewis's XI at Lord's, ready and willing to play a benefit game for Fred Titmus – (*back row, left to right*) Brian Rix, Elton John, me, Peter Cook, Ed Stewart, Nicholas Parsons and Ray Barrett. (*Front row*) Gerald Harper, Malcolm McFee, Dennis Cox, Vic Lewis, Wes Hall and David Frost.

My first visit to my second home.

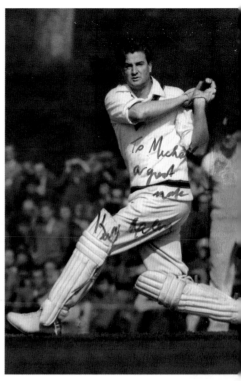

My dear friend and hero Keith Miller. Neville Cardus said he was 'the Australian *in excelsis*'.

The interview with Shane Warne proved he was a fascinating man as well as the greatest spin bowler of them all.

Interviewing two Bob Hawkes for Australian TV. Max Gillies is the phoney one.

Mary and I support the Royal Institute for Deaf and Blind Children in Sydney, a wonderful and inspiring organisation.

Above: In training for a bus trip to a charity football game. Distributing the drinks is Doug Hayward, my dear, late friend, who was the model for John le Carré's *The Tailor of Panama.* After he had sobered up.

Left: On the cover of a McCartney album. My true claim to fame.

Matthau and Lemmon – a magical double act.

He asked us to dinner. I said I was too tired. Mary has never forgiven me.

The man who nearly decapitated me in his act – afterwards Tommy Cooper asks Mary if she would still love me if I was headless. Jimmy Tarbuck thinks it's funny. Two of our great comedians. Jimmy was hosting the show when Tommy tragically died.

Spike Milligan was a regular guest. You never knew what to expect.

Vincent Price, my co-star in *Madhouse*, was a civilised man.

Sarah Miles said she didn't mind doing nude scenes providing everyone else also took their clothes off. She told me this while wearing a see-through top that intrigued the nation.

Sean Connery – a rare interview.

He was the one I most regretted never having interviewed. In my opinion he was, and remains, the greatest singer of popular songs there has ever been and his recordings contain collaborations between songwriters, musicians, arrangers and the singer that will stand for all time as the classic repertoire of twentieth-century popular music.

If Sinatra was the man I most wanted to interview and failed so to do, then the female equivalent was Katharine Hepburn. Richard Drewett wrote to her every year and she would reply that one day she might come to England and appear on the show. When Richard left *Parkinson* to work with Clive James he kept up the correspondence, which is how Clive ended up interviewing Ms Hepburn. I envied him that. She was a fascinating woman who captivated every leading man she starred opposite.

Peter O'Toole said that when they starred together in *Lion in Winter* he fell in love with her. 'I would have killed for her,' he said. Their first meeting had been unusual. Ms Hepburn came backstage to congratulate O'Toole on a stage performance and caught him peeing in the sink.

I asked why actors peed in the sink and O'Toole said because it saved time, and besides most dressing rooms in theatres were toilets. Yul Brynner offered a more plausible explanation. He was telling me about how he sacked a stagehand during a run of *The King and I* because the man whistled backstage. He did so, he explained, because backstage you have to concentrate and not be distracted from the job ahead.

'It's like flushing toilets. It's the only thing the audience can hear. That's why backstage an actor always pees in a sink,' he said.

The other female star I would have loved to have talked to was Marilyn Monroe. Sadly, she wasn't around at the time, so I pursued my interest vicariously by interviewing people who had worked with her.

Jack Lemmon said she could be a nightmare sometimes, going more than thirty takes to get a scene right. When they starred in *Some Like It Hot* he would save himself during the first dozen or so takes, knowing that she would take her time getting it right. When it came to the famous sleeping berth scene between Marilyn and Lemmon, he said she did it first time and Billy Wilder said, 'Print it.'

'What happened? I wasn't ready,' said Jack.

Tony Curtis told me what Billy Wilder said to them – as soon as Monroe got a correct take, that was the one they would print. Wilder said, 'You guys had better know what you're doing. Don't be caught with your finger in your ear.' Curtis said she was a 'fruitcake'. He went further. 'Billy Wilder said she was a mean seven-year-old girl and that's as good a description of Marilyn as any,' he said.

My favourite Tony Curtis story was of the very early days in his career when the young Bernie Schwartz with the thick Bronx accent found himself plucked out of acting school and taken to Hollywood where his good looks quickly established him as the new glamour boy of the movies. He left behind in New York some wonderful actors, incuding Jack Lemmon and Walter Matthau, who had to prove their ability on stage before Hollywood beckoned. Lemmon told me he was walking through New York one day when he heard his name called. On the other side of the road, across four lanes of traffic, was Tony Curtis, at the time Hollywood's hottest property, in town to promote his latest movie.

'Hi, Tony. How's it going?' shouted Jack.

'Great, just great,' yelled Curtis.

'How's Hollywood?' bellowed Jack.

'It's great, Jack. I've got something to tell you,' shouted Curtis.

Lemmon cupped his hand to his ear and Curtis shouted across four lanes of traffic: 'I've fucked Yvonne de Carlo.'

28

DUST IN THE CREVICES

In writing this book I have discovered how many times in my life I have sought mentors; older people, men and women, to give me the benefit of their experience. When I first played club cricket it was in the company of older men. When I started my career on the *South Yorkshire Times*, I was educated by an older and experienced journalist, Stan Bristow, who diligently and patiently taught me the ground rules of my trade. Throughout my life in journalism – both in newspapers and television – I chose the company of those people who had already achieved what I aspired to, and much more besides.

Some of my most memorable and fulfilling encounters have been with so-called senior citizens. More often than not they bring to the interview a capacity for plain speaking, having passed the point where they care about professional or personal inhibitions. Most importantly, because they feel ignored by society, they welcome any chance to be heard.

I am currently an ambassador for the government's 'Dignity in Care Campaign', which aims to improve the way old people are treated. As we become more and more obsessed with 'yoof', so we tend to brush aside the older generation, relegating them to a foot locker of priority, hoping they curl up quietly and die. What we

232

ignore is the link between young and old, seen at its most important and profound in the relationship between child and grandparent, and at its most practical in the way the older generation can act as an inspiration and mentor to the young.

As I write, there is debate in the media about whether or not Harrison Ford, aged sixty-five, is too old to play Indiana Jones in the latest adventure epic, whereas the real lesson to be learnt from Mr Ford's longevity as a film star is how he has kept at the top of his profession for so long. What has he absorbed about his craft that might prove useful to the young actor hoping to make the grade in a tough business?

In my life I have been lucky enough to meet men and women who have not just been successful in their chosen professions, but have led full and vigorous lives and often felt able to explain their experiences in the most inspiring manner. One such was Professor Jacob Bronowski, a member of the team who developed the atom bomb and who went on to write and present one of the towering achievements of television documentary, *The Ascent of Man*.

Professor Bronowski was my only guest when I interviewed him. His use of language was so precise that if you took a transcript of our talk and removed my questions it read as beautifully constructed prose. At the end of the interview, which held the audience spellbound, I asked him if we should take any notice of anything he had said.

He replied, 'Should you listen to me? Yes, you should. Not because you have to believe any single thing that I say, but because you have to be pleased there are people who have lived happy and complete lives, who feel they can speak out of a full heart and a full mind, all in the same frame.'

It seemed to me that thought precisely explained and justified my fascination with older people.

Dame Edith Evans was another who put to shame many younger actors with her unflagging energy and optimistic disregard of growing old. She triumphed over advancing years by refusing to be ignored. Mind you, it would be a brave man who even attempted to deny Dame Edith her rightful place in the order of things.

Whenever we had her on the show she would arrive in a Rolls-Royce, wearing a new dress from Norman Hartnell and a fur cape. She looked and behaved as what she was – a star. Having arrived, she would immediately head for the elderly BBC commissionaire treatment of old-age pensioners. If only Mr Parkinson could one day wangle it so she appeared on the same show as the prime minster, Harold Wilson, she would give him a piece of her mind.

On about the second or third time I had witnessed this performance, I gently ventured the thought that there was perhaps a discrepancy between the picture she painted of herself as an impoverished pensioner and arriving in such a regal manner. She fixed me with a disdainful glare. You had to be careful with Edith. She could become terribly imperious.

'What do you mean?' she asked in that marvellous voice.

'Well, whenever you arrive you go on about the old-age pension and yet you are wearing a new dress by Norman Hartnell and a fur stole,' I said.

'Yes?' she said, her look daring me to continue and, like an oaf, I did.

'Well, I suppose what I am trying to say, Dame Edith, is that you complain about the pension and yet arrive in a Rolls-Royce,' I said.

She glowered at me for what seemed like an eternity; the look she reserved for blithering idiots. Then she said, 'Would you have me arrive in a Mini?' She gave Mini the same emphasis as she did 'handbag' in *The Importance of Being Earnest*.

She was eighty-five years old when she made her talk-show debut on *Parkinson*. She told me, 'I don't like to be noticed, you know, except when I want to be noticed. If somebody raises his hat when I get out of a car, I bow in turn, but I don't like being looked at because I'm not acting, you see. But when I'm acting to be looked at, then you must look at me.'

We didn't manage to get her on the show with Harold Wilson but she did appear with Ted Heath.

Before the show Mr Heath asked if we could arrange for him to see an interview he had recorded that was being shown on BBC2. We showed him into a viewing room and Dame Edith followed on behind. She wasn't invited but who was going to tell her?

As Heath endeavoured to watch the recording, Dame Edith kept up an incessant stream of conversation, mainly consisting of an offer to give Mr Heath elocution lessons. She became aware that Mr Heath was not giving her his full attention.

'Edward,' she demanded, 'what are you doing?'

'Actually, Dame Edith, I'm watching an interview I did a short time ago which is now being shown,' he said, relieved that at last he might get some respite from the unending chatter.

Dame Edith looked at the set for a minute or two and then asked, 'Edward, exactly when did you do that programme?'

'I recorded it two or three days ago,' he said.

She looked once more at the box, then turned to the politician.

'Edward, you are still wearing the same shirt,' she scolded.

We lunched once at her home in the country. She cooked the meal herself and, in my honour, had made Yorkshire pudding. The slight problem was she forgot the self-raising flour, so it lay on the plate the colour and consistency of a rusty wheel. We ate up, nonetheless.

At the end of the meal Dame Edith closed her eyes and fell asleep. We assumed this was the signal she'd had enough of our company and we were to depart.

After her first appearance on the show we added her face to the list of stars in the opening title sequence. She wrote to me – green ink, blue paper – saying she never went to bed on Saturday night without watching the opening of the show. 'Just to reassure myself I am still alive,' she said. She watched me walk down the stairs to see if she approved of my appearance – 'Get rid of that brown suit, it neither fits nor flatters,' was one note. Then she would switch off and go to bed. 'Can't watch the rest. Past my bedtime,' she wrote.

She was a joy to interview, although, truth be told, you didn't interview her so much as follow wherever she led. Once, in the middle of talking about how she feared that when she died she would not be remembered, she offered up this thought on old age: 'The trouble with growing old is you tend to fall down a lot. I've learned the trick though. When you fall down at my age the great secret is not to try and get up too quickly. Just lie there. Have a look at the world from a different angle.'

She died aged eighty-seven and what we who had known her thought of her was marvellously summed up by her biographer, Bryan Forbes. When she was taken ill, Forbes broke the news to his children. One of his daughters asked him if she would die, and Bryan said it might happen. His daughter said, 'But Dame Edith can't die, daddy, she's not the type.'

Another hero I came to know through the show was Alistair Cooke. He was not a modest man. He had a very strong sense of self and a tendency to dominate any conversation, no matter what might be the subject under discussion. But he was not boring. Indeed, he was one of the most entertaining and fascinating men I have ever met. He was also one of the greatest journalists of his time and no one reported more perceptively and entertainingly on an adopted land than Cooke on America. His *Letter from America* on BBC Radio, which lasted for fifty-eight years, was a weekly masterpiece in the art of what might be described as 'conversational journalism'. His reporting in the *Guardian* was an exemplary demonstration of the journalist's craft. In fact, in Cooke's case he turned a craft into an art form.

To paraphrase Kenneth Tynan, if there is a tightrope bridging the gap between being a good journalist and a great one, Alistair Cooke would make the trip in white tie and tails with a cocktail in one hand and a quill in the other. Not only did he hobnob with presidents, but he knew Chaplin, adored Garbo, worshipped Duke Ellington and, most impressive of all, was able to argue the case for Sugar Ray Robinson being, pound for pound, just about the best fighter who ever made the ring.

My admiration for this polymath reached new heights when browsing through a second-hand record stall in Manchester and finding a recording called, I think, 'An Evening with Alistair Cooke at the Piano'. I struggle to recall the title only because the record was nicked from my collection some time later. My consolation is that the thief must have been a fan of Mr Cooke's and therefore the record found a good home. On it Alistair Cooke is heard yarning, playing piano, singing and whistling. At one point, while he was whistling and playing a blues on the piano, the recording was interrupted by Buck Clayton, the splendid jazz trumpet player, who put his head round the door of the studio to see who was making the noise and said, 'Boy, that's a mean piano and a dirty whistle.' Cooke regarded this as a tremendous compliment. I saw it as yet further proof of my hero's versatility and felt a warming pride that I had worked for the same newspaper as one of the few men in the entire world acquainted with the work of both Isaiah and Irving Berlin and able to write about the two of them with the same enthusiasm.

He told me that when he first arrived in America he hated the place. 'I suffered from the delusion, which is universal among the English, that Americans are Englishmen gone wrong.'

He said this belief was summed up by a book, a satire on English condescension towards America, which contained the line: 'It has to be admitted that practically every old Etonian knows more Latin than the average West Virginia miner.'

He said he believed the fatal moment in recent American history was paradoxically the moment of highest euphoria, Kennedy's inauguration speech, in which he said: 'We will support any friend, oppose any foe, make any sacrifice, suffer any hardship for the protection and preservation of liberty.'

Cooke said, 'This was the peak moment of America's delusion that it really could be the policeman and that it had a duty to be. Since they couldn't use the bomb, it meant they would have to have conventional forces of about eight hundred million to cope with their ambition. That was the beginning of the end to me.'

He told me this in 1972 and his words are even more prescient today.

Discussing American idealism, he quoted his favourite journalist, H.L. Mencken, who defined an idealist as: 'A man who, on noticing that a rose smells better than a cabbage, assumes it will also make better soup.'

Cooke defined American humour as 'the humour of the soured immigrant' and recalled the great humorist, S.J. Perelman, who wrote the early Marx Brothers movies. Getting out of a cab in New York, the cab driver said to him, 'Have a nice day, Mr Perelman.' Perelman said, 'Listen, don't poke your nose into my affairs. I'll have any kind of day I want to.'

Cooke said the wittiest man he knew was Herman Mankiewicz, the screenwriter who wrote *Citizen Kane* and provided the story for *It's a Wonderful World*. He said Mankiewicz had a running feud with a Hollywood producer who was a terrible wine snob, given to saying such things as, 'I think this wine is a little virginal.' Mankiewicz, on the other hand, judged booze by quantity rather than quality.

Cooke said, 'He went to a dinner party at the producer's house and by the time he got to the table was already drunk. But he got through the meal until it came to the sweet, which was a great baked Alaska, and the sight of this flaming thing was too much. Mankiewicz threw up over the table and everyone tried to ignore it. They turned to their neighbour and said, "You were saying?" and things like that. As he slid under the table, Mankiewicz looked up at his host and said, "Well you have to admit at least the white wine came up with the fish."'

Sir John Gielgud appeared on the show, along with W. H. Auden. Try proposing that combination to the people who run television today and see what happens.

Gielgud told a story about his dislike of cats. He was appearing in *The Vortex* with Lilian Braithwaite when, in the middle of a very melodramatic scene, a cat came on stage. Sir John said, 'Of course, the audience screamed with laughter and Lilian Braithwaite, keeping in the play, said, "Oh, for God's sake, put that cat out of the room." So I took it up very gingerly and, because I hated it, threw it out of the window. It immediately came in again by the door, whereupon I was so distracted and despairing I threw it into the audience. I don't know what the front row thought, but I never saw it again,' he said.

Auden had just published a new collection of poems called *Epistle to a Godson*. I asked him what was the purpose of a poet and he said, 'As a poet one has a political duty, which is to try, by one's example, to protect the purity of the language. Because when words lose their meaning then I'm quite sure physical violence takes over.'

Gielgud's face was plump and healthy as a ripe apple. Auden's was ridged and wrinkled like a beach at low tide. I found myself inspecting his face as I was talking to him and I swear there was dust in some of the crevices.

Ralph Richardson was another fascinating ancient. Like Dame Edith, he set his own agenda during a conversation. There was no stratagem ever devised by any interviewer to persuade him to follow your line of questioning. When he was interviewed by my dear friend Russell Harty, he took control of the studio, asking Harty the origin of his name, wandering round the place talking to the crew, and finally arriving at a window painted on the back set. It showed London at night and Sir Ralph commented on the magnificence of the view. It was a memorable, wonderful performance.

We had him on the show a couple of times, once with Enoch Powell and the second time, celebrating his love of motorbikes with Barrie Sheene, then the world motorcycle champion. We had Barrie's bike in the studio and I shall forever remember the sight of the old actor knight assuming the racing position and making engine noises, like Toad in *The Wind in the Willows*, while I tried to ask him questions.

Sir Ralph's fascination with motorbikes was only matched by his love of comedians. He told me he thought Charlie Chaplin the greatest actor of all time and, if he wasn't, then Little Tich was.

His knowledge and enthusiasm for music-hall comedians was shared by Enoch Powell, and we were well into what I thought was a fascinating conversation between two very different men, when Sir Ralph looked at his watch and said, 'Well, I have to be off.' When I asked why he was in a hurry, he said, 'We have talked enough. The audience is fed up with us. And we must never overstay our welcome. In any case, I need a drink.'

On one occasion we went for lunch to Scott's restaurant in Mount Street. This was before its latest transformation, when it was the old established seafood restaurant, lately moved from Piccadilly to Mayfair. Sir Ralph turned up in mac, scarf, hat and umbrella in spite of the fact it was a pleasant day in early summer. He removed his hat but not his coat or scarf as we were shown to our seats. I had the impression he was auditioning the restaurant.

He called the manager over. 'Terribly dark in here. Can't see the menu,' he said.

The manager immediately increased the wattage, causing shuffling noises and no little complaint from shadowy booths where middle-aged men sat with much younger companions.

'Warm in here,' said Sir Ralph. Instead of pointing out he was fully dressed for the arctic on what was a passable summer's day, the manager said he would turn the heating down.

Having now set the scene to his specifications, Sir Ralph removed his coat and scarf and got down to business.

The menu arrived.

'Take that back,' he said. 'Don't need a menu in Scott's. I will have a grilled Dover sole and so will Mr Parkinson, boiled potatoes and a few green beans I fancy.'

Then he turned to me and said, 'Maybe you want chips? Never eat them myself but I will order them on your behalf.'

I hadn't said a word. I was still marvelling at this seemingly batty old man bossing the universe.

He ordered a very agreeable Montrachet and, when the food arrived, ate every chip he had ordered for me. Then he called the wine waiter over and had a scholarly discussion about the comparative merits of marc and grappa before ordering two large marcs.

We lurched into Mount Street in mid-afternoon, whereupon Sir Ralph discovered, next door to the restaurant, a shop selling expensive baths. The shop was looked after by a Sloaney young woman wearing a Hermès scarf. Sir Ralph said he was particularly intrigued by a round bath on display in the window and could he sit in it to see if it was big enough. The girl nodded uncertainly, whereupon Sir Ralph sat in the bath and said to the girl, 'I wonder if it takes two people. Would you join me?' And she did. By this time there were a few people standing outside the shop witnessing this demonstration of saving water by bath sharing.

After producing this second moment of theatre, we moved off down Mount Street towards an art gallery which, Sir Ralph told me, had a couple of paintings by Georges Seurat he wanted to look at. When we arrived the owner, recognising Sir Ralph, approached and started the sales pitch.

He was interrupted by the actor who launched into the most fascinating account of Seurat's place in the history of Impressionist art, particularly in his development of pointillism, again gathering a sizable audience. Having completed the third act of his entertainment, in the art gallery, he swept out and asked me back to his place for a drink.

On the way we passed a brand new BMW limousine, complete with chauffeur, parked outside a restaurant. Sir Ralph tapped the window and said to the bemused driver, 'I've got one of these but it only has two wheels.'

He lived in a beautiful Nash terrace opposite Regent's Park, complete with lift. Upstairs in the kitchen, the wall was plastered with the lines of his latest play. This, he said, was one of his aids to learning his part. We finished a bottle of gin, whereupon he went to a lift with folding doors, put the gin bottle on the floor, shouted something down the shaft and despatched the lift to the basement. Five minutes later the lift arrived back on the first floor containing a replacement bottle.

When I eventually and unsteadily departed his company and had time to consider the day, I realised that at no time had we discussed what he might talk about on the show, which had been the purpose of our meeting. What I also realised was that the lunch and all that followed had been designed by an impresario with the express purpose of thwarting my ambition. The entire performance, starting in the restaurant and concluding at his home, had been calculated to divert my attention from finding out anything about my guest other than that he was a master of illusion.

After the interview at the BBC, and as he departed the Green Room, this remarkable man stopped at the door, turned and said, 'Do you know what's wrong with a lot of actors today?'

We said we had no idea.

'They don't know how to die,' he said. 'If they are shot they die like this,' and he lurched across the room before slithering in melodramatic fashion down the wall. 'In fact, they should die like this,' he said, crumpling in concertina fashion until he lay on the floor looking like an empty suit.

He rose to his feet, doffed his trilby and wished us all a good night. When he left the room it was like a light going out.

29

THE TOUGHEST JOB
IN THE WORLD

In 1975, having written a biography of George Best, I was returning from a book signing in Glasgow when the taxi driver said, 'Do you know the Big Yin?' I said I didn't. We were passing a theatre at the time. 'That's yer man,' he said, pointing at the billboards, which said 'Billy Connolly in the Great Northern Welly Boot'. 'Drive on,' I said.

One of the occupational hazards of doing a talk show is that you are always meeting people who have an uncle who is a better singer than Pavarotti, and know a milkman funnier than Les Dawson.

We stopped outside a row of shops. 'Won't be a minute,' said the driver. He returned with a long-playing record entitled 'Billy Connolly Live' with a picture on the front of a man with a haystack of hair and what looked like bananas on his feet. 'Play that and you'll want him on your show,' he said.

I left it on a table in my house and thought no more about it until one day Andrew, my eldest boy, asked me if I had listened to the recording. I said I hadn't. He said I must. 'He's hilarious,' said Andrew.

As I listened to Billy turning the story of the Resurrection into a parable of drinking and football in Glasgow, I knew I had stumbled across a comedian of great gift. This is not hindsight. I was convinced that once he appeared on the show he would become a major new star. I was as certain as I was when I saw George Best's first game and knew I had witnessed the debut of a great performer.

Billy's first appearance caused a sensation. He told a joke about a man murdering his wife and leaving her bum sticking out of the ground so he would have somewhere to park his bike, which nowadays would have the Political Correctness Riot Squad battering down the doors at the TV Centre. In those less sensitive times the joke was accepted for what it was, a satire of the battle of the sexes in the tougher parts of working-class Glasgow. It would be silly to say that Connolly's subsequent career was built on that one joke, but it certainly provided what later came to be called 'a water cooler moment' and set Billy on his way to stardom.

He appeared eight times on the show and on every occasion the viewing figures soared. He was a cast-iron box office magnet. When I was hosting my talk show in Australia, I persuaded Billy to join me and so began a lasting relationship with a country we both came to love.

Australia in the late seventies was a lot more conservative than it is today and Billy's appearance alone was enough to invite extreme reactions. They ranged from the appearance of Connolly look-alikes to the rage of a policeman who rushed on stage at one of Billy's concerts and detuned his guitar. To have such a feeble conclusion to such a dramatic invasion was a bit like being nuzzled after being charged by an angry bull.

We went out for dinner in Sydney, with Billy in striped coat, pointy boots and shoulder-length hair, and when we entered the restaurant, we realised we had to negotiate a long bar before reaching the dining room. This would have been all right except the bar had been requisitioned by about twenty very large and drunken rugby players.

'G'dayparkoyerpommiebastard,' was OK. This meant they were being friendly. They didn't know what to make of Billy but, while they were thinking about it, we slipped past. As I was trying to find the group of people we were joining for dinner, I felt a tap on my shoulder and turned to discover that a large blond Australian rugby player, not quite as big as the Sydney Opera House, had managed to get between me and Billy. 'Can I help you?' I feebly asked, at which point I heard Billy say, 'Hey big man.' As the rugby player turned, Billy said in a loud clear voice, 'Why don't you fuck off?'

The Aussie took a while to digest this suggestion and as he was pondering whether to hit Billy or tuck him under his arm and throw him across the restaurant, the maitre d' ushered us quickly to our seats. The rugby player then positioned himself in the entrance to the restaurant, making dramatic gestures at our table indicating Billy Connolly's end was nigh. Eventually he was taken away by his friends. At about two in the morning, as we were being driven home through Kings Cross, a garish and louche part of Sydney but jammed with traffic and sightseers even at that time, Billy jumped out of the car. He walked across to a five-way junction and started directing traffic with flamboyant arm gestures and hair flying as if conducting a symphony orchestra. He quickly transformed a normal traffic jam into a showbiz event, attracting the attention of two patrolling policemen, whom I saw approaching over the brow of a hill.

I went to Billy, who was by now working the audience.

'Big Yin, the law approaches,' I said. I pointed at the policemen, who were heading our way in a slow but purposeful manner.

'I see them,' said my pal, in a manner that suggested he was looking forward to the confrontation.

'Billy, these guys don't muck about. They'll bang us up and you have a concert tomorrow night and we don't need this kind of publicity,' I said.

He looked at me, smiled, and said, 'Can you dance, Parky?'

I nodded.

'Can you foxtrot?' he asked.

I nodded again.

'Can you dance the lady's part?'

'Anything you want to get out of here,' I said. I started humming 'Let's face the music and dance'. I was singing 'There may be trouble ahead . . .' as I tried to steer my dancing partner to the car ahead of the police. We just about made it, mainly because the officers found it difficult to negotiate a road which, by now, was full of people doing the foxtrot.

The next night at the Sydney Opera House, Connolly gave one of his greatest performances. Certainly the best I have ever seen. He held the stage for nearly three hours, telling an audience, aching and weary with laughter, 'I have some good news and some bad news. The good news is I have not finished with you yet. The bad news is they've just closed the car park.' And they had, but no one seemed to care.

Watching him over the years, I have seen his style develop and mature as he grows older and more reflective. There were times when I glimpsed a secret sadness and when I asked about it he said, 'One day I'll tell you the story.'

In the end he told it to his wife Pamela who wrote a fascinating account of an abused child who became an alchemist, transforming grief to laughter. When they ask me what he is like, I always say Billy Connolly is many fascinating men, all worth knowing.

Comedians intrigue me. They have the toughest job in the world. I have lost count of the number of actors who have told me how much they envy the comic's skill and nerve in commanding an audience. I grew up watching music-hall comedians Sandy Powell, Jimmy James, Albert Modley, Frank Randle and the like. Both Richard Drewett and, particularly, John Fisher shared my love for and fascination with funny men. John Fisher wrote a book entitled *Funny Way to Be a Hero*, which is a classic account of the great music-hall comedians of the twentieth century. He also wrote *Always Leave Them Laughing*, a biography of Tommy Cooper.

With most comedians you can detect the difference between the man and the performer. In other words, even though most comics are unable to resist the urge to make companions laugh over dinner or when playing golf – Jimmy Tarbuck is the classic example – there is still a difference between the amusing companion and the stage performer. With Tommy Cooper there was none. The Cooper on stage was the one you encountered in real life. I could never work out if he was one of the brightest men I ever met or the silliest.

Hearing that Tommy was to speak on my behalf at a Foyle's Literary Lunch, Trevor Howard called me and said he would also make a speech if I would introduce him to Tommy. After the meal Howard and Cooper sat in a corner talking about their particular skills with Howard telling Cooper he thought he was a great actor.

This perplexed Cooper, who said, 'I'm just playing myself.'

Howard would have none of it. He made the point that what actors did was interpret other peoples' creations, but what Cooper had done, like Chaplin before him, was create a character any playwright would have been proud of, and brought it to life on stage.

I sat quietly listening, wishing I could have captured every moment on camera. While fascinated by Howard's analysis of Cooper's genius, I was still unable to decide whether Tommy's apparent bafflement was real or play acting.

We eventually managed to get Tommy on to *Parkinson* in 1979. It was a Christmas special. Tommy was to top the bill in a packed show. He wasn't an easy interviewee because he paid little attention to what you asked, preferring to steer the conversation into comfort zones where he could perform magic tricks or answer a question by putting on a silly hat. The finale was to be the famous guillotine illusion where I stick my head under the blade and Tommy pretends to chop it off.

In rehearsal he walked on wearing a fez. On the show he came on with a saucepan on his head. The conversation went:

ME: 'What's that you've got on your head?'
COOPER: 'A bucket.'
ME: 'That's not a bucket, it's a saucepan.'
COOPER, LOOKING SURPRISED: 'Is it? I've got the wrong hat.'

This was the start of a memorable encounter. It went better than we dared hope until the guillotine illusion, which, I later learned, could have provided a spectacular and bloody finale to the show.

John Fisher, my producer, is a magician himself, a member of the Magic Circle, indeed a Gold Star Member, which means he knows how these things work. As I stuck my head in the guillotine, John, watching from the floor, suddenly saw that Tommy had forgotten to set the safety catch on the apparatus.

John wrote in his biography of Cooper: 'We were only a few gags away from the moment when the blade would have fallen and seriously injured, if not worse, the talk-show host.'

John Palfreyman, Cooper's technical assistant, managed to creep on set and put the catch into its proper position. I have often wondered, if the worst had happened, would the audience have laughed, as the people did when Tommy died on stage at the London Palladium.

Jimmy Tarbuck, who was hosting that show, said as soon as Tommy collapsed he knew he was dead. The curtains closed over Tommy's body but left his feet sticking out in view of the audience who started laughing. They thought it was part of the act. His death rattle was picked up by the microphone. It sounded like the noise he made before saying 'just like that' and further deceived the audience into believing that what they were seeing was all part of Tommy's act.

Jimmy Tarbuck, himself one of our finest stand-up comics and a good friend, was deeply affected by the experience. Like all comics, he held Tommy Cooper in something approaching awe. He said, 'The thing about us comics is that we fall into categories; there are those who say funny things and those who do funny things. It's a scheme to make people laugh. Tommy Cooper was the rarest comedian of the lot, a genuinely funny man off and on; he couldn't help it, a total natural. There wasn't another like him in my time and I doubt there ever will be.'

Eric Morecambe joked on the show about a near-death experience. He said when he suffered a heart attack and was lying on a stretcher in A & E, the man who had taken him to hospital and who had been told how serious his condition was, came to say goodbye. He said, 'Do you think I could have your autograph . . . before you go?'

I have never seen a better double act than Eric and Ernie. We had them on the show with Raquel Welch, at the time possibly the most beautiful woman in movies. We wanted her to stay on after her interview and join in the talk with Eric and Ernie but her agent would have none of it. He didn't want Eric looking at her ample bosom, adjusting his glasses, and asking, 'Is it a fella?' She was a sumptuous woman and I asked her if she had always been beautiful. She said it had taken a while before 'the equipment' arrived but when it did she began to 'strut her stuff'.

When Eric and Ernie came on Eric said he wanted me to know that his equipment had never arrived, which probably accounted for the fact he'd never had any stuff to strut. Eric was responsible for delivering me a home truth. It came after Mary had accused me of having a boring dress sense and bought me a leather jacket, which she insisted made me look years younger.

I hated the thing but said I would wear it to the office and see what the reaction was before even considering appearing on television wearing the damned thing. So I sat through a meeting at the BBC wearing this smooth black number, convinced my team were being polite and holding back the sniggers. I finally escaped and headed for the lifts, eager to get home and burn the garment. The lift doors opened to reveal Eric Morecambe, who looked at me, did the trick with the glasses, and said in a loud voice, 'Parky, you look like a tall wallet.'

We organised some classic reunions on the show. We brought together the *Beyond the Fringe* team of Jonathan Miller, Alan Bennett, Peter Cook and Dudley Moore, and we reunited the Goons with Peter Sellers, Harry Secombe and Ray Ellington in the studio and Spike Milligan fooling around in Australia.

On one trip to Australia I was staying at the same hotel as Harry and Spike and Billy Connolly.

'I'd love to meet Spike. He's one of my heroes,' said Billy. I told Spike and we all arranged to have lunch. Spike and Billy hit it off and were soon swapping routines. After a couple of hours I was literally exhausted with laughter and could take no more. I went to the gents where I found Harry Secombe leaning against a stall, tears streaming down his face.

'Can't stand it. I've laughed so much I think I'm going to have a bloody heart attack,' he said. We didn't return. We didn't have the energy. We left them to it. Two great funny men creating a duet of humour.

Spike was an unpredictable man. He suffered with depression and could be difficult, not to say impossible. He could also be generous and warm and wonderfully funny. I interviewed him many times, the best not on television but radio when I was doing a programme at LBC. It was a live show and, during a break, we were told that a strange man who said his name was Milligna, and that he was an unfortunate typing error, was at reception, and wanted to speak to me. What is more, Mr Milligna was wearing what looked like pyjamas under his overcoat.

When Spike arrived at the studio he explained he was recovering from a bout of depression in a nearby nursing home and, hearing me on the radio, thought he would come and have a chat. We put him on the show and he was brilliant.

Pete and Dud were regulars on the TV show. Like Tommy Cooper, Peter was destroyed by drink. I remember seeing them on stage performing *Behind the Fridge* and Dudley was literally holding Peter up and propelling him around the stage. It seemed to me Dudley was assured of his talent for music but less certain of his ability as a funny man compared to what he considered to be the wittier and more erudite of the Fringe team. In fact, in my view, he was the most talented popular entertainer of the lot. Few could resist his boyish attractive persona; none could deny his great talent as a musician. He was one of the best jazz pianists – certainly the most swinging – this country has produced.

He also had a wicked sense of humour. During the seventies my friend Douglas Hayward opened a restaurant in London called Burke's. Now and again Dudley would come and play piano for the diners. One night I arrived late and a little drunk for a dinner party and Dudley was playing as I entered. At the end of his number he announced he was glad to see I had finally arrived, particularly as the audience should know that I was a better singer than an interviewer.

This was news to me as well as the audience.

Therefore, said my friend, he would like to invite me on stage to sing my favourite song which was 'Moon River'. I like 'Moon River', indeed any song written by Henry Mancini and Johnny Mercer has a lot going for it, but it wasn't my favourite. I calculated I knew enough of the lyrics to get by and, in any event, was so emboldened by drink I frankly didn't care. Dudley gave me that mischievous grin, suggested a key and away we went.

The first indication things were not as they should be was when he started mucking about with the key so I sounded worse than, in fact, I was. It was a bit like being accompanied by Les Dawson. I started to panic and looked in desperation to my pal. Again that lovely twinkly grin as he held my gaze and nodded toward the nearby tables. Still singing 'Moon River', I looked where he was indicating and there sat Andy Williams with his head in his hands.

30

WHY DO ACTORS DO IT?

Peter Sellers said he would do a one-man show, provided we could have lunch and talk things through. Our meetings consisted of Peter talking in great detail about how he had fallen in love with various leading ladies, including Sophia Loren. He also spent a considerable time with Patricia Houlihan, one of our senior researchers, who reported that, while nervous, he seemed to be looking forward to the interview. He had never done a one-man interview and the research showed he had a fascinating story to tell. It was a big event. Sellers was a huge star. In Britain he had established an everlasting reputation because of *The Goon Show* and films such as *The Ladykillers* and *I'm All Right Jack*. In Hollywood he reached new heights of international stardom with *Dr Strangelove*, and by creating the bumbling Inspector Clouseau in the Pink Panther movies.

Come the eve of the show and I was called at home by Theo Cowan, a wonderful and funny man who was Peter's press agent.

'You will be aware that while my client possesses an incomparable talent, he can also behave in a reprehensible manner,' he said. 'Therefore I have to tell you he won't be doing the show for reasons I don't quite understand. I have tried to change his mind but he seems adamant. I give up. If you ring this number you may talk to him yourself. If a Chinaman answers take no notice. That will be my client pretending to be someone else, which he is very good at.'

I called the number and the Chinaman answered. After a minute or two he became Peters Sellers and said he couldn't do the show because he didn't like being interviewed and was too nervous to walk down the stairs. I said we had announced the show and that we didn't have a replacement, so what did he suggest I tell the British public as they watched sixty minutes of blank screen. He said I didn't understand. I said I was willing to be sympathetic if he told me the real reason for not appearing.

There was a pause and then he said, 'I just can't walk on as myself.'

So I said, 'Well, walk on as someone else.'

He said, 'Can I?'

I told him he could walk on disguised as a tomato if that was what it took – which is how Peter Sellers came to walk down the stairs on his one-man show dressed as a German soldier.

Once he removed the disguise and became Peter Sellers he was brilliant, giving the audience an astonishing display of his virtuosity and so obviously enjoying every minute, it begged the question, what was all the fuss about in the first place?

I have spent a lifetime talking to actors, asking why they chose such a strange and risky profession, without ever finding a consensus. Why would anyone seek a job where the majority of practitioners are out of work for the greater part of their careers, and even when lucky enough to be in work, spend most of their lives pretending to be someone else? Beats me.

Robert Redford was one of the most famous and glamorous actors in the world when I first interviewed him. *Butch Cassidy* and *The*

Sting had taken him to the stratosphere of stardom and recognition. I met him in his dressing room and offered to escort him into the studio, which was bulging with his fans. He said he would make his own way there. We waited for a while, then began to worry. Something had obviously gone wrong.

We found Redford at the door to the studio, trying to persuade the commissionaire that he was on *Parkinson*. He didn't have a pass, so the official said he couldn't enter. 'They're hanging from the rafters in there,' he said. 'He's interviewing Robert Redford, that's who,' he added, by way of explanation.

'But I'm Robert Redford,' said Redford.

'They all say that,' said the commissionaire.

He told me that shortly after making *Butch Cassidy and the Sundance Kid* and feeling mighty pleased with life, he was waiting to cross a street in Los Angeles when a group of kids drove by and started waving. He gave them a big smile and as he did so they wound down the car window and said, 'Robert Redford, you're such an asshole.'

An even bigger question than why be an actor is what is acting?

Robert Redford said James Cagney was his hero, a man who told me he never took acting lessons. 'Why take lessons when acting is a perfectly normal thing to do? You hit your mark, say the words and that's it,' Cagney said.

Robert De Niro came on the show after playing the boxer Jake Lamotta in *Raging Bull*, and told me he had to be the part to play it. He put on sixty pounds to make the movie, and when he made *Taxi Driver* he worked as a cabbie in New York. Sir Ralph Richardson said that in order to act you had to dream yourself into the part and James Stewart said that movie acting was about creating moments. Sir Alec Guinness said he learned about acting by watching a bird in a zoo – every time he looked away and then looked back, the bird had changed its position – while Dirk Bogarde said he made a film with Alan Ladd and at the end of the shoot asked Ladd if he'd had a satisfactory day. Ladd replied he had had the best day an actor could have. Bogarde asked what had happened. 'I just did a great look,' said Ladd. Dirk said from that point on he built his film career on one thought: create a relationship with the camera, a look.

Sarah Miles talked about the kind of acting that required nude scenes. She said she had only one rule. If she stripped off, so did the crew. She said, 'In fact everybody becomes very happy when they're all stripped off. We have a lovely time.' Sarah caused a sensation by appearing on the show in a see-through top, which I endeavoured to ignore while the director struggled unsuccessfully for a shot that would not enrage one half of the population while arousing the other half.

David Niven said he enjoyed acting because it meant having a good time. Of all the stars I interviewed, it seemed to me that Niven made the best of what it had to offer. He was in Hollywood in the years between the thirties and the sixties when eight hundred million people every week bought tickets to go to the movies worldwide. He returned to Britain to join up at the outbreak of war. It changed him, as it did the entire surviving generation, but he didn't lose his debonair approach to his craft. His book *The Moon's a Balloon* is one of the funniest and most engaging memoirs ever written by an actor and his appearance on the show to talk about it gave us one of the most entertaining one-man shows.

Yet before the show, I doubted if he would make it down the stairs. We had adjoining dressing rooms and with about ten minutes to go, I heard the sound of Niven being violently sick in the next room. The retching lasted for about five minutes and sounded so bad that when it stopped I knocked on Niven's door. He looked pale and I asked him if he was all right. He said he felt marvellous and why did I ask? I said I had heard him being sick. 'Oh that,' he said. 'It's nothing. I throw up every time before I go on.'

I had a lunch or two with him and he was the most marvellous companion. After one meal we were driving back to his hotel when he ordered the driver to stop opposite Charing Cross Station. He said, 'I want to show you something.' We left the car and stood looking back at Trafalgar Square.

'Look at Nelson and tell me what he has in his right hand,' he said.

From where I was standing it looked like Nelson was holding something other than his sword, and that instead of keeping a watchful eye on London was engaged in an altogether more absorbing activity.

We were soon joined by a group of tourists. 'What are you looking at?' asked their shepherd.

'Something you won't find in the tourist guides,' said Niven.

His last appearance on the show was a sad event. When I visited him in his dressing room he confessed he was having a bit of difficulty speaking. He said he was slurring the odd word and sometimes sounded as if he was pissed but hoped I would understand it was due to tiredness and not drink. When we came to do the interview it was worse than I had imagined. There was obviously something radically wrong, something that could not altogether be accounted for by fatigue. Sitting next to David, willing him to answer in that fluent, self-deprecating manner that had become his trademark, I felt a terrible sadness and an awful foreboding.

After the interview had been broadcast I received a call from a nurse who said she thought David had suffered a slight stroke. Predictably, some viewers called the BBC complaining he was drunk. It was, in fact, the early manifestation of motor neurone disease, which eventually killed him.

Unlike David, who was far too professional to drink before a performance, there were those who sought drink or other drugs to give them the confidence to walk down the stairs. Shortly after making the marvellous Robert Altman movie *MASH* its two stars, Donald Sutherland and Elliott Gould, appeared on the show. At the same time we booked Al Capp, the creator of the comic strip *L'il Abner*, who was also a political commentator of great skill and conviction. It was the time of Vietnam and Capp was on one side of the political divide and Gould and Sutherland on the other.

They told me they were eagerly awaiting the moment they could confront Capp and challenge his views, but they made the mistake of partaking of a substance that, whatever it was, might have given them confidence but also rendered them soporific. Consequently, they treated their interview with me as a casual encounter before the main event, and were in no fit state properly to challenge Capp, who wiped the floor with them while I looked on in quiet satisfaction.

Thirty years later I interviewed Donald Sutherland on my BBC radio programme. When he came in the studio, he asked me if I recalled the last time we had met. We laughed at the memory. He said, 'I guess I owe you an apology. It wasn't me, it was Gould who was to blame.'

Oliver Reed was another who felt the need for a drink or two before an interview. Somehow I always managed to handle him, except for one occasion when, demonstrating his prowess as a boxer, he punched a hole in the set. When he played the part of Flashman in the movie, he had to fight a bare-knuckle champion played by Henry Cooper. Henry told me that they carefully choreographed the sequence and then broke for lunch, with a view to completing the filming in the afternoon. Henry said that when Oliver reappeared he was wearing a mischievous look and it was obvious he was tiddly.

They started filming the fight and straightaway Oliver ignored the choreography and planted an unexpected right hook on Henry's chin.

'What happened next?' I asked.

Henry said, 'I gently chastised him.' A magnificent euphemism for the actor being knocked on his back, a sadder and wiser man.

Oliver Reed was a wonderful screen presence, an actor with a powerful star quality, and it was a pity he allowed drink to dominate his life. He was once misbehaving on Michael Aspel's talk show when another guest, Clive James, asked the question we all wish we had asked. He said, 'Why do you drink so much?' The look of bafflement and confusion on Oliver's face was not an answer, but an unforgettable moment.

My worst experience with a drunk occurred early in my career. When interviewing an MP for Granada Television, he fell asleep. It was the last part of the show so I couldn't link to another item. I ploughed on, both asking and answering the question. I would say, 'What kind of a week has it been for the party?' and then follow up with, 'I suppose if I was the prime minster, I would say that the economic situation is not good and the prospect of a three-day week a potential disaster,' and so on. The MP's only contribution was the sound of gentle snoring.

There were only two occasions I can recall on *Parkinson* when we had a debate about whether or not a guest was unfit to appear on the show. The culprits were the newscaster, Reginald Bosanquet, and the football manager, Brian Clough. Brian had been at some presentation lunch in his honour and my producer asked me to visit him in his dressing room to see what I thought. I both liked and admired Brian far too much to allow him to go on television and make an ass of himself, and I told him so. It worked. He got a grip of himself and we got away with it.

Reginald Bosanquet said he was going to interview me on the show and ask me all sorts of personal questions. I said he could try but all I had to do was sit there while he misbehaved. 'I won't help you out. You're on your own,' I said. He took the point and we struggled through without incident.

I cringe whenever I see that notorious encounter between Terry Wogan and George Best. I think Terry was badly served by his producer, who allowed George on to the show when he was clearly stupidly intoxicated and incapable of making any sensible answer. The people who thought it funny should understand they were laughing at a sick man, an alcoholic, in the throes of an illness that eventually killed him.

That said, I must admit that another demonstration of Oliver Reed's drunken behaviour did provide me with a great deal of merriment. Sadly, it was on radio and not television and the full impact of what happened could only be properly enjoyed by those who saw as well as heard it. It was a show, to celebrate the opening of a London radio station, which I was presiding over in the company of special guests, among them the American entertainer Elaine Stritch and Oliver Reed.

Oliver wasn't on time for the opening of the show and we were told there had been a snag with transport. The problem was that Oliver had persuaded the driver to stop at a pub en route where he was having a few drinks. The next bulletin involved Oliver meeting up with a group of workers digging up the road and inviting them to join him in another pub. A further report had him fifteen minutes from the studio in a car full of labourers who were coming to the studio as his guests.

I was talking to Elaine and she was in mid-flow when the studio door burst open and there, naked except for a pair of green wellies, stood Oliver Reed. Elaine looked up in mid sentence, smiled and said, 'Dear Oliver, I must tell you I have seen bigger and better,' and continued her story.

Apart from checking for sobriety, the only other concern I have before an interview is in finding out what the guest might not want to talk about. If it is something I judge to be mere tittle-tattle or deeply personal, then I am happy to go along with their request. There are times, however, when I have to point out that the matter they don't want asking about is a necessary part of the interview.

When I asked Rex Harrison the question, he said he didn't want to talk about his wives. I said he had been married eight times and if we didn't talk about this it would leave a big gap in the conversation. He agreed.

When I talked to Julie Andrews I questioned her about working with Harrison. She said he was inclined to flatulence. I asked her to elaborate and she said that there were times when performing *My Fair Lady* that she was reduced to helpless laughter because every time she opened her mouth to speak he farted.

Mary, my wife, was often mistaken for Julie Andrews. One evening I arranged to meet her in the BBC bar. I was late and Mary was cornered by a man who mistook her for Julie and went rambling on about how he worked with her mum and dad and how much he enjoyed her in *Mary Poppins*. Mary was too polite and good-natured to put him right and, in any event, he was the sort of fan who never paused for breath. I arrived in the middle of this, completely unaware of what had gone before. I went up to Mary and said, 'Come on, let's go home and have an early night.'

The man looked at her in horror and said, 'You're not having it off with him, are you?'

When I asked Charlton Heston what he would prefer not to talk about he said, 'The chariot race in Ben Hur.' I thought this was most strange. 'Why on earth not?' I asked. He looked conspiratorially around before beckoning me closer.

'It was fixed,' he whispered.

31

WITH LOVE, JOY AND LAUGHTER

It was the mid-seventies. Things could hardly have been better. The show was attracting audiences of eight million viewers and more, I had a highly successful column about sporting matters in *The Sunday Times*, we had a beautiful family house on the River Thames and three boys growing up in a robust and noisy manner. Mary was a star in her own right on television and we were proud of her. Then my father died.

When he retired from the pit we brought my parents from Yorkshire to live nearby in Oxfordshire. It pleased my mother to return to the county of her birth, it delighted my father because his wife was pleased. His main ambition in life was to make her happy. His other was to make his three grandsons into professional cricketers and he put them through the routine he designed to ensure his son played for Yorkshire.

Play forward, play back. Nothing flash. Never cut until late July and only then when you've made 50. When bowling, remember it's a side-on game. Look after umpires and they will look after you and only marry a girl who can sit through a Roses match without yawning. He took them on holiday to a resort where he introduced them to the science of Roses beach cricket, and with his mastery of this particular form of the game undiminished, created a demoralised and disgruntled opposition. It was still a bit like a team captained by Napoleon taking on Captain Mainwaring and his platoon.

Seeking revenge one year the Lancastrians suggested a game of water polo. This posed two serious problems for my father. Firstly, he couldn't swim and secondly he had a heart condition, which was supposed to limit his range of physical activity. Typically, he solved both problems by ignoring them. To this day my sons speak with awe of their granddad's performance, which they described to me as 'playing while drowning', as well as him recovering by the side of the pool by taking the tablets prescribed for his heart condition and telling them, 'Don't tell your grandma.' The heart condition was exacerbated by pneumoconiosis, a lung problem sadly common among miners of my father's generation. More than fifty years underground had taken their toll but he refused to let disability compromise his life.

We went one day to Stratford-upon-Avon – my mother's choice of excursion – and somewhere between Anne Hathaway's cottage and the theatre we lost the old man. He had a terrible sense of direction and I imagined him distressed and floundering in a strange town. My mother said we mustn't worry. All we had to do was ask where the nearest cricket ground was. When we found it, there he was in a deckchair, sitting near the sightscreen, the happiest man on the planet. He loved all games, and was very good at most of them, but he loved cricket the most. He judged everything and everyone by the game. The only time I ever saw him lost for words was when someone confessed they neither knew nor cared about cricket. Then he would shake his head sadly, baffled that a great part of his world – for cricket was surely that – could mean so little to any other sane human being.

In many ways the manners of the game, its courtesies, the humour of cricket, defined him as a human being. I was never told fairy tales as a child. Instead I heard about Larwood's action and Hobbs' perfection. Before I ever saw him play I knew all about Len Hutton. Stories extended into football and the first time I witnessed Stanley Matthews in the flesh I knew which way he was going, even if the full-back didn't. The stories of these gods, and many, many more besides, I heard at my father's knee.

He was a remarkable man with a marvellous facility to adorn an anecdote.

It was he who told me of the full-back whose fearsome sliding tackles carried him into the wall surrounding the ground, causing the spectators to start wearing goggles at home games for fear of being blinded by flying chips of concrete. Frank Barson, the Barnsley centre half, he assured me, once ran the entire length of the field bouncing the ball on his head, beat the opposing goalkeeper and then headed his final effort over the crossbar because he'd had a row with his manager before the game.

Moreover, the old man swore he managed to see Len Hutton's 364 at The Oval by convincing the gate attendant that he was dying of some incurable disease and his last wish was to see Len before he took leave of this earth. I never swallowed that one until once at a football match, where the gates were closed, I witnessed him convince a gateman that he was a journalist and I was his runner. I was seven at the time, and it was the very first occasion I watched a football match from a press box.

Whenever I smell cut grass and hear the sound of bat and ball I think of him. He was at his happiest in England and had no wish to go abroad. My mother had more expansive ambitions.

At the time of my father's retirement neither had travelled overseas nor had they been on an aeroplane. We decided to send them first class to Madeira. I arranged for a limousine to take them to the airport. It was one of those ancient Rollers with a glass panel separating the driver from his passengers. The chauffeur opened the door to the rear seats, an offer my mother accepted, whereas my father sat up front with the driver. My mother's look of disapproval as they headed off to the airport was nothing compared to her thunderous demeanour when we met them off the plane two weeks later. She strode ahead with my father, obviously in the doghouse, trailing behind with all the luggage.

The story she had to tell started when they boarded the plane at Heathrow. They had settled in their seats when the steward asked if they would like a drink before take-off. Mother ordered a sherry and father a pint of bitter. When the steward said they didn't serve pints of bitter, but my father could have a glass of champagne, he said, 'Champagne? I can't afford champagne young man.' The steward pointed out that the champagne was free. 'Free?' exclaimed the old man. 'Well that's different.'

It is necessary to tell this next part of the story in my mother's voice. Imagine pursed lips: 'Do you know, your father drank just about all the champagne they had on board? Worst of all, he was so tiddly that after they had served lunch he called the steward over and asked if he needed any help with the washing up. Well, I've never been so embarrassed in all my life.' Worse was to follow when, upon arrival at their destination, my father became involved in a dispute over a tip with the local porters, who were on the point of taking all the bags off the bus and calling a general strike before the tour guide settled the difference out of his own pocket and allowed the holiday to begin.

Their next holiday was a cruise on an ocean liner. I bought my dad a white linen jacket and black bow tie, which would be suitable if they were invited to the captain's table. I knew they would receive an invitation because we had arranged for it to happen. It arrived for the third night of their voyage, a cocktail party followed by dinner with the captain. My father was dressed before my mother so he said he would go ahead and see her at the cocktail party. Attired in white jacket and black bow tie he set off. When my mother arrived twenty minutes later she was horrified to see him standing by the door just about buried in mink wraps and other garments. Apparently, he had been dithering at the door when a couple mistook him for the doorman and handed him their coats. From that point on, the longer he stood there the more garments were deposited in his arms until, when my mother arrived, he was literally buried in fur.

'Gormless,' said my mother. 'That's what he is, gormless.'

He didn't travel well and yet his great ambition was to go to Australia to follow an Ashes series. He greatly admired the Aussies, believing they were antipodean Yorkshiremen, part of the same tribe, loving beer, plain speaking and cricket. When I first visited Australia and went to the Sydney Cricket Ground and saw the Hill and the lovely old pavilion, I knew what he meant and what he had missed.

He loved coming to the show and moved effortlessly around the Green Room, chatting to anyone who would listen, engaging Hollywood stars and waitresses with the same easy, unaffected manner. Everyone who met him felt they had known him for a long time.

He formed a special bond with Mary, filling the gap in her life caused by her father's early death, and becoming her mentor and her champion. She, in turn, felt a deep love for him.

When he was very unwell and in hospital it was to Mary he confessed his deepest fear. 'I don't want to die here,' he said.

So she brought him home and for a month or more he lay in palliative care, while we watched his life ebbing away like a disappearing tide.

I would sit with him and look at his hands lying outside the sheets. His hands always fascinated me. They were strong and well shaped and the palms and fingers were those of a working man, calloused and rough to the touch. I would lay my hands on his, mine unmarked, soft and smooth, and I would remember as a child the love and security I felt when he took my hand. For some reason this memory made me feel ashamed and filled my mind with the unbearable thought that his hands represented all he had done to enable me to enjoy a view of the river and an easy life. I imagined one day I might write a book about his life and mine and call it *Like Father, Like Son?* On the cover would be a picture of our hands, the miner and the layabout.

He died as he had lived, without making a fuss.

When the undertakers came for him they brought him downstairs in a blue rubber bag and he looked so small and insignificant I turned my head away. In that moment I accommodated his death by pretending it hadn't happened. Nor could I share my mother's grief because I couldn't face my own. That was when my mother started writing her book, as a tribute to the man she loved. It was typical of her intelligence.

I began to drink even more than normal, which was to say, a lot. The more I drank, the more depressed I became. I went to see a psychiatrist who probed away but didn't tell me anything I didn't already know. My drinking didn't interfere with my work. I didn't drink for twenty-four hours before a show and never ever on the day itself, at least not until the show had ended.

It was Mary who caused me to change.

She said to me one day, 'You know the worst thing about you and drink?'

I asked what she thought it was.

'It makes you ugly,' she said.

Her words rang in my brain ever after and, without ever causing me to become teetotal, made me forever cautious of further excess.

One day, about two years after my father died, I came across a picture of him as a young man, a group photograph of the village cricket team outside the pavilion on the ground where I first saw him play. He looked eager, athletic and handsome and the image broke the dam of my grief and I started crying. I cried for an hour or so, tears of love and regret, of pride and guilt. When I stopped I felt purged and later came to realise that when my mother reached the same moment, she stopped writing her book. Like me, she was then able to remember him with all the love, joy and laughter he gave to us when he lived.

32

STORM IN A
BBC TEACUP

I started getting the professional seven-year itch in 1978. By the end of the year I had done more than two hundred shows and was exploring the possibility of expanding what had become a highly successful and popular part of BBC's Saturday night programming.

I remembered being in America, a long time before I started doing the talk show, and, switching through the channels in my hotel room, coming across an early *Johnny Carson Show*. Carson announced that Ella Fitzgerald and the Count Basie Band were among the guests and that was enough to grab my attention. Then he introduced a new Hollywood star, George Segal at the very beginning of his career. Mr Segal turned out to be a fabulous guest, not only talking entertainingly but revealing a real talent as a guitarist. Carson kept him on beyond his allotted time to the point that he closed the show by saying to Ella and the Count, 'Can you come back tomorrow night?'

This seemed to me to define Carson's power as a talk-show host, as well as demonstrating the flexibility of the five-night-a-week format.

After seven years of trying to find a headliner or two for every show, I felt it would make a pleasant change to expand the format.

STORM IN A BBC TEACUP

Broadening its boundaries would enable us to create – as Carson and others in America and elsewhere had done – a nightly familiarity between show and viewer and explore a wider range of guests and subjects. I had talked to Bill Cotton about my ideas in general terms. We'd sometimes meet in his office after the day's work and chat over a drink or two. Like me, he could not explain why the five-night-a-week show had never been tried on British television and felt sure it would work. John Fisher, my producer, was also keen. Bill went to the Managing Director of Television, Alasdair Milne, who bought the idea.

The plan was to replace the ailing current affairs show *Tonight* with *Parkinson*. *Tonight* had been running for three years with an average audience of 2.5 million viewers per night. Bill Cotton reckoned we could increase that figure to between six and eight million. We decided the show would be done at the Mayfair Theatre in London and a couple of flats were organised to accommodate John and me, since we would literally be living over the shop.

Alasdair Milne told the Board of Governors at their meeting in October 1978: 'I am convinced that this would enable us to freshen schedules that are, after ten years of being tinkered with, beginning to look stale; and we introduce to British television a new kind of evening programme which should prove attractive to the audience.' The Director General, Ian Trethowan, had been consulted and had given the go-ahead. We thought it was a done deal but we had reckoned without a foxhole of disgruntled journalists in Lime Grove, questions in the House of Commons and dramatic intervention from the Board of Governors.

What seemed like a good idea at the time turned into a bureaucratic nightmare, and the beginning of the end of my relationship

273

with the BBC. There were rumblings in the media about trouble ahead but it wasn't until a meeting of the Governors on 8 February 1979 that the full-scale conflict began. At the time I had no means of knowing what was exactly happening at various meetings of the Governors. It is only now, when we are allowed access to the minutes of those meetings, that we discover exactly what went on. Reading them is to be given a glimpse of the Establishment at work, as well as a demonstration of the clunking wheels of bureaucracy turning and the media manipulation of politicians.

All I can do is offer a sketch of events, which demonstrated how a programme idea developed into a crisis, with questions being asked in parliament, threats being made about how the BBC is funded, and a proposed shut-down of the entire network by a strike of journalists. At the hub was the phrase 'trivialisation of the airwaves', which, according to some, was what would happen if my show replaced *Tonight*. It was first used by the Vice-Chairman of the Governors, Mark Bonham-Carter, at a board meeting in February 1979. He said that the idea of using me as a sort of 'English Jack Paar' would be a mistake, a move towards 'trivialisation'. The fact that Jack Paar had retired seventeen years earlier, to be replaced by Johnny Carson, appears to have escaped the attention of the vice-chairman of the governing body of the largest broadcasting organisation in the world.

Ian Trethowan said that *Parkinson* commanded a sizeable audience and it was time for a change, given the fact that current affairs had not worked satisfactorily in his experience of more than ten years. The BBC Chapel of the NUJ threatened a walk out. Vincent Hanna, a former colleague on *The Sunday Times*, used his political contacts to stir up trouble in parliament. That doughty defender of the working class, Dennis Skinner, asked the Home

Secretary, Merlyn Rees: 'Does my right honourable friend agree that it would be a good idea if he met the Director General again and urgently told him that it is not only members of parliament, but many millions of people outside who are concerned about the removal of certain current affairs programmes and their replacement by chat shows?'

With – if we are to believe Dennis Skinner – the nation in fear and trembling, the *Observer* reported: 'BBC television current affairs men are threatening to resign over plans to drop the *Tonight* programme in favour of a nightly chat show hosted by Michael Parkinson. The proposal, already agreed in principle by the Board of Governors, has provoked one of the bitterest BBC storms in recent times. Mr Alasdair Milne, Managing Director of BBC television, is trying to diffuse the revolt.' The *Observer* issued a dire warning: 'Everyone will expect endless interviews with Peter Ustinov and that's not what current affairs are about.'

Four days later the BBC Governors met for a crunch meeting. Immediately prior to their gathering yet another layer of bureaucracy met to have its say. This was the Television Programme Policy Committee, which included one of my fiercest critics, Lady Faulkner, widow of the former Northern Ireland prime minister Brian Faulkner. The minutes of the meeting record: 'Lady Faulkner hoped that Michael Parkinson could be "broken in" as a serious interviewer.' At the time of this fatuous utterance I had been interviewing people for nearly thirty years, which was probably the length of time Lady Faulkner had not been watching television.

According to the minutes, this observation brought a reply from the Director General: 'He felt it was Michael Parkinson's present image that had disturbed Governors and that they would not have objected if they had been told that Robin Day would be fronting the new programme. But Robin Day would not be able to draw in the extra millions that were the object of the exercise – people who did not normally watch current affairs.'

Bill Cotton said I was a journalist and reporter with substantial current-affairs experience and that, although my present brief was with light entertainment, it did not mean I was typecast.

A few hours later the entire matter was discussed by the Board of Governors. Mark Bonham-Carter said he was not impressed by Bill Cotton's presentation. He warned that if the new programme went ahead and came to grief, the Board would not treat the matter lightly. He said he meant 'no disrespect' to those involved; a solecism fit to serve as an epitaph for the whole absurd débâcle.

While all this was whistling around our heads we went on producing shows with such 'trivial' guests as Luciano Pavarotti, Henry Kissinger, André Previn, John Mortimer, Bernard Levin, Christian Barnard and Denis Healey.

The Governors chucked us a bone, a chance to do two shows a week, Wednesday as well as Saturday. I seriously thought about leaving. It had been a demoralising experience for all of us on the show and, in the end, we felt betrayed by a mixture of weak management and clueless governance. The extra show was not a good idea. It simply meant we were booking two headline shows a week instead of one, which often meant a dilution of the Saturday line-up. Moreover, because the BBC was short of studio space, we had to do the mid-week show at Guy's Hospital.

This establishment included a small but attractive theatre which, according to legend, had been built by mistake. The story was a famous surgeon who had operated at the hospital bequeathed a theatre in his name whereupon they built not an operating theatre, as the surgeon intended, but one to accommodate thespians and

333

33333

3333333

strolling players. It seemed to me that the confusion of its creation made it the perfect venue for our extra show.

For a long time I felt resentment at the way we had been treated but, at the same time, I was buoyed by the notion that, if the BBC didn't want us, there were other options. During the débâcle I had been approached by an Australian businessman, Colin McLennan, who sold some of the early shows to ABC Television in Australia, where they had done well. He thought it might be a good idea if I went to Sydney and did a series of shows interviewing prominent Australians for the ABC. I didn't have to think twice. I had always wanted to go to Australia, particularly if someone else was paying the fare.

I set off anticipating a one-off visit to a remote haven where I might lick my wounds. I soon discovered Australia was no place to feel sorry for yourself, particularly if you happened to be a Pom. But its optimism and enthusiasm recharged me. I fell in love with Oz and its people. Thirty years on it is my second home.

33

LEARNING MY ABC

While the BBC debated whether or not cultural life as we knew it in Britain in the 1970s would be destroyed by a talk show, an entrepreneur was busy buying up the back catalogue and selling it to Australia. We had long thought that the galaxy of stars on offer would make the show attractive to buyers overseas but the BBC commercial arm of the time thought otherwise. When approached by an American businessman, Michael Baumohl, the man in charge of selling the BBC abroad said he doubted if an English talk show would have an international appeal. When it was pointed out to him that James Cagney, Fred Astaire, Bob Hope, Bing Crosby, Luciano Pavarotti and the rest were great international stars with massive box-office appeal, particularly in rich and expanding English-speaking markets such as Australia, the man from the BBC offered the thought that maybe the Aussies would have difficulty understanding my accent. Mr Baumohl persisted in doing the deal anyway, and Colin McLennan, the Australian entrepreneur who had identified the market, flogged the shows to Australia, where the natives had so much difficulty understanding me that, over the years, they bought the entire *Parkinson* catalogue, including more than a hundred shows we recorded in Australia.

The ABC, the Australian equivalent of the BBC but without the money, took the first series of twelve shows and they proved so successful they agreed with Colin McLennan's suggestion to bring me to Oz to record a series with Australian guests. I flew out to meet Colin in Singapore ahead of landing in Australia.

In those days the 747s had the bar on the upper deck and a small bedroom alongside, which is where I lay my head before arriving in Singapore. I had been asleep for no more than an hour when I developed an itch on my chest and belly. Looking down I saw I was being invaded by a swarm of nipping creatures, which turned out to be bed bugs. I called the hostess who found a first-aid kit and smeared me with a yellow antiseptic cream, which looked delightful when matched with my pink silk shirt with the Concorde collar, which, I assumed, would knock 'em dead in Oz.

There was mild panic among the staff because, not only was I a designated VIP, but they also knew I was a journalist, who might sell his story of the calamity. I was whisked off the plane at Singapore and found myself in the back of a white Rolls-Royce with a pleasant young man who said he was PR for the airline. He wanted to offer profuse apologies and told me a story about the bed linen having been infected in some foreign laundry and he hoped I would understand and not make too much of it, particularly as he had arranged with the hotel to pick up the bill for my stay and pay for everything, and he meant everything, and, by the way, sir, we asked the hotel to provide you with a VIP reception reserved only for very famous people, and we hope you will be pleased.

At this precise moment, we turned off the road into the driveway to the hotel across which was hung a huge banner with the message: 'WELCOME NORMAN PARKINSON'.

I arrived in Australia not knowing what to expect. 'G'day, Parko,' said the immigration man. That was the first time I heard the antipodean version of my nickname. As we drove into Sydney and I looked about me, I was amazed by the quality of the light. Every building was clearly etched, its contours diamond bright and clean cut against the azure blue sky. In my mind I contrasted it with the landscape I grew up in, the Lowry churches and factories diffused with the sky in a soft blur. On television the newscasters wore vivid, bright colours, the women had American teeth, and everyone glowed with exercise and well-being.

Alan Whicker once told me that the quickest way to come to terms with a strange land was to watch telly and listen to the phone-ins for a couple of days. I took the advice of the master and discovered a land a lot more complex and sophisticated than I had imagined, yet at the same time a country with growing pains, sometimes gawky, lacking in self-confidence. The Australia of the seventies was not the assured, self-reliant, wealthy nation of today.

Listening to the phone-ins was also a way of finding out what Aussies made of a Pom coming out to show them how to do interviews, which was the way my trip was perceived by one or two of the phone-in hosts, who were generally scathing about the notion. One called me a carpetbagger, another a ratbag, and yet the general feeling was typically Aussie. 'Give the Pom a fair go,' was how they summed it up.

I was installed in the Sebel Townhouse, an establishment that the *Sydney Morning Herald* once described as: 'a place where the best stories are even now unpublishable and people still joke about selling the carpets for their cocaine content'. It was even better summed up by another regular guest, Billy Connolly, when he said: 'It is not the best hotel in terms of rooms, or food, or ambience or anything you get a star for. What makes it unique is it's the only place I've stayed in where you never hear anyone say: "Oh, you can't do that sir."'

I stayed there for so long they named a room after me. They offered it to Michael Aspel when he visited Sydney. He said he would only take it at a large discount. They pulled the hotel down a couple of years ago to make room for apartments. It should have had a preservation order slapped on it. Where else in the world could you sit in the bar in the company of the aforesaid Billy Connolly, Elton John, Marc Bolan, Warren Mitchell, George Best and David Frost, as happened one night?

The next morning I went to breakfast and sitting in the far corner of the room was Bob Dylan. Doing the job I do I am not in the habit of autograph-hunting, but this was someone I wanted to meet because he didn't do talk shows and it might be my only chance. So I went across and bade him good morning. He looked up and grunted. Whereupon I launched into my overture to the autograph request, which included telling him how much I admired his talent as a musician, singer, composer and general all-round special human being. All this I said to the top of his head and, when I had finished, he looked up and drawled, 'Two eggs sunny side up and orange juice.'

'Certainly, sir,' I said.

We set up in Colin McLennan's office with two experienced journalists, Chris Greenwood and his wife Barbara Toner, making up the production team. Barbara was an Aussie, Chris had worked in the country on television talk programmes, and together they were a formidable package. Barbara, who later went on to win a deserved reputation as a novelist, had a sharp and decisive mind and a tongue to go with it. She didn't do polite conversation, nor did she suffer fools at all.

We were once at dinner in Melbourne with an exceedingly pompous and boring television executive, soft-soaping him for a deal we were making, when Barbara struck, having accidentally spilled salt on the table.

'Throw some over your shoulder and make a wish,' said the boring producer.

Barbara closed her eyes and did as he said. When she opened her eyes she said, 'It didn't work.'

'How do you know?' asked the man.

'You're still here,' said Barbara.

We needed to make a quick impact because our first run was limited to seven shows. We identified three Australians whose appearance on the show would be regarded as masterstrokes. They were Kerry Packer, Sir Don Bradman and Bob Hawke. Hawke, later to be prime minster, was then the head of the Australian Labour Movement.

Bradman was *the* prize. Along with Sinatra, he was the man I most wanted to interview. I wrote him a letter to which he replied saying that if ever I came to Adelaide, where he lived, he would shout me lunch, but he really didn't like being interviewed, and would therefore politely have to decline our request. News that Don Bradman had turned us down was used by some journalists to suggest I was angry at the rebuff and couldn't understand why he had said no. What I had said was that I was disappointed and why should I not be? I pointed out that Bradman was the greatest batsman the game had ever produced, that he was the genius against which every other player would be judged and that it was a pity he didn't give the public a chance to hear his story from his own lips. I offered the somewhat flamboyant thought that in musical terms it was a bit like Mozart saying 'no comment' when asked about his contribution to music.

I should have kept my mouth shut. The more I tried to explain the more the media made mischief. Nor did it help when, at the same time, I wrote an article for *The Sunday Times* in London based on an interview with Harold Larwood. Larwood was the fast bowler who was England's spearhead in the infamous Bodyline series of 1932–3. He was the weapon used by the England captain, Douglas Jardine, to nullify Bradman's genius and win the Ashes by the simple expedient of bowling at the batsman's head. The plan succeeded but the echo of anger and disapproval resonated through succeeding generations of Australians.

I met Larwood in Sydney, where he had lived for a number of years, and had lunch with him and Keith Miller, plus a few other heroes. He said Bradman was the greatest batsman he ever bowled against and the only chance you had was to get him out early on. Otherwise he would destroy you. He said in the 1930 Test series, when the Aussies came to Headingley, the England team worked out he was vulnerable to the short ball when he first came to the crease. According to Larwood, the second ball he bowled at Bradman was a short-pitched one, which he nicked and the wicket keeper caught. 'We thought we had him but the umpire disagreed. Mind you, we got him out soon after,' said Harold.

I fell for it. 'How many did he make?' I asked.

'Three hundred and thirty-four,' replied Harold, with a grin.

Sir Donald took exception to the anecdote and wrote to the editor saying I had cast doubts on his sportsmanship. I certainly had not intended so to do and had merely treated Larwood's anecdote as it had been told, to enhance the Bradman legend rather than diminish it. It didn't make any difference. The mischief-making continued and I never did interview Don Bradman. Some might wonder why I dwell on the story of my failure to persuade Bradman on to the show, why I placed so much importance on getting a mere cricketer into our studio.

I did so because anyone who regarded Bradman as simply a gifted sportsman is missing the point. Sport played a large and important part in establishing the Australian identity and Bradman provided the evidence of the nation's ability to produce an athlete who had his own place in the pantheon of the greatest sportsmen of all time. In a country where sport really matters, and which has produced so many great international sporting heroes, Bradman remains the towering icon.

Even without Bradman, the first series of shows proved more successful than we had ever dared to hope. The ABC put it out on Saturday evenings and it flourished like no other Saturday evening show on ABC had done in recent history. Our success had much to do with the type of guest – the Don notwithstanding – we were able to attract. Our biggest coup was Kerry Packer. He was not only, along with Rupert Murdoch, Australia's most powerful media mogul, he was also Australia's most controversial figure, adored and loathed, feared and respected in equal measures. He was the head of a family who had lived the Australian dream, coming from nowhere to a position of such power that members of it could treat the country as a personal fiefdom, an observation that might seem exaggerated until you hear the story of Frank Packer and the winner of the Melbourne Cup.

Frank Packer, Kerry's father, was the man who built the family fortune based on publishing and television. The family owned Channel 9, which, during my time in Australia, was the country's favourite channel. Frank Packer owned a horse that won Australia's big race, the Melbourne Cup. At dinner on the night of his triumph as an owner, a guest told Packer he had not yet seen the race, whereupon Packer rang the television station and ordered a bemused duty officer to take off air whatever was on air at the time and replace it with a rerun of the big race, to the general bafflement of the millions watching at home who couldn't work out why the Melbourne Cup suddenly reappeared in the middle of their favourite soap.

What made Kerry Packer particularly interesting was that his phenomenal success in consolidating and building upon his father's enterprise was unexpected. He had been marked out as 'the idle playboy' by the media and it was generally assumed that when Frank Packer died his eldest child, Clyde, would take over. But Clyde and his father fell out a year before Frank Packer died, Kerry took over and proceeded to expand the empire to the point where he became Australia's richest man.

That apart, I had another reason for wanting to interview Kerry Packer. He was in the process of creating World Series Cricket, which at the time I, along with many other lovers of the traditional game, regarded as an act of vandalism.

When he arrived at the studio, he managed to split his pants while getting out of the car. Kerry Packer was a very big man and it was a considerable split that required the combined talents of the wardrobe department to mend. My first view of the great man was sitting in wardrobe, minus his pants, seemingly not the slightest bit fazed by his predicament. He was a fascinating interviewee, articulate, combative, humorous. He told the story of his family's rise in fortune. It started when his grandfather, flat broke in Tasmania, went to the races and found ten bob, which he put on a horse. It won at twelve to one so he bought a ticket to New South Wales with the winnings, where he started a career in the newspaper industry.

'Ten bob on a racecourse. That's how it all started,' said Kerry Packer, who was worth a billion dollars at the time.

Things warmed up when he discussed World Series Cricket. I told him I didn't like the idea. He said I hadn't the right to visit Australia and put the Establishment's point of view. I said the MCC would find ludicrous the idea that I was the Establishment. He said I was a Yorkshireman and all Yorkshiremen were 'unreasonable' about cricket. He was trying to rile me and he succeeded. In the end he was right about World Series. His concept of one-day cricket changed the game for good, and for the better. Kerry Packer fundamentally shaped the modern game, and cricket – particularly its players – owes him an enormous debt.

So do I. His appearance on the show, his frankness, his argumentative style, made an enormous impact, and the door opened. Bob Hawke came on the show. Jack Fingleton, the former Australian cricketer and writer, bet him fifty dollars he would be Australia's next prime minister. Bob Hawke said not a chance. Jack waited just three years to collect his money.

I interviewed artist Lloyd Rees, who talked about coming to Sydney for the first time in 1916 and seeing the gap between the two points where the Sydney Harbour Bridge was eventually built. 'Nature puts awful temptation in the way of humanity,' he remarked. It was Lloyd who gave me a privileged insight into the world of art. I opened one of his last exhibitions, which the critics praised for his ethereal depictions of light, pointing out how his painting had gradually refined from the more conventional style of his early years. I asked him what he made of their remarks.

'They know nothing,' he said. 'Shall I tell you why I paint the way I do?' I nodded. 'Because I am going blind and I paint what I see,' he said. And then he added, 'But don't tell them. It will make them seem foolish.'

A natural history expert, Harry Butler, talked about the damage English settlement had caused to a land protected for so long by what he described as 'the gentle custody' of the Aborigines.

Sir Robert Helpmann, the actor and ballet dancer, described by *The Times* as 'a dancer of mimetic genius and theatrical flair', remembered prancing round his house as a child covered in mosquito nets. He was a country boy and when he moved to Sydney he went to Bondi Beach wearing a pair of Oxford bags, popular in England at the time, but not yet acceptable men's wear in Oz. He was set upon by a crowd of men who picked him up and threw him into the surf, leaving him to crawl out 'like a drowned rat'.

'You couldn't wear a pair of suede shoes in those days without being attacked for being effeminate,' he said.

He lived to see Sydney become the gay capital of the world. A couple of years ago, on the eve of the Gay Mardi Gras, Mary and I were in a lift about to leave our Sydney hotel when we were joined by two men entirely dressed in rubber – one in a suit, the other a dress – who were joined together at the wrist by a pair of handcuffs. 'G'dayparkoowyergoin?' said one. That was many years after I first met Robert Helpmann, who perfectly summed up my feelings about my first visit to Australia when he said, 'Someone asked me the other day, do I regard Australia as a cultural desert? And I said how could I think it so when it has given birth to Dame Nellie Melba, Dame Joan Sutherland and me?'

Another clue to the effortless and pleasant way I was accepted into Australia was given by a wonderful old actress called Enid Lorimer, who was born in London in Victorian times and had emigrated to Australia as a young girl. When I met her she was in her eighties, but an imperious figure, still possessing her English accent. She reminded me greatly of Dame Edith Evans. One day I asked her why she, the archetypal English woman, had chosen to live in Australia.

She said, 'Because the English invented the word snob and the Australians don't know what it means.'

34

TWO BAGGY GREENS

Australia gave me a much-needed injection of enthusiasm for the job. All the palaver and politicking at the BBC had left me jaded and discontented, but my experience in an altogether more relaxed environment down under produced renewed optimism, not for staying any longer than necessary at the BBC, but for making the best of it while I was there.

I was greatly helped in this ambition by a move of office, which meant sharing with a group of amiable lunatics assembled to make a programme called *Not the Nine o'Clock News*, subtitled *When Pamela Met Billy*. The first week they moved in I arrived at my desk to find a bloody hand hanging out of my filing cabinet. In weeks to come, opening a cupboard might reveal a false leg or an inflatable banana. You never knew. Nor did sharing an office spare me from their irreverence. On one show they featured a sketch depicting me interviewing Geoffrey Boycott, both with impenetrable Yorkshire accents and exceedingly boring dialogue.

I thought I would have a word and arrived early the morning after the show to be sure to catch them as they arrived at the office. I was standing there, with a large stick in my hand, when the door opened and Rowan Atkinson scuttled past me, going sideways like a crab, while at the same time touching his forelock and muttering, 'Sorry but it wasn't my idea . . . terribly sorry.'

The two shows a week compromise looked what it was, a compromise, neither one thing nor t'other, and no matter how hard I tried, there had been a significant shift in my relationship with the BBC. Hitherto I had been confident of the support of the organisation, now I wasn't. I had seen its flaws, been disappointed by its weakness. I was on the lookout for alternative employment. Australia gave me that opportunity. I returned to produce a new series for the ABC, which proved more popular than the first and succeeded so well it had the two major commercial companies, owned by Kerry Packer and Rupert Murdoch, bidding for my show.

I thought long and hard and eventually settled for the Channel 10 deal put forward by Rupert Murdoch. It was a five-year agreement and meant spending at least six months a year in Australia. I was joined by James Erskine, an ambitious former medical student, now working with my agent Mark McCormack. It was the beginning of a business partnership and friendly relationship that has lasted until the present time. James is now my business manager.

I brought Mary and the children out to Australia before I signed the contract to see what they thought. They loved it. We bought an apartment looking down the harbour to the Heads in the same block as Danny La Rue, who entertained the most amusing and exotic house guests. One morning I was sitting by the communal swimming pool when Liberace appeared as if in a Ziegfeld movie. He was wearing a purple silk beach robe with ivory piano keys stitched onto its large lapels.

'Hi, I'm Lee Liberace,' he said.

'I know,' I said.

He indicated the keyboard on his lapels. 'These are just in case you didn't,' he said.

Princess Anne and Captain Mark Phillips agreed to appear on our show. This was big news, a great coup for Channel 10, who redecorated a large dressing room, draping it with silk and hanging a royal coat of arms that had been used as a prop in a courtroom drama. We were told Princess Anne drank only Coca-Cola from small glass bottles. They were not sold anywhere in Australia except Adelaide so we ordered a special shipment. When Princess Anne arrived and was asked what she would like to drink she said, 'A mineral water, please.'

We were informed it would be acceptable if we invited Princess Anne to an informal lunch at our apartment. Mary and her friends went into overdrive. What to wear? How informal is royalty? The office driver was told to sit outside Princess Anne's hotel to see what she was wearing when she left en route to our apartment. Was it a trouser suit, a frock, a sundress? When the Princess arrived it was with the minimum of fuss and palaver and she put everyone at ease with her direct and friendly manner.

Everything was going perfectly until, recalling one or two of the civic functions she had attended, she told a story about a man who drank the contents of his finger bowl.

Someone observed, 'When he saw the slice of lemon he must have thought it was a gin and tonic.' Whereupon the Princess declared one did not put lemon slices in finger bowls.

I looked at Mary and she looked at me because sitting in our kitchen were finger bowls containing slices of lemon. They were despatched over the balcony into the garden, causing consternation among the bodyguards concealed in the shrubbery who were not used to being bombarded by citrus fruit.

It was a happy time. My boss at Channel 10, Greg Coote, was

kind and supportive. We had assembled a team of bright and funny Australians, led by David Mitchell and David Lyle, who made work an agreeable pastime. However, the move was not without its problems. For one thing, to get value for their money, Channel 10 wanted the show stretched to ninety minutes. This meant an extra booking per show and, given we were doing more than thirty shows a year, it involved going farther afield for some of our guests. We imported Alan Alda, Joan Fontaine, Zsa Zsa Gabor, Kenneth Williams, Adam Faith, Lee Marvin, Harry Belafonte and just about anyone else who had a current passport. We brought back stalwarts including Jack Fingleton, Spike Milligan and Billy Connolly.

Jack rang me from his hotel room on the morning of one show.

'I've been thinking of what might make my appearance more interesting,' he said. I asked him what he had come up with. 'Ever had anyone croak on your show?' he asked.

Fingleton was a fascinating man. He was a journalist by trade, working in Canberra as a parliamentary correspondent, and he had played his cricket for Australia in Bradman's era. Jack became friendly with many politicians and a few prime ministers, including Ben Chifley, who loved cricket and was persuaded by Jack to receive Harold Larwood as a new Australian.

The background to this situation was fascinating. The Bodyline tour threatened diplomatic relations between England and Australia. Douglas Jardine, who devised the leg theory, which caused the outcry, was an accepted member of the cricket establishment and well able to survive the storm. Larwood was a professional cricketer in a game with an amateur ethos, in the days when Gentlemen and Players had different dressing rooms, separate exits and entrances. Larwood was trade. He was hung out to dry and made the scapegoat.

Hurt and disenchanted, he left the game and hid away in a shop

Right: Elton John gave me this picture of George Best. It has a wistful quality I find appealing.

Below: My old sparring partner before our third contest when he lost his cool. He is a fascinating and complex man and maybe the greatest heavyweight of the lot.

Me and my sons, including Kenny Lynch, whom I adopted after finding him in a shoebox near White
Hart Lane.

Relaxed in Oz.

One of my favourite photos of Mary.

David was something of a regular on the show. His wife told me he was called 'Goldenballs' when more than nine million were tuned in.

We waited a long time for Madonna but it was worth it.

Way back in 1971 – a singalong with Elton and Michael Caine.

The first show on ITV. The critics said we would struggle to get the big names so we opened with Tom Cruise.

Win some, lose some. Meg and I did not hit it off and it showed.

Stevie Wonder gave me his harmonica to round off a perfect evening.

There was a mutual antipathy between Dame Helen Mirren and me when we first met. Then things got better. A wonderful actress and an intriguing woman.

Opposite above left:
A BAFTA in 1999.

Opposite above right:
A knighthood in 2008.

Above left: Billy Connolly
– several fascinating
people.

Above: Time to go –
Peter Kay suggests a new
career.

Left: 'Goodnight and
goodbye.' The final line-
up – 23 November 2007:
(*left to right*) David
Attenborough, Michael
Caine, Jamie Cullum,
Billy Connolly, Judi
Dench, me, Peter Kay,
Dame Edna Everage and
David Beckham.

Left: John William Parkinson, beloved father, with Freda Rose Parkinson, a mettlesome woman.

Below: The engine of my ambition.

in Blackpool and didn't even put his name above the door. He was found by Jack Fingleton who, although he had played against the Bodyline team and suffered many a battering from Larwood, persuaded him to emigrate to Australia. The Aussies had a clearer view of what had happened. They saw the patrician Jardine as the architect of their downfall and loathed him for what they believed were his unfair and unsporting methods. Larwood they regarded as the sword in Jardine's hand, yet they admired him as a great fast bowler.

Jack told me the marvellous story about Larwood's visit to the prime minister's residence. He introduced the two men and left the room. After about ten minutes the prime minister came out. Jack asked how the meeting was progressing.

'I think it's OK,' said Chifley. 'But I have to tell you, Jack, I can't understand a bloody word he's saying.' A while later Larwood appeared, looking slightly concerned. Jack asked him what was wrong.

'He's a nice man,' said Harold. 'But I wish I knew what he was talking about.'

Jack followed Larwood back into the room and for the next half hour acted, discreetly, as interpreter for two people divided, as they say, by a common language.

Jack and I first met when we worked together at *The Sunday Times* and became good friends. I hadn't seen him again for several years until I came to Australia and was asked to speak to the National Press Club in Canberra. At question time, after my speech, Jack stood up and, pretending he had never met me, reduced the formality of the proceedings to rubble. His question, which lasted five minutes, included the observation that, although I was a Pom, I was at least a Yorkshire Pom, which wasn't so bad, although I came from Barnsley which, as everyone knew, had the highest illegitimacy rate on the planet and, what is more, was the birthplace of the groundsman who prepared the wicket at Headingley where Fred Trueman twice bowled out the Aussies to win a Test match, which was clearly a fix, since the only way we could beat Australia was by cheating . . . and so on and so on. All this delivered out of the corner of his mouth and with twinkling eyes.

He was a funny, wise, cantankerous and loveable old man, and among the best half dozen writers about cricket there have been. He gave me two of his Australian cricket caps, two baggy greens, which I still have and treasure, unlike Keith Miller's last Test sweater, which Keith gave to me during one drunken lunch in Sydney. It was washed by a daily help and shrank so badly it would hardly fit Frankie Dettori, never mind a physical specimen such as Miller.

Of all the athletes I have met in a lifetime of observing sport and writing about it, Keith Ross Miller is the one who fits my definition of the athletic ideal. Neville Cardus described him as 'the Australian *in excelsis*'. John Arlott said that if he could pick one man to hit a six, take a wicket or make a catch with his life depending upon it, he would choose Keith Miller. But he was not simply a connoisseur's cricketer. He was beloved by all who came within range of his formidable personality. Women adored him, men envied him. To walk with him around Lord's during a Test match was to experience royalty on the move. We once set off before lunch and by the time we had completed the circuit, taking in conversations with programme sellers, bookmakers, barmen and the hundreds who saw him hit the ball on to the roof of the stand at Lord's in the forties, it was tea time.

Keith was shaped by the country that reared him, but forever conditioned by the war. He flew fighter bombers over Germany, once making a detour from a mission to fly over the birthplace of Beethoven, his favourite composer. The only photographs in his study were of the Australian services team playing at Bramall Lane, Sheffield, the year after the war, and a picture of Guy Gibson VC, DSO, DFC, sitting in a field of red poppies.

Even heroes have their heroes.

Keith Miller was deeply affected by the Second World War. It changed him.

The way he played his cricket in the immediate postwar years was as much a celebration of surviving the war as it was the product of an impulsive nature and a lifelong desire never to be bored by either a person or a game. Keith Miller held life in a passionate embrace because he had seen the alternative.

It was famously Miller who defined the way that sport has become distorted to the point where people have forgotten that what they are watching or playing is a pastime, an entertainment, a tarradiddle. He told me how much he hated the word 'pressure' when applied to athletes doing their job. 'They don't know what pressure means,' said Keith. 'I'll tell you what pressure is: it's having a Messerschmitt up your arse at twenty thousand feet. That's pressure.'

I interviewed one of my favourite Australians, Rolf Harris. Rolf is a neighbour of mine and throughout our years of friendship I have grown to admire not only his great talent as an all-round entertainer but also his support for various good causes I have been involved with, which he has undertaken with typical enthusiasm and no though of remuneration.

He said he wanted to talk about his father, who had died shortly before our interview. He had a video of father and son on stage during one of his Australian concerts and said he would like to show it on air. When we played the tape during the interview, he burst into tears. He was still obviously grieving and broke down at the sight of his beloved parent.

The problem facing the host on an occasion such as this is to think of a way of enabling the interview to proceed without a gruff exhortation to 'pull yourself together man' or some other equally insensitive instruction.

As he wept and the clip ended, the audience came face to face with a man who, a moment ago was happy and jolly, and now was distraught with sorrow. I said, 'You said your father liked a laugh. Tell me a funny story about him'. Fortunately, it worked, and Rolf, ever the professional, found a story to guarantee the interview ended in laughter and not tears.

For three years or more I continued to work at opposite ends of our planet – six months doing *Parkinson* in the UK, six months in Oz – and because of ratings requirements suffered two winters every year. The Australian one wasn't too bad, but it was far from a perfect arrangement. I also experienced what eminent Australian historian Manning Clark once described as 'the tyranny of distance'. Australia is a long way from anywhere, particularly Europe, and I felt myself becoming increasingly detached from my backyard. This growing sense of disassociation was most apparent during the Falklands War. I watched developments on Australian television, which, every night, offered an hour-long assessment of how the operation was developing. I would sit and watch with an unnatural detachment, as if watching Mars fight Jupiter.

My state of mind was not helped by the fact that the longer the shows continued, the more difficult it became to provide the stars the channel demanded. Greg Coote left to work in Los Angeles, where he now heads up one of Rupert Murdoch's production companies. There were rumours Murdoch would likely relinquish his interest in Australian television as a condition of his American citizenship. One day Ken Cowley, Rupert's right-hand man in Sydney, suggested lunch. We dined at a quiet Italian restaurant away from the media crowd. I thought this bloke is going to sack me. I had always fancied the big pay-off, the financial poultice for bruised pride, but something – I don't know what exactly – made me determined to fight any attempt to get rid of me. So I kept up a stream of incessant chatter about this and that, pausing only to order more wine.

At the end of the meal – both of us pleasantly sozzled and being driven back to the office – I asked Ken if his intention was to let me go. He said it was. I said he was right if he thought the weekly talk show had maybe had its day, certainly at thirty ninety-minute shows a year, so why didn't we do some specials and fill in the rest of the contract by making documentaries. Being a good and fair man, and a pal, he agreed.

Princess Anne was one of the studio specials and the documentaries took me all over Australia, an all-expenses paid journey around a fascinating, awesome and beautiful country.

In Darwin we went hunting with a man whose job it was to tag baby crocodiles. We filmed at an aboriginal cattle station where they rounded up the beasts by helicopter and where I met a saintly woman, a nurse, who cared for the men with an intriguing blend of modern and folk medicine. She swore that a native paste made from pulped ants was superior to penicillin.

One day I stood on an outcrop of rock in Kakadu National Park doing a wrap to camera when the director made the casual observation it would make a more interesting shot if there was something happening in the background. As it was, all we could see was forest stretching to infinity.

We had a park ranger with us. 'You want action?' he asked. 'Then get ready to roll when I fire my gun.' Whereupon he discharged his weapon into the air and immediately the sky behind me was filled with birds of every colour, blue and yellow, white and pink. They blotted out the sun. It was amazing, so much so that I just stood, open-mouthed, and watched the feathered rainbow, quite forgetting to do my piece to camera.

While we were in the Top End, as the Aussies call the Northern Territory, I was asked to be guest of honour at an event organised by the local press club. As I was filming at the time, I asked if it would be a lunch or a dinner. They said dinner. I said that should be OK, I could do a full day's filming and then meet them in the evening, about what time? Four o'clock, mate, they said. 'We like to eat early.' I said I couldn't make it before six in the evening and they said that would be all right and they would make sure they didn't drink all the grog before I turned up.

When I finally arrived the party was in full swing. A greeter sent out to escort me into the hall collapsed in the doorway trying to negotiate a step that wasn't there. As I entered the room the piano player attempted to play my signature tune. In the words of the great Eric Morecambe, he did play all the right notes but not necessarily in the right order. The assembly was, quite rightly, beyond caring about hearing a boring speech but were battered into submission by the chairman, who quietened the rabble with the unforgettable exhortation: 'Come on, ladies and gentlemen, give the Pom a fair go. After all, it's better than a poke in the eye with a burnt stick.'

That moment sealed my love affair with Australia.

35

THE FAMOUS FIVE

David Frost first approached me about bidding for the morning television franchise when I was in Australia working for the ABC. Whenever David calls, it means one of two things – either lunch or a new television company. One way or another he has played an important part in my television career. *That Was the Week That Was* turned television on its head and, both technically and editorially, inspired my generation of producers and presenters. It was brilliantly cast and imaginatively directed by Ned Sherrin. The list of writers has never been equalled on any programme since and the entire enterprise found its perfect front man in David Frost.

His interview programmes in the late sixties and early seventies, particularly his confrontations with the crook Savundra and the formidable Enoch Powell, created a new genre of television; serious journalism as an entertainment event. David has the rare talent of being able to transform complicated research into simple questions. He also has the showman's instinct for the dramatic pause or gesture and a comedian's timing. As I grew up in television, I watched and admired him. I couldn't quite fathom the jibes and sneers he sometimes attracted. On other hand, he has the consolation of having outlived most of his critics.

His entrepreneurial skills also set him apart. He created two television companies, he beat the American networks in the bid for the Nixon interviews, and he is the only English interviewer to become a major star on American television.

He told me that his idea for the breakfast consortium was based on the United Artists concept, where we would pack the bid with as many stars as possible. Eventually his dream became reality and he signed up the so-called 'Famous Five' . . . Angela Rippon, Anna Ford, Robert Kee, David and the author of this book. Our chairman was Peter Jay, formerly Ambassador to the United States, and former Economics Editor of *The Times*. Lord Richard Marsh, once head of British Rail, was also on the board.

We embarked on the ludicrous rigmarole of trying to win the franchise. This involved convincing the IBA of our credentials by speaking to and answering questions from community groups about our intentions. It seemed to me that, no matter where we travelled, we were pursued by a lobby group of cyclists whose main argument against breakfast television was based on the theory that it would make motorists late leaving the house in the morning and, in speeding to work, they would cause a serious threat to the pedal-pushers. The alternative theory was that cyclists themselves might become hooked on the box and, in trying to make up lost time on their journey to work, might crash and cause serious damage to their persons. This theme of our roads becoming flooded with kamikaze motorists and cyclists in a zombie-like trance induced by watching breakfast television was repeated again and again at our various meetings.

It was difficult to stay awake, never mind keep a straight face, as this catalogue of impending doom was laid at our feet. You might imagine we were asking permission to build a nuclear reactor rather than give people the chance to watch telly in the morning.

Equally baffling was the assumption that morning television meant people *had* to watch, would be compelled to do so. You wanted to say, 'You don't have to watch the bloody thing,' but that would not have gone down well with the IBA, or the media who kept a keen eye on proceedings.

One story suggested that the Famous Five were spending lavishly on first-class rail fares to places such as Darlington. David decided he would set the example and travelled second class, an exemplary sacrifice. However, he forgot to cancel the Bentley he had ordered to meet him at our destination. I shall forever treasure the memory of David walking briskly down the platform being shadowed all the way by his limousine and attempting to shoo it away with muttered instructions to 'bugger off'.

It was at this meeting that a member of the public – at long last – put the crashing car/cyclist question into a proper perspective. During the inevitable debate he stood up and said, 'Where I come from we've had breakfast television for years and never had a problem with crashing cars.'

Thank the Good Lord and hallelujah we thought. We asked him where he came from. 'Hong Kong,' he said, a place of water and sampans. It was as if Spike Milligan was writing the script.

John, now Lord, Birt coached us for our appearance before the IBA. It was at this time the phrase 'mission to explain' was first used. Little did we know the battle cry would soon become the epitaph. We won the franchise and rejoiced. Peter Jay brilliantly marshalled us through the final interviews and we celebrated at David's home.

That was the good news. The bad news was that the IBA delayed the start of TV-am, allowing the BBC to nip in ahead of us. They had a two-week start, and a combination of Frank Bough's woolly jumpers and Selina Scott's seductive charm attracted a substantial audience while we were still recruiting key staff and working out who fitted with whom.

It's fun recruiting star names, but the problem arises when you pair one with another. It was suggested that Mary and I do the weekend slot, which seemed a straightforward decision as we had worked together before, and it also made economic sense because we could share a taxi to work. Robert Kee was our most experienced and distinguished journalist and, once we had decided the first hour should be news based, he was the obvious anchor, along with Angela. This left David and Anna to carry the main show, an interesting proposition but not without its problems.

The five of us seemed to get on well together, there was a commendable lack of conflicting egos, but I always had the feeling that Anna was less comfortable with the deal than were the rest of us. I sensed she had doubts from the very beginning, not that TV-am might not work, but whether or not she really wanted to be involved in the hurly-burly. Her on-screen relationship with David wasn't working, either. The promised 'sexual chemistry' was apparent only by its absence. In fact, Cinemascope would have been necessary to accommodate the gap between them.

The opening show featured an interview with Norman Tebbitt, the then Employment Secretary, the debut of *Through the Keyhole*, the weather presented by a bluff naval type, Commander Philpott, who would have been more at home on the poop deck of the *Cutty Sark*, and a visit from special guest, John Cleese, who turned up wearing pyjamas, which he thought perfect dress for a breakfast show. We just about got away with it.

The *Guardian* said our debut was 'brittle, sharp, gaudy and feeding off its own adrenalin' – not exactly a rave review but gentle compared with what came later. Pairings apart, our major problem was that we had recruited a lot of people on both the technical and editorial side who lacked the experience to bring a new company to the point where it could produce more than twenty hours of live television every week. We got by because there were stalwarts in every department – men and women who looked as if they lived with permanent jet lag – who kept us on air.

I cannot remember a single day at TV-am when there wasn't a crisis of one sort or another. The ratings showed we were attracting only 500,000 viewers each week-day morning, compared with the BBC's 1.8 million. Mary and I did better at the weekend, but the BBC didn't have a breakfast show on Saturday or Sunday. The media started the drum roll of doom, there was unrest among a tired and confused staff, advertising starting falling away.

Anna was unwell and had a week off. I was paired with Angela and the ratings showed an improvement. The management believed we should continue to work together. We were told the suggested change was necessary because advertisers had asked for my partnership with Angela to be extended. Peter Jay was opposed to the idea and Anna refused to budge. This gave Jonathan Aitken, who, along with cousin Tim, was the company's major shareholder, the chance to get rid of Peter Jay. A week after the change of pairing had been suggested, Peter Jay was sacked and Jonathan Aitken took over.

From that moment TV-am, as it had originally been conceived, started to fall apart. The advertisers took flight and our financial situation worsened. Anna and Angela told the media what they thought about the board's decision to get rid of Jay and were sacked. I threatened to resign and spent a day or so thinking things over while the media camped outside the house and patrolled the river in hired boats in case I decided to make a swim for it.

I was asked by Richard Marsh to attend a meeting at the office where he would attempt to explain the board's decision and inform me of important new developments that, he hoped, would make me reconsider resigning. There were pickets outside the building and an agitated and worried assembly inside – people uncertain about the future, which, to my consternation, they appeared to think hung on the outcome of the meeting.

What followed were possibly the most bizarre few hours of my entire life. Let me introduce you to the cast of characters. Jonathan Aitken was tall and languid with perfect manners and an elegant charm. This was Aitken the Golden Boy, a man of probity and substance, some time before he was unmasked as a liar and a scoundrel. Cousin Timothy had neither time nor inclination for the courtesies of life, nor was he diplomatic. 'What's up with you?' he asked Richard Marsh, who presented himself to the meeting in some discomfort in the area of his groin.

Marsh said he had just had some minor surgery, which was causing him a little pain. As a matter of fact, he said, he was suffering the after effects of a vasectomy. He looked towards me for some kind of encouragement, knowing that I had had a similar and well-publicised operation a few years earlier. I kept staring out of the window into the well of the office where it seemed the entire staff had congregated and were looking up to the room in which we were meeting, wondering what we were talking about.

Sir Richard was urged to get on with it by a generally unsympathetic Timothy Aitken and he proceeded to tell us, or rather me because the Aitkens already knew, that he had been informed by the IBA that, following the dismissal of Angela and

Anna, the departure of any other member of the original Famous Five would cause the IBA to rethink the franchise. He gave us this news in between moans of pain as he shifted his position in the telling. At one point he lay on the floor, stating it was the only position in which he could get relief for his discomfort.

The proposition therefore was quite clear-cut. If I resigned, there was a distinct possibility the franchise would be readvertised and TV-am disbanded. Is that what I wanted? It seemed to me I had to choose between the sacking of two colleagues or the collapse of the entire company and the possibility that five hundred people would be put out of work. If that was really the case, my decision was an easy one. I am not sure to this day if Richard Marsh and the Aitkens were bluffing.

Certainly, there were rumours that David Frost was next on the Aitkens' hit list and the fact he survived gives some credence to the IBA threat being real. I knew of Jonathan Aitken's antipathy towards David because I was invited to a meeting in which he gently raised the subject of how I might feel about David being moved aside. My reply was unequivocal.

While all this was going on, David Frost married Carina, the Duke of Norfolk's daughter, and I was his best man. Throughout the wedding feast I found the Duke looking at me in a slightly puzzled manner. Whenever we had met previously, he had always mistaken me for someone else. 'Let's do some dry stone walling,' he would say to me, or 'Let's go out and chop down a few trees,' or 'How are the horses?' During my speech I could sense him staring at me, wondering what on earth a son of the soil, an estate worker, was doing as David's best man.

David went to Venice on honeymoon and the next morning picked up the *Observer*, which carried the headline: 'Aitken to sack

Frost'. Anna and Angela were not pleased with events. Anna famously threw a glass of wine over Jonathan Aitken; both Anna and Angela accused me of weakness in not carrying out my threat to resign. When I accepted an offer to join the board, Anna saw this as the pay-off for what she regarded as my betrayal.

In fact, I joined the board out of curiosity and it is fair to say that what I saw hastened my own eventual departure from TV-am, and put me off big business forever.

Greg Dyke took over and, according to legend, saved the station with Roland Rat. David hung on but the rest of us gradually dispersed. Robert Kee, always an amused and civilised observer of the chaos of our lives, drifted away; there was no room for him in the new and thrusting company run by Dyke and later Bruce Gyngell.

When I had time to look back it was without sorrow or regret. It was a fascinating adventure in which those of us hitherto innocent of the ways of big business caught a glimpse of a treacherous and slimy world. There was anger and betrayal but also a lot of fun and fulfilment.

In the final analysis we achieved the impossible and turned a racing certainty into a seaside donkey. What we were handed when we won the franchise was the right to broadcast adverts between the hours of 6 a.m. and 9 a.m. every morning, seven days a week. In other words we were given the keys to a fortune. How could we fail?

But we did.

If I have a lasting memory of that episode in my life it is, at the darkest time, standing by the window of my office overlooking the canal below and glancing left to see David, in the adjoining office, gazing at the waterway.

He looked at me and smiled.

'Who goes first?' he said.

36

FROM ELTON JOHN TO SKINNER NORMANTON

I had been a castaway on *Desert Island Discs* in 1972 and had found it to be a profoundly depressing experience. I had expected more of an event. This, after all, was *the* accolade of broadcasting to be sought after and treasured. When the Labour politician Herbert Morrison died they found his list of music in his belongings. Morrison, a politician of substance in Attlee's immediate postwar government and a man of high achievement, nonetheless sought, and was denied, the privilege and honour of being a castaway on Mr Plomley's mythical island. Nor was he the only one who went to his grave unfulfilled through the lack of Plomley's beckoning finger. All of which explains my disappointment when I found the experience such a dispiriting one.

The problem was Plomley himself. He seemed bored with the show, not the slightest bit interested in the guest's story, more in favour of a long lunch at the Garrick with a bottle of wine before the interview took place in what seemed like a broom cupboard at Broadcasting House. What particularly disappointed me was that he couldn't be bothered to play the music in the show as we recorded it, preferring to edit it in later.

When Plomley died in 1985 the show had been running for forty-three years. It had become so associated with the man who devised and presented it that there were suggestions it should not be revived. David Hatch, the then Controller of Radio 4 and later Sir David, took a more pragmatic view. He believed it was a popular programme not because of who presented it but because it was such a titillating idea. He decided to continue with a new man in charge, and asked if I could take over.

I told him my reservations and he confirmed he wanted me to do it my way; to pick the guests I wanted, to play music into the show during the interview, to explore opinions as well as life stories.

David predicted there would be trouble ahead in the shape of Diana Wong, Plomley's widow, who now held the rights to the programme and was involved in the choice of presenter in that she was offered a list of names for approval. According to the *Evening Standard*, Diana Wong was in favour of John Mortimer getting the job, with the newscaster Richard Baker as her second choice. Her reaction to me was one of unequivocal rejection. She told the *Sunday Express*: 'I don't think he's civilised enough', an opinion that might have done serious psychological damage to a more sensitive soul. There was more. Commenting on my appearance on the programme thirteen years earlier, she said my choice of records was 'embarrassingly awful' and added: 'I don't think he's very sensitive', which was a bit rich coming from someone who had just given a severe kicking to someone she had never met.

I bit my tongue. I wasn't about to get involved in a slanging match with Plomley's widow, nor explain to the nation my opinion of the man I was replacing. I didn't have to. The media obliged. *The Times* talked of Plomley's 'complete inability to conduct an interview'. Curiously, it argued, this was what gave the programme its charm. Derek Drescher, my producer on *Desert Island Discs*, who had also been Plomley's producer, said, 'People used to say that Roy was good at drawing people out but he wasn't. If somebody wasn't talking he was lost.'

Alan Parker, the director of *Midnight Express* and *Birdy*, was my first guest and I offered him the chance to criticise the shortcomings of the British film industry, an invitation he was delighted to accept. The media cautiously accepted that, although my style was different, it wasn't likely to cause an outbreak of hostilities in the Balkans.

Bruce Oldfield, the dress designer, was my next guest, and I asked him if he thought designing frocks was a proper job for a man. It was a deliberately provocative question, designed to wrong foot Bruce and perhaps annoy him. It didn't upset Bruce half as much as it did some critics, including the BBC Review Board, which criticised me for being too obtrusive and 'not nearly interested enough in the music'.

This last observation was particularly witless, given I had introduced music back into the interview and had done so with a purpose. If Plomley had seen the programme as a chat with music, I very much saw it as a chance to explore exactly what music meant and what part it played in the castaway's experience, to analyse the soundtrack of their lives, if you like.

But if the Review Board criticism was barmy, what followed was even more stupid and incomprehensible. This time it was our old friends on the BBC Board of Management who, at their meeting in 1986, voiced concern that 'all the guests who had so far appeared on the programme under Michael Parkinson's chairmanship had indeed been born in Yorkshire'. This was offered to substantiate their opinion that the show was suffering a 'Yorkshire bias in the choice of castaways'. In fact, of the six guests up to that point, Alan Parker came from Islington, Nigel Kennedy was born in Brighton, Bruce Oldfield in London, Dennis Taylor in Northern Ireland and Roy Hattersley in Derbyshire. Only Maureen Lipman was guilty of having been born in Yorkshire, although that was the last thing on our minds when we booked them.

With this latest ludicrous episode added to what had gone on in my last days at the TV Centre, I could be forgiven for believing there was a plot to scupper my career at the BBC, or that the entire organisation was run by madmen. In fact, what was really happening was a rearguard action of the broadcasting establishment against what it perceived as the desecration of a hallowed institution. Fortunately, the public didn't see it that way. The ratings climbed. David Hatch – no lover of the establishment himself – was totally supportive. He told the critics as far as he was concerned there were not enough Yorkshire-born people on *Desert Island Discs* and he looked forward to hearing many more. Indeed, he said his ambition was eventually to make it compulsory that everyone working on Radio 4 was born in Yorkshire.

Mr Hatch himself was born in Yorkshire, and liked a laugh.

My stint lasted nearly one hundred shows and two years and I left of my own accord. To be frank, I never intended a long run. I knew there would be resistance to my appointment and planned to see that die down, make a point and then move on. I certainly didn't want to spend the rest of my life hosting a parlour game, which is what, in fact, it is.

I was having too much fun at the time hosting another parlour game, *Give Us A Clue*. Of all the many television shows I have done, aside from the talk show, this was among the most enjoyable.

Lionel Blair and Una Stubbs, later followed by Lisa Goddard, were not only a delight to work with but also the most entertaining and agreeable companions. I did a couple of turkeys as well. *Parky* was a feeble attempt at a mixture of satire and talk and I'm not sure, even now, what *All Star Secrets* and *The Help Squad* were about, although *Secrets* did involve one great comedy moment featuring Bernard Manning and a feisty member of the public.

After chatting to Bernard I invited questions from the audience whereupon one formidable-looking lady stood up and denounced Bernard in vigorous fashion. She told him he was not only a male chauvinist pig, but a bully, a racist and, generally speaking, a disgrace to civilisation and mankind. At the end of her tirade she stood her ground, looking challengingly at Manning, awaiting a response.

I feared the worst. Instead, Bernard looked at her admiringly and, taking in her ample figure, said, 'By gum, lass, but I'll bet you've crushed some grass in your time.'

Sir Paul Fox, my mentor at the BBC, now boss at Yorkshire Television, asked me to do a series of one-man shows for his company. When he was in charge at the BBC, Paul had been a particular fan of the longer interviews with such people as Muhammad Ali, Professor Jacob Bronowski and Fred Astaire. We obliged with Richard Harris, Anthony Hopkins, Walter Matthau and Jack Lemmon, Robbie Coltrane, Adam Faith, Tom Jones, Billy Connolly, Terence Stamp and many more, including Elton John.

The Elton John interview was something of an event because we had an exclusive with him at what might have been the lowest point in his life. He had recently undergone throat surgery, which made his future uncertain, he was living apart from his wife Renate – a wedding greeted with much mirthful cynicism by the media –

and was under constant siege from the tabloids. The *Sun* ran a sequence of stories accusing him of soliciting and drugging rent boys as well as having his dogs' barks silenced because they were disturbing his sleep. All lies.

I called him to see if he would come on the show and talk about his troubles. He agreed and then, just before the show, cried off, saying he was too ill. I called once more and he agreed to try again. This time he turned up, wearing a tracksuit and baseball cap and with a heavy, dark stubble, looking more like a down and out than a rock star.

I had known Elton for many years. We used to go to watch Watford together when he was chairman of the club. I would sit next to him while rival fans abused him about being 'queer' and 'taking it up the rear' and other such pleasantries, and I would marvel at his fortitude and good humour in the face of the most appalling provocation. But this was a different Elton, almost a defeated man. When he talked about his marriage to Renate he said they were having a trial separation. A year later they divorced.

Mary and I had been guests at the wedding in Australia in a pretty church on a hill overlooking Rushcutters' Bay. I think we might have been the only couple present who were not stoned. I remember that an insect, crawling up one of the stone pillars in the church, attracted an inordinate amount of attention from guests who gazed in awe at the creature's progress, no doubt seeing a golden snake gliding across a rainbow, or some similar hallucination. The fans held their boogie boxes blaring out Elton's greatest hits at the open windows as the organ played the wedding march. I commissioned a painting, by Australian naive artist Narelle Wildman, of the wedding party outside the church, and gave it to the couple as a wedding present. I wonder who has it now?

When I see Elton nowadays, happy in his relationship with David, secure in his position as one of the giants of rock'n'roll, I sometimes recall that hunched and pained figure I interviewed in Leeds and marvel at the strength and self-deprecating humour that saw him through the crisis to his present state of prosperity and content.

He sued the *Sun* and won. The paper published a full front page apology and reportedly paid Elton a record one-million-pound settlement. At the end of the show Elton suggested he should perform 'Don't let the sun go down on me'.

In the fifteen years between leaving TV-am and returning with the talk show to the BBC, I practised the Michael Caine theory of employment. This involves accepting anything legal that is offered in the certain knowledge that a lot of it will be forgettable, even risible, but also understanding that every time you go before a camera or a microphone you learn something about your craft.

I did a morning show for LBC Radio, a sports programme for Radio 5 Live, took over from Keith Waterhouse as a columnist on the *Daily Mirror*, returned to writing about sport as a columnist for the *Daily Telegraph*, worked with the enchanting Mariella Frostrup and Penny Smith on *Going For A Song*, commenced a twelve-year stint on *Parkinson's Sunday Supplement* on Radio 2 where, with producer Anthony Cherry, we created a weekly haven for fans of the Great American Songbook.

Tim Rice and I developed a publishing company called Pavilion and indulged our passion for books about cricket. We also published the work of a then fairly unknown artist called Jack Vettriano. Tim bought one or two of his paintings for a song. I passed on the chance. Nowadays it will cost you upwards of £50,000 for one of Jack's paintings.

It was in this busy period that I made my debut as an actor. I was sent the script of a television play called *Ghostwatch* by Stephen Volk. I was to play the part of the host of the eponymous television show about the supernatural, which, one awful night, was invaded by a malignant spirit. The play attracted an audience of more than eight million but sadly also made news headlines when a young man committed suicide after watching the programme. His family claimed he had been affected by what he had seen on television and the consequence was the play was never repeated until very recently when it appeared as a DVD.

Much to my amazement and delight I was nominated for a BAFTA. It wasn't exactly my acting debut. Previously I had appeared in *Brookside* and in *Madhouse*, a horror film starring Vincent Price, which involved him setting fire to himself in a TV studio as I interviewed him. Don't ask why because I never did work it out.

Vincent was a joy to work with, an urbane man with a deep knowledge of art and a great lover of racehorses. When he was making *Dr Phibes* at Bray Studios he would take his lunch alone, sitting by the River Thames wearing his hideous make-up. When passing pleasure boats full of eager tourists were informed by their guide that these were the studios where many horror movies were made, Vincent would appear on the bank and, taking a sandwich from his picnic box, he would shove it slowly into a hole at the side of his throat.

Richard Curtis gave me a part in *Love Actually*. I had to interview Bill Nighy, playing a mad rock'n'roller with shameless exhibitionist tendencies. These included exposing himself to me during the interview. The audience just saw his back and, of course, he didn't really show me his willy but there were those who believed he did. For some time I was approached at social gatherings by attractive young ladies who would ask me what the gorgeous Mr Nighy was like to work with and would then ask, 'But what is he really like?' in that nudge-nudge-wink-wink kind of way. After a while I stopped trying to explain to them that filming movies is make believe, and found a one-word answer that stopped any further pursuit of the truth. 'Frightening,' I would say.

My most difficult co-star was a koala bear. While in Australia I was asked by Quantas to make a commercial, which required me to sit next to a koala bear and attempt to involve it in polite conversation. We started work in a mock-up of a 747 at 8 a.m. and by midday I was starting to hate my furry friend. Koalas eat eucalyptus leaves, which contain a narcotic, and therefore spend most of their lives either asleep or stoned or both. Nor are they particularly cuddly. They have long and powerful claws with which they can shred the bark from trees and cause serious damage to human tissue, as I witnessed when one turned on a model at an earlier publicity event. In addition, my koala was also a bedwetter. Whenever we awoke him for a take he would have a pee and we would have to change the seat covers.

The entire business became a tedious farce, made worse by the attempts of the trainer to devise ways of getting the creature to cooperate. His best suggestion was that just before we went for a take he would prod the koala with a stick, hard enough to wake it up. I pointed out the flaw in the scheme. The first person it would see after being so rudely aroused from its slumbers would be me, and I had already seen what damage koalas could cause when angered.

Eventually, at about six at night, with the set stinking of pee and everyone frazzled, except the koala, we had what we wanted in the can. I was sitting there, thinking this was not what I had in mind when, all those years ago, I decided I wanted to be a film star, when a woman with a tape measure leaned across me and started measuring the koala's inside leg.

'What are you doing?' I asked.

'Measuring him for a pair of trousers, of course,' she said rattily, as if I was stupid.

'Why?' I asked.

'Because I'm making him a suit, that's why,' she said, as if talking to an imbecile.

'I don't want to appear thick,' I said, 'but I must ask. Why are you making him a suit?'

'Because tomorrow he's off on a personal tour to Japan,' she said. She then added, in a whisper, so the koala couldn't hear, 'He'll feel a bit strange. It's his first time abroad.'

What gave me the greatest satisfaction during this period was getting back to full time sports journalism. I wrote a column for the *Daily Telegraph* sports pages, then edited by David Welch. It was David who invented the idea of the sports supplement and, with the encouragement of the paper's editor, Max Hastings, assembled a group of journalists of matchless talent, humour and style. It was a good time to work for the *Telegraph* and my ten or more years there were the happiest and most fulfilling of all my years in writing about sport.

I revived the style I had developed at *The Sunday Times* twenty or more years before, recalling the heroes of my youth including Skinner Normanton, the hard man of Barnsley FC, whose deeds stirred admiration as far afield as Malaysia, where I was asked to attend the annual dinner of the Kuala Lumpur Skinner Normanton Appreciation Society. I was writing about a lost and nostalgic world and comparing it with the super smooth multi-million pound industry soccer was becoming, and it struck a chord.

Nothing summed up better what I was trying to achieve, nor illustrated more clearly the change in the game since Skinner's time, than the obituary I wrote when he died in 1995. I reprint it because it tells you much about the way a game and society has changed and explains a lot about heroes and why they matter.

Skinner Normanton died peacefully aged 68. Between 1947 and 1953 he played 134 times for Barnsley and ended his career with a brief spell at Halifax. He retired to his garden where he grew sunflowers and turned out occasionally for the local team when they were a man short.

Sydney Albert Normanton was a local legend when he played at Barnsley. He was the hard man of the side, the minder for ball-playing colleagues of delicate disposition. There wasn't much of him but every ounce counted. He was destructive in the tackle, as unrelenting as a heat-seeking missile in pursuit of the enemy.

If I close my eyes I see two images. The first is a still photograph with Skinner posed in the manner of the day, arms folded and one foot on a leather football. His hair was short and wavy, parted near the middle and rigid with Brylcreem and his legs were as sturdy as pit props with bulging shinpads and bulbous toecaps that glowed with dubbin and menace.

My second memory is more like a black and while film of the time with Skinner taking a penalty in a Cup tie and running from the halfway line before toe-ending the sodden football which became a blur as it passed the motionless goalkeeper, crashed into the underside of the crossbar and rebounded on to the back of the goalkeeper's head and into the net.

The goalkeeper was poleaxed and took several minutes to recover and it wasn't until much later that the iron crossbar stopped quivering from the impact of the shot. For a while it hummed like a male voice choir.

He was a local celebrity. Mothers would tell their children to stop mucking about or they would send for Skinner. He gained a wider audience many years after he retired when I first wrote an article about him.

I don't know what it was about the article that captured the imagination. I think it might have been the name. If you wanted to invent a local football hero of the time, someone who worked in the pits during the week and spent Saturday afternoons kicking lumps off the opposition, you'd invent a man called something like Skinner Normanton.

Whatever the reason, his fame extended far beyond his beloved Oakwell. I have been asked about him during all my travels throughout the world. There was something in the name that was irresistible to Brits living abroad, particularly when they were feeling homesick for Saturday afternoons and kick-off time.

Many people believed him to be a mythical character like the Great Wilson of the *Wizard*. I remember Yorkshire Television producing him as a surprise guest on a programme I was doing in Leeds. They brought him into the studio and announced him in triumphant fashion as if they had found Lord Lucan or were about to produce the Loch Ness monster on the end of a lead.

He was smaller than I remembered and was wearing a blue suit with a nipped-in waist. The hair was as immaculate as ever and he looked like he was going to church. I had never seen him in his Sunday best. When he spoke his voice was soft, the manner modest, even shy.

It was difficult to convince people that this gentle and diffident man had at one time put the fear of God up any member of the human race who didn't wear a Barnsley shirt. He played at a time when the game drank deep from its tap roots and although there were many more skilful and talented than he there was no one who better represented what you were up against if you took on a collier from Barnsley.

I was thinking that they ought to name the new stand at Barnsley after him. The Skinner Normanton stand would be a constant reminder that no matter how much we merchandise the modern game we must always remember what it is we are really selling. Nowadays they talk of image. There was a time, when Skinner was a lad, when it had a soul.

Reading it again is to be warmed by memories of a happy childhood in a land a long, long way from the one I now live in. I was happiest when I was writing for a living because I could push the rest aside and dwell in a world of my own recall.

37

GARDEN SHED
COMEBACK

The way back to the BBC and a revival of the talk show began in my garden shed. In 1995 a young BBC producer, Tony Moss, recalled watching the Muhammad Ali interviews as a child and wondered if they were as good as he remembered them and, if they were, would they be worth a second showing and would I be willing to introduce them. We couldn't afford to film in a studio so we set up in my garden shed, blacking out all the windows, creating a dark and dramatic setting for my recollections of interviewing the great man. The public and the critics liked what they saw and the BBC ordered more.

We repackaged the interviews with Peter Cook, Richard Burton, Orson Welles, David Niven, Tommy Cooper and Frankie Howerd into a five-show series. Jack Tinker, in the *Daily Mail*, wrote: 'The entire series . . . was in itself a revelation of just how far interviewing techniques have fallen since he all but disappeared from our screens in any creative capacity. He was undoubtedly the master of the chat trade.' Giles Smith, wrote in the *Independent*: 'The compelling repeats . . . lift out of the screen like treasures from a Golden Age, before television chat shows turned into *Hello!* with some of the longer words left out.'

There was another series and rumours of my return with a talk show, although no one made an official offer.

In the meantime, I was having a good time at Radio 2 where, under the amusing and benign leadership of Jim Moir, the station was transforming itself from a fossil into the most popular of them all. Moreover the column in the *Daily Telegraph* was winning awards. So it was in a contented frame of mind that I passed my sixtieth birthday and looked ahead to a tranquil future watching cricket and having the odd cocktail, ideally with Oscar Peterson providing the soundtrack to my gentle drift into senility.

One programme changed all that. Because of the success of the repeats, and in order to see me in a setting other than a garden shed, BBC producer Bea Ballard asked me to host an evening celebrating sixty years of BBC television.

I later learned I was not first choice. There was a thought Noel Edmonds might be the man and some disquiet that someone last seen on afternoon television on *Going For A Song* was suitable for a show of this magnitude. But Ms Ballard is a very determined lady and she had her way. I tried to sound confident about the job I had to do but its significance made me slightly nervous. For one thing the studio audience would be entirely composed of BBC executives and stars, past and present, and if that wasn't daunting enough, I realised, as did Bea, that it was not so much a job more an audition, the chance to prove that I was due a return to the BBC mainstream.

We worked hard at it, left nothing to chance and I got through it without falling down. At the party afterwards people kept sidling up making agreeable cooing sounds. Bea was approached by executives who thought I should be doing something with the BBC, but what? Bea was unequivocal. 'Bring back the talk show,' she said. And, after a while, they did.

We started with Paul Merton, Barry Manilow and Sir Anthony Hopkins, who spent most of his time imitating his great hero, Tommy Cooper. We booked imaginative pairings, as we had done in the seventies – Billy Connolly and David Attenborough (a triumph); John Prescott and Phil Collins (they both played drums). We went for the exclusive one-man show – George Michael talking about his escapade with a policeman in a gents' toilet in the USA.

George said he would do the interview if we could meet beforehand and have a chat over a quiet dinner. We went to the Ivy, which was a bit like having a secret meeting in the middle of Wembley Stadium during a Cup final.

When we met he said, 'I have to tell you I have always wanted to appear on your show. Just think, I had to flash a policeman to get on.'

I told him, 'Say that as soon as you come on set and we're off and away.'

And he did, and we were.

The ratings were wonderful, the critics kind. We won the first of four consecutive National Television Awards, followed by the Comic Heritage Gold Award, the Broadcasting Press Guild Award, a Variety Club Award, the gold award from the music industry and a BAFTA. About the only award we missed out on was one from Crufts. It was a rich and heady time, particularly as, during the seventies, doing a series of shows now described by the critics as 'classics', we won not a sausage.

It was especially pleasing to have a second chance at interviewing some of the stars we had missed out on first time around, such as Woody Allen. He had been top of my list since the time in the sixties when he was every talk-show host's favourite guest and a regular on *The Eamonn Andrews Show*. It was a very different Allen now. This was Allen the film-maker whose catalogue of movies puts him in very select company.

It was also a controversial Allen, no longer the cuddly, friendly, funny guy but the man who had a much-criticised relationship with his stepdaughter Soon-Yi. We were told this was an area he would not want to discuss. I said that I wasn't the slightest bit interested in people's private lives, but Mr Allen's career had been seriously affected by his affair with Soon-Yi, because Middle America disapproved and stopped going to his movies, and that justified a line of questioning. The interview was going well until I raised the subject. He was displeased but he didn't flounce out. I tried to justify the enquiry and he did his best to get rid of it as soon as possible. I think there might have been a discussion after the interview with his publicist, but the show went out as we planned.

We always refused to accept any pre-conditions on an interview. That is why I never interviewed Barbra Streisand and why it took many years before I finally interviewed Madonna.

I had moved to ITV before we managed to persuade her to do a one-woman show without any pre-conditions. She turned out to be so bright, frank and funny it made you wonder what the previous debate had been about. Hers is an extraordinary story of determination and hard work and the perfect antidote to the celebrity pap fed today's wannabes. Anyone wanting to succeed in the music business, or indeed any other business, should watch the interview and learn what it really takes to get to the top.

One of the fascinations of working with divas is in finding out the duties of the entourage. What, exactly, do all those people do? Observing Madonna, in a recording break, surrounded by her worker bees, I was fascinated to see that one assistant, armed only with a cotton bud on the end of a stick, was trained in a manoeuvre, which, as far as I could make out, was designed to make certain Madonna's nose was free from bogies.

Clint Eastwood was another star I had been trying to interview ever since the show began. He came over to publicise *Mystic River* and the deal was he would do the show if I interviewed him at the National Film Theatre. I had particularly wanted to meet Eastwood, and not simply because he has a wonderful screen presence and is a marvellous director, but also because of his love and deep knowledge of jazz. He directed Forest Whitaker in *Bird*, the biopic of Charlie Parker, uses jazz often on the soundtracks of his films and has a son, Kyle, who is a jazz musician.

After we finished the interview, I collected Mary and took her to meet Eastwood, a most agreeable and pleasant man. We were chatting away, Mary transfixed by his lanky, easy charm, when he said to me, 'I'm going out to have dinner then on to a jazz club to see my son Kyle play. Would you and Mary like to join me?'

And I said, 'Thank you but I'm feeling knackered and I think I'm going to have an early night.'

As we left his company Mary said, 'I can't believe you said that.' Nor could I. She moans about it to the present day.

I interviewed Oprah Winfrey, the most self-possessed woman I have ever met, who seemed to glow with success. George Clooney appeared to me to have all the charisma and old-fashioned charm of James Stewart and Henry Fonda. So did Tom Hanks, Kevin Costner and Kevin Spacey, but Clooney, in particular, created the kind of interest among the female staff I had only witnessed once before, when Robert Redford appeared on the show in the seventies.

But the biggest star of all, the one who created most interest among both sexes and gave us the highest rating we ever achieved on the comeback series, was David Beckham. He appeared with Victoria, along with George Best and Elton John, and the show was watched by more than nine million viewers. It was the top entertainment show on British television that week and made headlines that, in a sense, lasted forever. It was Victoria's admission that she called her husband 'Goldenballs' that caused the media frenzy. The moment she said it I looked at David and he gave me a wry smile as if to say: 'That's me labelled for the next twenty years or more.'

Another time he was on the show we had adjoining dressing rooms. I answered a knock on my door and discovered David standing there with just a towel round his middle.

He said his shower wasn't working so could he use mine? After the shower he stepped out of my room and into the path of a BBC secretary who was walking down the corridor carrying an armload of papers. When she looked up and found herself confronted by a half-naked David Beckham, she gave a little cry and an involuntary jerk of her arms, which sent her papers spilling on to the floor.

David and I helped her pick them up, and when she eventually continued her journey and passed me, flustered and blushing, she said, with a tut, 'And me, a married woman.'

The appearance of George Best alongside David was particularly emotive. In the world of football, George was David's godfather – George, the first rock'n'roll footballer, the original superstar, David then at the very apex of his fame and fortune. George, a recovering alcoholic, David so fit he gleamed with health. Most poignantly of all, George, for all his celebrity, earned, at most, two hundred quid a week from soccer and David was worth millions.

I first met George when he was on his way to superstardom and at the epicentre of what constituted Manchester's party scene in the sixties. He wasn't handsome; he was beautiful – blue eyed, black haired and slim as a railing. He was designed for the sixties. He could have made a living on looks alone but what set him apart and made him special were his gifts as a footballer. He was, and is, the best all-round player I ever saw. He had more ways of beating an opponent than could be imagined. He had speed and agility, was two-footed, good in the air and was the most certain finisher of them all. Those were his virtues as an attacker. As a defender and creator, he was a fearless tackler and a precise and imaginative distributor of the ball, either long or short.

Sir Matt Busby said he was probably the best player he had in any of the outfield positions and maybe a better keeper than Harry Gregg, though he dare not try him out in goal for fear of Gregg's renowned and awesome temper. Sir Matt was, of course, exaggerating but only to make a point that among all the players he had nurtured and watched, George Best was the most complete of the lot.

So where did it all go wrong? From the start really. The problem of being the first rock'n'roll footballer was that no one knew what was required to protect the athlete from the rock'n'roll life. By the time people came to understand that George needed shielding it was too late.

Whenever he felt like getting away from his life in a goldfish bowl in Manchester he would come and stay with us. He would always bring a mixed bag of balls for my three sons to play with and needed no persuading to arrange a game of soccer with them on the lawn by the river. One day, Michael, my youngest son, was asked at infants' school what he did over the weekend. He replied, quite truthfully, that he played football with George Best. He was made to stand in a corner for telling fibs.

Sometimes George would bring a girlfriend with him. He would always ring and ask if he could come down for a few days. When

I put the phone down I would count to ten and it would ring again.

'Mike, it's George again. I forgot to mention I'd like to bring a girl with me. Is that OK?' he would say.

I never worked out why he didn't tell me in the first place. On one occasion I thought I would tease him.

'And what's this one like George?' I said, after he had made his request.

'Oh you'll like her, Mike. Tall, slim, blonde hair and great knockers,' he said.

'George,' I said. 'You have just described every girl you ever went out with.'

One night he went clubbing and the next morning Mary and I were in the kitchen when a pretty girl, dressed as if she was on her way to Ascot, suddenly appeared. She said she had met George at Tramps and hoped we didn't mind that he brought her home. Then, addressing Mary who was washing up, she said, 'Would you like me to help with the hoovering?'

When Nick, my son, opened his gastropub, the Royal Oak in Paley Street, George came down and we decorated a corner with a photograph of George and David Beckham taken at the *Parkinson Show*. Many of Nick's customers have a soft spot for Manchester United and every year the old boys, mainly the team George played in, would come down and have a charity dinner. One day a sponsor said he would give an extra ten thousand quid to charity if I could persuade George to turn up. I called him and, typically, he said yes. In all the years I knew him he never refused a charity request, nor did he ever let me down.

He wasn't drinking at the time because he had lately been confined to hospital with his liver problems. He had never been to a reunion and he had a wonderful time. All his friends were delighted to see him and all were unequivocal in their opinion he was the greatest of them all. The next day he called to say he'd had the best evening for years. I said he should try being sober more often. He told me to fuck off, but pleasantly. I said to Mary that maybe George was going to stop drinking, that maybe he would recover and save himself.

A week or so later he was taken to hospital and shortly thereafter died.

The picture of George and David still hangs in the Royal Oak and he is never far away from my thoughts.

I asked him once on the programme, given the chance to live his life again, what he would change.

'Not a thing. I keep reading people who describe my life as a tragedy and I don't see it like that at all. I have no regrets,' he said.

But he left us too soon and I still miss him.

While defending him as a soak was sometimes difficult, admiring him as a great athlete and loving him as a friend never was. Whenever I interviewed George I would wonder if it might be for the last time.

I had the same feeling when I interviewed Luciano Pavarotti. I had interviewed him a couple of times in the seventies when he was young and charming and possessed a voice of incomparable power and beauty. To sit near him as he sang was one of my most privileged moments. That was then. The Pavarotti who was assisted into the studio in 2003 was a sad parody of a great singer. He had come to plug his new album but wasn't really in a fit state for public appearances. He had been ill, there was talk of financial problems, and he looked very much like a man performing out of desperation rather than joy.

His entourage shunted him into position on the set. He was hugely overweight, heavily made up and wearing a hat he refused to remove. It was suggested I take the interview to him rather than ask him to walk on to the set. But the most disappointing decision of all was that he would mime and not sing live. When I talked to him he was sweating heavily and the dye from his hair was threatening to streak his brow. It was like watching a great monument disintegrate before your eyes.

On the other hand, there is nothing more gratifying than the great artist who adapts his talent to accommodate the advancing years and in old age remains as popular and revered as when he was a young shaver. Tony Bennett is a favourite singer of mine and a man who, although now in his ninth decade, remains the benchmark for any aspiring interpreter of the Great American Songbook. I have been friendly with Tony Bennett for more than thirty years. We met first at Doug Hayward's where he was a customer, and then consolidated our friendship through the ubiquitous Sammy Cahn.

I was staying with the Cahns in Beverly Hills at the time of the Oscars. In fact, I was doing a profile for *The Sunday Times Magazine* on Faye Dunaway, who had won an Oscar for her performance in *Network*. I met her in one of the bungalows at the Beverly Hills Hotel, along with photographer Terry O'Neill. Not only did Terry photograph Ms Dunaway, he ended up marrying her. We were not invited to the Oscars ceremony, so Sammy Cahn asked a group of his friends to his house for an Oscar television viewing party.

Sammy Cahn's friends included Billy Wilder, Angie Dickinson, Jack Lemmon, Jack Jones, Tony Bennett, Sidney Poitier, in fact, most of the Hollywood stars who were not, for one reason or another, at the Oscars. I asked Billy Wilder why he wasn't there.

'Because I wasn't nominated,' he said.

'How many times have you been?' I asked.

'Six times,' he said, with a smile. Mr Wilder won six Oscars.

Later when the name of a famous song writer came up and Sammy said he was anti-Semitic, Billy Wilder said the definition of an anti-Semitic was someone who disliked Jews just a little more than is necessary.

The highlight of the evening came when Jack Lemmon sat at the piano and played some Gershwin tunes for Tony Bennett to sing. If Tony Bennett was simply an outstanding singer it would be enough, but he is also a generous and modest man with firm convictions and principles, particularly about race relations. He told me, during the BBC interview, of being demoted during the war because he had been seen having a drink with another soldier, who was black. In those hideous days of segregation this was an offence that resulted in him being reduced in rank and given the job of digging graves for dead soldiers.

Some time after the interview, on Tony's eightieth birthday, I went with Mary to his birthday party at the American Museum of Natural History in New York. I sat next to Harry Belafonte who told me that during the anti-segregation marches into the Deep South in the fifties there was no more committed supporter than Tony.

'He marched with us and, you know, the risk was great. I mean, forget what it could do to your career. Just being a white man marching with all those black people could get you killed. Tony never wavered,' he said.

Shortly after the birthday bash I was asked to present Tony with a Lifetime Achievement Award at Ronnie Scott's Club. The presentation took place after Bennett had treated the audience to a definitive reading of the Great American Songbook. It was one of those special moments when you know you are witnessing a performance that could not be equalled by any other human being. Everything was flawless, his musicality, his phrasing, the way he told the story in the lyrics. It was a masterclass. I said as much when I gave him his award.

I was having a drink at the bar later when I was approached by two young men who said they were actors and singers learning their trade and could they ask me a question. 'Of course,' I replied. One of them said, 'How long will it take me to sing like Tony Bennett?'

I looked at his guileless face and the eager anticipation in his eyes and said, 'Why don't you ask him yourself?'

I took them to Tony's dressing room where he was as accommodating and friendly as I knew he would be. I remember thinking, and not for the first time, of the privileges the job afforded me and how lucky I was to meet my heroes.

On the other hand, there was still one great man left on my wish list whom I had not encountered.

38

MANDELA'S COUNTRY

I had tried for many years to meet Nelson Mandela. As well as all the obvious reasons, there was a personal significance in my ambition. In the sixties I was made aware that I would not be welcome in South Africa because of what I had written and broadcast during the debate about whether or not we should play sport against the apartheid nation.

When I finally got the chance to meet him it was through Sport Relief, who asked me to interview Mr Mandela as part of a film about South African children orphaned by Aids. In 2002 I travelled to South Africa with Peter Salmon and Kevin Cahill, the tireless Chief Executive of Comic Relief, and a film crew. This is my diary of what happened:

Day 1:

The approach to Cape Town takes in both the beauty of Table Mountain and the unending miles of tin-shack townships. It is an ideal introduction to the extremes of South Africa. The Bay Hotel is on the Atlantic seaboard, overlooking a tempting beach. Soon, we are in another land of tin lean-tos and shebeens where children play on the earth floors and their elders stand outside, smoking a mixture of marijuana and mandrax – a sedative. It is their escape from reality.

We have been brought here by two fifteen-year-olds to see the kind of environment that is creating South Africa's appalling crime problem. There are fifty-five murders every day in this country and a rape every thirty seconds; in the Cape Flats, where we are filming, thirty thousand young men are involved in crime. Without the prospect of work, and often missing a male role model in their lives, the gangs are their families. Prison is their school, ideal preparation for a future career.

Initiation ceremonies involve murder and rape. The gang members we talked to thought nothing of describing how they shot someone, yet they were uneasy when I mentioned rape. I pointed out that, in the argot of gangster culture, women are referred to as 'bitches and whores' and asked if that is what they thought of their mothers and sisters. They seemed shocked at the thought.

To film in one block of flats, we needed permission from the local gangster chief. He was a tense twenty-eight-year-old, who had spent fourteen years in jail. He showed us his gun wrapped in a duster. He had a crown tattooed on his forehead between his eyes and four of his front teeth were missing. I was told he had had them pulled to be replaced with gold teeth. We were informed on the quiet that the real reason was it made him a better kisser.

The regrettable truth was that he was beyond saving, but the boys who took us to him are not. They are part of what is known as a diversion programme, using mentors – often former gangsters – for lessons in survival skills, a period spent in the wilderness, a vigorous schedule of sport and six months' community service to demonstrate that there is another way. Any young person seeing the programme through has his criminal record wiped clean.

I asked one of the boys, who had completed the course, what his ambitions were: 'To marry, have children and mow the lawn,' he said. A mundane ambition until you realise this was someone who, only a year or so before, had taken an axe to school to settle an argument.

Day 2:

That ever-present contrast between those who live in the land of luxury and those who live on the very brink of existence is nowhere more stark than in Johannesburg. The Saxon Hotel is where Nelson Mandela edited his memoirs upon release from Robben Island. By any standards, it is a sumptuous and luxurious place. Twenty minutes away, in our crew bus, accompanied by an armed guard, we drive alongside the Alexandria township, where more than three million people live in a hideous shanty town of bric-a-brac and tin. It looks like a gigantic scrap-metal dump.

We are stopped by a roadblock and politely but methodically searched by the police. Our guard's gun is taken away and then returned because his permit is in order. He is a big man, wearing a Newcastle United beanie. He asks me if I know Bobby Robson. I say I do and that he is one of the good guys. He asks if Newcastle United might adopt his club in the South African town of Newcastle. I say Bobby Robson is a nice man, but not that nice.

All this as we drive into the shanty town of Zama Zama.

We are here to film a team of women looking after victims of Aids, not just the sick but also the children orphaned by the ghastly pandemic. Nearly five million South Africans are infected with HIV/Aids. That is ten per cent of the population. Every day, 1,500 more people are infected. In the hut where the women meet, an undertaker's list of coffin prices is pinned to the wall. Grace Sibeka heads the team. She was a cost clerk before she was made redundant at the age of forty. Since then, she has dedicated herself to working in her community. She takes us to the tiny rented room in a dilapidated garage that is used as a nursery for children aged between two and six who have been orphaned by Aids. The disease has orphaned eight hundred thousand children in South Africa; Grace has fifty of them. More than two-thirds of them are HIV positive.

It is impossible to be the dispassionate assessor, the balanced journalist in such a situation. The children sing and dance for us, grab our legs, hold our hands, show off, tumble and chatter – like children do. They don't know the trouble they are in. Not yet. We know, but feel so helpless. I am so angry that I buy the premises. Now, they don't have to worry about the rent and we can start building a proper school.

Day 3:

Today, Grace takes us to meet Given. He is sixteen years old and still at school. His mother died of Aids two years ago. She was a single parent. Given is now mother, father, protector and provider to two younger brothers, aged thirteen and ten. The boys sleep in one narrow bed in what is no more than a corrugated shed with a primitive paraffin cooker, a small stove and a picture of the Virgin Mary on the wall. They have no running water and no electricity. There is no money for food or clothes. They exist because of Grace and her organisation.

Winter is coming and cold winds swirl through the camp. The brothers scavenge for newspapers. Paper is their only source of fuel. Given is an intelligent boy who wants to continue his education. It is his only hope, his only means of escape. I ask him what he wants to be. He says, 'A doctor.' I look at Grace as she translates his answer and she reads my mind. Later, she tells me, 'You should not be surprised. We must never stop hoping.'

That evening, with the sun going down, we film Given and the local football team in action. Our bodyguard, the Newcastle United fan, is on the touchline, no doubt scouting for talent. The teams play in a haze of dust that, added to the drifting smoke from the evening fires, filters the view across the township to the setting sun. Our bodyguard says, 'There is an African saying: "At this time of day, everything is beautiful."'

Remembering Alan Whicker's advice about listening to phone-ins for a crash course on a new country, I switched on talk radio. They were interviewing young South Africans living in the townships. One was asked to describe himself: 'Broke, black and living in a shack,' he said.

Day 4:

We film outside the hut where the women have their headquarters. It has been a long time since I walked and talked to a film camera. Long enough to forget how difficult it is. I used to do it for a living. Now, trying in vain to make it seem natural, I am reminded of why I gave it up.

We send the bodyguard off for food. He comes back with

chicken and chips, which we eat in the women's hut. I am not hungry and push my food away, half-eaten. I suddenly realise what I have done and look guiltily at Grace. She picks it up and takes it into the back room, where children have gathered, certain of rich pickings. They are as aware of our wasteful ways as we are insensitive to their abject poverty.

We save the most harrowing filming to the last.

Maria, a twenty-six-year-old mother of two small children, is dying of Aids. We have met one of her children, the four-year-old, at the school run by Grace. We film the child being picked up from school by Lorraine, another of the helpers. She has been looking after Maria for ten months. Before that, she cared for Maria's mother, who is dying in a hospice. Like all the women involved in the scheme, Lorraine deals with death and grief on a daily basis. It takes an awful toll. You can see it on her face.

Maria lies huddled under a blanket, curled into the foetal position, head against the concrete wall. Lorraine introduces me; Grace sits in a corner of the room behind the camera.

How do you interview a woman who has a few weeks to live? I ask her about the drugs I see on the bedside table. Lorraine says Maria has pulmonary TB and the drugs help – but she doesn't take them because she has to take them with food and she gives the food to her children. Maria looks at me with black, deep eyes, waiting for the next question. I don't have one. I can't imagine any follow-up to her answer.

Grace says from behind the camera, 'Ask her what her children will do when she dies.' I do as I'm told. Maria shakes her head in mute despair. I find myself apologising. I can't handle it.

Outside, Grace says, 'You were too emotional in there.'

'And you weren't?'

'Not so I couldn't be of help.'

Then I see clearly her sense of purpose, the strength and detachment required to be compassionate without ever being overcome with pity.

Day 5:

Nelson Mandela is taller than I expected, straight, pencil slim, elegant. He apologises that his dodgy knee won't allow him to walk down steps for a photographer. It is not yet 9 a.m. and already he has had two meetings. I ask one of his three PAs when his day finishes. 'When he has worn us out,' she says. He is eighty-four, but you don't have to make allowances. He doesn't.

Mr Mandela knows the effect he has on people, but seems careful not to abuse that power. He is effortlessly good-natured, even when his office is invaded by a film crew. The cameraman is on his hands and knees looking for a socket in what he takes to be an empty office when, from behind, comes the unmistakable voice of Nelson Mandela. 'Is it not customary to say good morning to an old man?' he asks. Noticing that Anna Gravelle, our director, is the only woman in our team, he tells her, 'Remember, you must not let the men dominate you in your profession.'

He has beautiful manners, even when establishing the rules for our interview. 'Mr Parkinson, I have to tell you before we begin that I am deaf,' he says.

'I hope, sir, you will be able to hear my questions,' I reply.

He looks at me directly and smiles. 'I will hear the ones I want to answer.'

Day 6:

After we have filmed the interview with Nelson Mandela, it is time for summing up. If you woke up in the morning and pondered the crisis of South Africa, you would not bother getting out of bed. The problems of unemployment, crime and Aids seem insoluble.

Maybe the answer lies with the kind of initiative Sport Relief is getting involved in. Maybe the tiny ripple created by Grace Sibeka and her helpers spreads outwards and has significance far beyond where they work in Zama Zama. Certainly, the example set by those remarkable and selfless women is something we can all learn from.

Before we depart, Grace gives me a letter to give to Mr Mandela, asking him to visit Zama Zama. 'If he came, it would be glorious,' she says.

'He's a busy man,' I say, thinking he must have hundreds of similar requests every day.

She senses my caution. 'Do you know what Zama Zama means?' Grace asks. I shake my head. 'Keep trying,' she says.

39

TIME-SLOT WARS

I imagined finishing my career at the BBC, of being the only man in the history of the organisation to qualify for two brass buckets from a grateful Light Entertainment Department. (This was the Beeb's version of the carriage clock and presented, I was assured, to only a few, though no one knew why.) Then, in 2003, I read an article suggesting the BBC was moving to regain *Match of the Day* from ITV. The commercial network had pinched the programme, and Des Lynam, from the BBC with great fanfare. It hadn't worked for various reasons, one of which was outlined by Des Lynam, who said: 'There's nothing wrong with the show that moving *Parkinson* to a different time-slot wouldn't put right.'

We were very strong in the ratings against it. Nonetheless, the BBC wanted to re-establish a relationship with football and saw *Match of the Day* as an important statement of intent.

I asked the question what would happen to *Parkinson* if *Match of the Day* returned? They said what was I worrying about? Not much, really, I said, except it seemed to me that if they had one show that went out after 10 p.m. on a Saturday night – which was the best time for it, as had been proved over many years – and they bought another show that could only go out after 10 p.m. on a Saturday night called *Match of the Day*, there might be a problem.

Oh, we'll deal with that, old chap, don't worry, they said. But I did worry and as the deal went through and the start of the new football season approached, I began to press for answers.

Looking back, I think that if, during that time, someone had sat me down and talked through the situation and invited thoughts on a solution, things might have turned out differently. As it was, I was presented with a fait accompli and told they were thinking about alternative slots for *Parkinson*. There weren't any. At least, none that made any sense. Friday night was out because Jonathan Ross had that spot. How about moving it to Wednesday against *Coronation Street*, they said? How about I sign my own death warrant, I said?

The fannying and dithering went on to the point where one top executive – I will spare his blushes by not naming him – actually ran away from me in the car park at the BBC and fled to his office, rather than have me ask him if he'd done anything about my predicament, as he had promised to do. Lorraine Heggessey, Controller One, tried hard but there was no solution. She bravely suggested Saturday night at 9 p.m., the best offer so far, except I have never seen a talk show as a peak-time event. It has, like all shows, a natural habitat and that is late evening.

As events teetered and swirled, I began to suspect there was a gathering opinion within the BBC that maybe the best way out was for me to retire. At the time I was sixty-nine and not contemplating putting my feet up, particularly at the behest of an organisation that thought it made sense to replace a successful programme with one it had regularly trounced in the ratings. It wasn't me who needed a rest. It also occurred to me that it had not occurred to them that I might take the show elsewhere and, as I was gently fuming, my agent John Webber called and said ITV was interested in talking.

341

I met Nigel Pickard, the Programme Controller of ITV, and he said if I wanted to move the show to ITV he would be delighted to accommodate it. I called Sir Paul Fox, my old boss at the BBC, and asked his advice. 'Go to ITV. Go back to where you started,' he said. So I did. John negotiated an excellent deal. I asked if I could choose my producers, pick the research team and, most importantly, choose the guests and have control over editorial content, all of which meant producing the show as we had done for many years. Nigel agreed.

I was sorry to leave the BBC but I didn't see how I could stay. As I said at the time, they flogged my playing field and I had no alternative but to find a new one. I asked my son Michael, who was, by now, already producing television shows, Steve Lappin, whose work at the BBC I greatly admired, and Chris Greenwood to form the nucleus of the production team. We decided that, instead of opting for an independent production, we would hand the show to Granada, which gave me a warm feeling of returning to the womb, except I didn't realise how much the company had changed.

Simon Shaps, who was in charge of production at Granada, had not been privy to the deal done between John and Nigel Pickard, nor did he want the show, as I was to discover when, shortly after arriving at our new home, I was invited to meet him and his off-sider, Jim Allen. We went to the Ivy for lunch, which I imagined was to be a cosy getting-to-know-you occasion. I soon became aware Simon Shaps wasn't happy with the deal, particularly the question of editorial control. I said it sounded worse than it was but all it guaranteed was our freedom to produce the show as we had done for twenty years or more. This seemed to discomfort Mr Shaps who, at one point, produced a copy of the contract, which I feared he might start quoting at me.

I was not at all prepared for this. I had anticipated a pleasant lunch, yet seemed about to have an argument with my new boss. I decided to stop the nonsense immediately. I told Mr Shaps that if he didn't put the contract away, I would roll it up and shove it where the sun don't shine. I went back to the office and told the team that if ever Mr Shaps came to ultimate power in the network we could start packing our bags.

It was not an auspicious start. The media was generally downbeat. Overnight I had gone from the Man Who Had Made a Triumphant Return And Shown Them How To Do a Talk Show to a Man Well Past His Sell By Date Who Should Give It All Up. One paper alleged I had 'defected' from the BBC and printed a list of other well-known defectors, which put me alongside the spies Burgess and Philby, Robbie Williams, who left Take That, and Judas Iscariot.

There were also suggestions we would not be able to attract the big names. We answered that with our first show, which starred Tom Cruise, Billy Connolly and Kelly Holmes, who had just won Olympic gold. The commercial breaks meant we had to look more closely at how we edited the show, which allowed for forty-seven minutes of talk and not sixty, as it had been at the BBC. The easy solution was to reduce the guests from three to two, but we decided instead to cut the length of interviews and edit with a keener eye.

Michael began redesigning the set and the configuration of the studio. I sincerely believe that what we ended up with was a product that, at its best, was as good as, if not better than, it had been at any time during its entire history. Charles Allen, then ITV's Chief Executive, transformed a grotty reception room into a stylish hospitality area, which he used to entertain bankers and investors after the show. Nigel Pickard could not have been more encouraging. The show was working well. We were more than competing with

Match of the Day, we had a talented young production team, and everyone – well nearly everyone – was making agreeable noises, but the overwhelming problem was that ITV was struggling.

A year after we joined ITV, Nigel Pickard was clinging on to his job. The man who brought Simon Cowell to ITV was now an increasingly beleaguered figure. Shows such as *Celebrity Love Island* and *Celebrity Wrestling* did nothing to improve either the ratings or the reputation of the company. Charles Allen went for a reshuffle. He appointed Simon Shaps as ITV's Director of Programmes and moved Nigel Pickard sideways. Shaps brought in his own Praetorian Guard. Nigel Pickard left to join the RDF Media Group as director of family and children's programmes, and I told the team to start the car.

It took a while for them to get rid of us and we made a few headlines in the meantime. The interview with Tony Blair was the lead story in the media for a couple of days. I asked the then prime minister about the war in Iraq and how he coped with having to make life and death decisions:

PARKINSON: 'You've been called a liar and a warmonger . . . what's your feeling when you read that? And also when you read of casualties and people blame you for those casualties, that's an awful thing to live with and I wondered how you coped?'

BLAIR: 'Well it's even more difficult for the people out on the front line doing the job.'

PARKINSON: 'Of course.'

BLAIR: 'And that's what you have to remember.'

PARKINSON: 'And you sent them there.'

BLAIR: 'Yep. And that decision has to be taken and has to be lived with, and in the end there is a judgment that, well, if you have faith about these things, then you realise that judgment is made by other people. And also by . . .'

PARKINSON: 'Sorry, what do you mean by that?'

BLAIR: 'I mean by other people by, if you believe in God, it's meant by God as well . . . the only way you can make a decision like that is to try and do the right thing according to your conscience. As for the rest of it, you leave it to the judgment history will make.'

The *Daily Telegraph* said: 'It was the frankest admission Mr Blair has yet made about how his religious beliefs influence his actions as Prime Minister, particularly the life and death decisions involved in military action.'

We had wanted to do a one-man show with the prime minister but Number Ten thought not, which left us with the question of who we put on with him. I thought Kevin Spacey, the film actor and artistic director of the Old Vic, would be an excellent companion. He was politically smart, articulate and no supporter of Mr Blair's friend, the President of the United States, George Bush. In fact, when Spacey and Blair came together in the studio and the prime minister started talking about the president, Spacey jokingly moved his chair to the other end of the set.

We discussed the link between acting and politics and I said it always seemed to me that Bill Clinton was a marvellous actor. Tony Blair described him as 'the best politician I have ever come across'. He then told a marvellous story of a summit in a foreign land where, for some unfathomable reason, the world leaders were required to make a photo call wearing local fashions. He said he was given three shirts to chose from, 'ranging from ghastly to unbelievably hideous'.

He said, 'I put on what I thought was the least worse, which was to say ghastly, and go to the summit meeting and meet Clinton who is wearing the worst of the lot, the unbelievably hideous one. So I go up to him and say, "Bill, that looks awful." And he says, "Yep," and I say, "Why?" And he says, "Tony, let me tell you something. When the folks back home in America see my shirt they are going to say, look at our Mr President, someone has made him wear that shirt just to be nice to all those people out there. But when the folks back in Britain see you in your shirt they might just think you chose it."'

The show rated six million, the critics were so kind you would have thought we were a flagship for the network instead of being on our way out. The fact was Simon Shaps still didn't want the show. They tried Al Murray and Dame Edna in my spot in an obvious search for a replacement. Their ratings did nothing to suggest they had achieved this, yet Murray was openly talked of as the man who would take over. When we asked what the difference was between his ratings and ours we were told that his programmes were watched by 'different eyeballs'.

Charles Allen departed and our last reliable supporter had moved on. Michael Grade took over as ITV's Executive Chairman and took me out to lunch. He told me the show was 'too expensive', yet when the last series of *Parkinson* was announced we were told that Elizabeth Taylor was the star guest the bosses most desired and we could spend £250,000 on getting her. There was obviously still plenty in the pot to finance barmy ideas.

It was decided *Parkinson*'s last series would start in the autumn of 2007 and I set off to Australia to watch the cricket – but not before a letter arrived informing me I was to receive a knighthood in the New Year's Honours List. I had no idea. I told the family.

Felix, my four-year-old grandson, asked, 'Will you wear a suit of armour?' In fact I turned up in the morning suit Mr Hayward had made for my last visit to the palace to receive my CBE. That time Prince Charles officiated, this time it was Her Majesty The Queen. Stuart Rose, the boss of Marks & Spencer, was also being knighted. I had not met him before and found him an attractive man with a ready sense of humour. After we had been instructed in how to advance and retreat from Her Majesty we were asked if we had any questions. Stuart Rose asked if they had a back door through which he could make his entrance. When asked why he replied, 'I'm trade.' Her Majesty asked how long I had been on television. I told her about fifty years and she laughed, sympathetically.

In Australia, England were the visitors, defending the Ashes so gloriously won in 2005. The Aussies had their revenge with a display of what can only be termed aggressive retribution, which, at times, was so overwhelming as to appear contemptuous. Our only consolation was we were beaten by the best cricket team I have ever seen, including the greatest spin bowler of all time, Shane Warne. I interviewed Warne at length for Australian television and it turned out to be the highest rating satellite television programme of them all.

Then I sang at the Sydney Opera House.

It would be wrong to claim it had been my ambition so to do, but when the chance occurred I was eager to experience the impossible. It happened when I was asked to write and present a live concert of film music at the Opera House, along with the Sydney Symphony Orchestra. As I wrote the script and paraded the glorious music by the Bernsteins – Leonard and Elmer – Vaughan Williams, John Barry, John Williams and Henry Mancini, and many more, it occurred to me that, with a slight finagling, I could

347

construct a means whereby I might justify singing in one of the world's most spectacular monuments to great music and celebrated performers.

Discussing great movie songs in the script, I told the story of 'As time goes by' and how it was written long before the film *Casablanca* was ever made and how, after the film had been finished, the studio wanted to replace it with an alternative song. Their decision was thwarted only because Ingrid Bergman had moved on to make a film in which she played a partisan freedom fighter and had had her hair cropped so short they couldn't match the shot. So 'As time goes by' stayed because of a haircut and became the world's favourite movie love song.

Many years ago I recorded the song with my friend Laurie Holloway when I was one of a group of celebrities asked to record a drinking song and a love song for a charity CD. The drinking song I chose was one my father taught me called 'Beer is best'. I had used the song again in a documentary I wrote for Yorkshire Television. I told my audience that all of this justified my singing it in a programme about film music. It led to me standing on stage at the Sydney Opera House singing these words:

> Beer is best, beer is best,
> Makes you fit, makes you strong,
> Puts some vinegar in your old King Kong.
> Beer makes bonny Britons,
> Beer will stand the test,
> What did Winston Churchill say?
> Beer is best.

You have to admire my nerve.

I told the conductor, Brett Weymark, I needed a pub pianist to accompany me and a battered upright pub piano. The piano was just right but the pianist was a skilled classical musician and not familiar with the vamping style of pub pianists. Brett stepped in. He had played in pubs to pay his way through college and knew how to belt out a tune. Together we battered the audience into submission.

The entire event was hugely enjoyable. To stand in front of a large symphony orchestra is a great privilege and to feel the music surge through your body was to be transported into a state of what can only be described as musical bliss.

It was a happy time until Andrew, my eldest boy, called. My mother had been taken to hospital. She didn't have long to live. We flew back to London straightaway and, as we waited for our luggage at Heathrow, I received a call saying she had died.

We went to the Radcliffe Infirmary in Oxford where she was laid out in a room with her hair swept back, her hands on the coverlet and three pink flowers across her bosom. I remember thinking how formal she looked, how much she resembled a carving on a tomb. And then I realised that the reason I was inspecting her like an exhibit was because, yet again, I was avoiding the possibility of grief invading my life.

I took her hand, and let the sorrow and the joy of being her son overwhelm me, and then I knew my mother had died.

40

THE ENGINE OF
MY AMBITION

Freda Rose Parkinson was ninety-six years old when she died. For all but the last two years of her life she was an industrious and opinionated citizen of the world in which she lived. When she was born women did not have the vote, there was civil unrest in the land with gunboats in the Mersey and troops on the streets, and George V celebrated being crowned Emperor of India by going on a tiger shoot. She lived in the most momentous century of human existence, through wars and poverty and radical change without ever a backward glance, and in the end she didn't die; she gave in.

She was the engine of my ambition. Her anger at being an intelligent woman yet deprived of a chance of a brighter future by a system that discriminated against all working-class children, but particularly women, burned through her life. Typically, she converted the energy it created into forging her son's ambition. She filled the house with books, took me to the movies and the theatre, opened up the prospect of a life beyond the confines of a pit village.

Similarly, she drove my father on, encouraging him to make the best of a life down a pit. For a while he went along with the idea but only because he loved her. I remember sitting at our kitchen table doing my homework while my mother sat holding a large book on mining engineering, bullying him through exams.

She loved him, and no other, but not like he loved her. My father loved my mother with a devotion that defied reason but was wonderful to behold. It wasn't that he forgave his wife her faults and accommodated her shortcomings. He simply didn't see them, which was even more remarkable considering my mother could be a troublesome woman. Her success at designing knitwear and selling her talents from a council house in a mining village only further convinced her that life had dealt her a lousy hand. It seemed to me she constantly wished she was somewhere else, somewhere a long way removed from our view of Grimethrope Colliery.

Like any working-class matriarch, she ran the house and our lives according to her rules. She had a fearsome temper and I remember on one occasion sitting in my wigwam in the garden with my father after we had sought refuge from one of her tantrums, and he suggesting – jokingly – I should go back inside and ask her to she join us to smoke a pipe of peace.

On the other hand, I never witnessed her looking less than glamorous; nor ever saw her without admiring the way she took pride in her appearance.

I drew strength and confidence from her example and grew into manhood very much the son of my mother. It took me a journey into later life to become more like my father, or I hope that is what happened.

Her happiest days were spent living in her cottage in Oxfordshire, which is where they relocated after my father retired. They relished their grandchildren, started travelling abroad and never missed a chance to attend a recording of the talk show, where my mother, who was a terrible flirt, would flutter her eyelashes at the likes of James Stewart and Henry Fonda.

She was a widow for a third of her life and dealt with her grief and her solitude in a typically practical and resolute way. She took a summer job working in a holiday home she had visited with my father; she delivered meals on wheels and visited care homes where she gave beauty treatments to old people. She told me they often wanted to be made up to look like a film star from Hollywood's golden period, the favourite being Carmen Miranda.

She travelled abroad with friends, never losing her enjoyment of savouring the world, and grew closer to her sister Madge and her husband Jim, who formed a bedrock of love and understanding for Mary and our family as well as my mother. She lived by herself and resisted any form of outside help, such as a daily home help, until she was in her nineties.

She walked a mile or more every day of her life and was in her late eighties before a series of events led to me persuading her to stop driving. The end came when, after parking in a deserted street in Oxford and finding herself boxed in when she returned, she endeavoured to shunt her way out of trouble. I was rung by a car-owner incandescent with rage at having his car battered by an octogenarian road hog.

Ever after she went by public transport, turning down any other sensible alternative, such as a taxi. She soon forgot the circumstances that led to her giving up driving and for the last ten years of her life would tell anyone within earshot that her awful son had taken away her car for no apparent reason and was an ungrateful cur.

It was because she was so independent and mettlesome that her swift decline into senility became so wretched to witness. It started with what might be termed ordinary forgetfulness in a person in

352

her nineties, and then she began telling us of imagined visitors – a child, a cat, a family who spent all their time getting drunk in the pub across the way, keeping her awake at night. Then she started wandering. A young policeman called me at 2 a.m. He had found my mother in her dressing gown walking the streets looking for my father. He had taken her home and made her a cup of tea. They were getting along fine. He sat with her until we arrived.

He was kind and considerate and treated my mother with a great deal of respect, something that was not always forthcoming from some of the professionals when my mother entered the care system. I always remembered the compassion of that policeman, and the memory of what he did was a major reason why, after my mother died, I became ambassador for 'Dignity in Care', and part of a campaign to improve attitudes towards the elderly.

As her mind deteriorated she became increasingly angered at what she recognised as her growing inability to run her own life. She who had delivered meals on wheels started receiving them. She objected to being called 'Dear' or 'Ducky' and other such terms of endearment, which she took to indicate she was slightly gaga. She hated being addressed in a loud voice when her hearing was perfect. In other words, she objected to being regarded as decrepit.

There were humorous episodes. She started imagining that my father had returned but was spending all his time getting drunk at the pub. She would wait up for him and, on one or two occasions, rang the pub, asking the baffled landlord to return her husband forthwith before she came across and sorted them both out. I tried to explain to her that she was imagining things, but she countered my arguments with an irrefutable logic. I told her that my father didn't drink so why would he be found in a pub getting sloshed? What is more, I said, Dad had died thirty years ago.

'Your dad's dead?' she said. She never called him 'my husband' always 'your dad'. I said that was the case.

'Well no one told me,' she said.

I was thinking about this when she delivered the line to which there was no answer.

'If your father is dead,' she said, 'then who did I climb over to get out of bed this morning?'

We took her home but we couldn't cope. She seemed even more confused and disorientated and her occasional bouts of incontinence made her ashamed and deeply unhappy. She went into a nursing home near where she lived with a view of trees and a garden with statues. One day, looking at a statue, she said, 'He's been standing there for ages. I don't know what he's doing.'

As her confusion deepened she imagined the garden was a schoolyard filled with children. She invented a post office, which she owned, and was constantly badgering me to drive her there. I would take her out in the car through the Oxfordshire countryside and she would say, 'One day I would like to live here.' She sometimes thought I was her brother, Tom.

Normal conversation was impossible so one day, knowing her love of Frank Sinatra and the Great American Songbook, I played a CD in the car. She sang every lyric just about word perfect. She, who could barely recognise her own son or remember where she lived, could recall every lyric she had memorised as a young woman.

In the end, as I say, she gave up. She didn't like what she had become, so she hid her medication under her bed and, most tellingly of all, stopped caring about her appearance. We went to Australia to fulfil a contract but I always knew I would receive the call bringing me back. And that is what happened but too late to say our final goodbyes. In effect we had already done that a year or so beforehand when we still recognised each other.

I owed her so much and this book is a testament to her ambition, which she regarded as being fulfilled, as I finally understood, when we took her to Buckingham Palace in 2000 to receive my CBE. When she reached the palace door and was asked for her ticket, she discovered she had lost it.

She looked at the man on the door, chin jutting and eyes blazing, and explained, 'But I'm Mike Parkinson's mum.'

I withered with embarrassment.

'Of course you are,' said the kind man, and let her in.

41

FINAL LINE-UP

The last series started like the first series had done thirty-six years earlier, with a visit to Doug Hayward's. My friend since 1970 didn't measure me on this visit. He couldn't. For some time now he had been suffering a form of dementia, reducing his mind to a rubble. I felt guilty because when I sat with him I was talking to a stranger and, in truth, I couldn't cope. Whereas once we talked just about every day, I found myself closing my mind whenever I began to think about him.

I am forcing myself to remember as I write and I find myself smiling. He was a funny and engaging man. In 1970 he used his contacts and persuasive charm to finance a movie about a park football team going to Mexico to play in their own version of the World Cup. When they returned, he asked me to write the script. The fee was a couple of suits. The footage was a mess. It didn't make sense. The only way to make it work was by having a commentator in shot to blag his way somehow through the missing footage. That's what we did and it won an award.

I returned one of the suits Doug made me for performing this miracle because the canvas showed through on a button hole. My tailor inspected the damage, took a felt pen from his pocket and coloured the canvas blue, to match the suit.

'That's done it,' he said.

'Is that how you treat your customers?' I asked.

'Only those who haven't paid for their suit,' he said. It was the start of a loving friendship.

Doug Hayward died in a nursing home in early 2008. He was a very remarkable man and a good and true friend. His funeral service was in the lovely Farm Street church near Doug's shop in Mayfair. I spoke in tribute, along with Sir Michael Caine and Sir Roger Moore and later, at the reception, other close friends, including Sir Jackie Stewart and Jimmy Tarbuck, paid their tributes, as did the loyal and talented team who worked with him, particularly Audrey Charles who held everything together in Doug's darkest moments. I loved him very much and I will miss him. At the reception I was approached by a mutual friend who said Doug had given him a suit for his birthday. It fitted perfectly and he was very moved. Some time later, attending a sporting event and leaving his jacket in the cloakroom, there arose a question about identifying his jacket. My friend told the cloakroom attendant that he would find his name stitched into the inside pocket on a Hayward label. The man looked, smiled, and handed my friend the garment. The name tag read 'Made for Telly Savalas'.

We met at the ITV offices on the South Bank to start the process of booking the first show of the last series. According to that morning's newspapers we were going to start the series by bringing back the Emu. Rod Hull's son was taking over his dad's act and, according to Paul Jackson, our head of entertainment, he could well make his television debut as a guest on the last series of *Parkinson*. Mr Jackson was speaking at the Edinburgh Festival and I can only hope he was joking.

The media took it seriously and it came up at every interview in the run-up to the first show. One journalist (hopefully a trainee) asked me the question and then followed it up by asking if there was anyone I had wanted to interview but hadn't. 'Frank Sinatra,' I said. 'Any chance of getting him on this series?' she said. I said I'd ask Doris Stokes, who represented Mr Sinatra nowadays, and put the phone down before she asked me for Doris's phone number.

The line-up for the first show was Michael Palin, Diana Rigg and David Frost, with Annie Lennox doing the music spot. The guests had all been stalwarts over the years. This did not impress our bosses. One wondered if David Frost was 'interesting enough'. Another remarked, 'They are all so old.' Such helpful comments made us wonder – not for the first time – if there is a link between open-necked shirts and being brain dead.

We recorded the show at the London studios. Television studios have their own character and I had a soft spot for Studio 1. Standing at the top of the stairs, waiting to go on, was my favourite moment. Mine was the only big band in captivity. It was my indulgence and I loved the sound it made. The musicians, led by Laurie Holloway, were some of the best in the business. Their sound was a physical thing. I could feel it on my back as I walked down the stairs.

Michael Palin reminded me of my final appearance back in 1982 when I left the BBC for the first time. At the farewell party he had presented me with a Spear & Jackson No 5 shovel, as used by Eric Outhwaite, the Most Boring Yorkshireman of All Time, a character he created for an episode of that sublime series *Ripping Yarns*. The shovel has a brass plate with the inscription 'To The Second Most Boring Yorkshireman in the World'. It went well with the Light

Entertainment Depatment's brass bucket. At the time I was thinking of opening a hardware shop.

I asked David Frost if he could remember his first interview. He said it was when he was working for Anglia Television in the early sixties and he interviewed a scientist about a new insecticide, which devastated every living insect. David asked him if he was not concerned that such a toxic potion might also harm human beings, to which the scientist replied, 'We will cross that bridge when we come to it.'

Recalling his historic interview with President Nixon, David remembered a bizarre moment during the week of the interview. Nixon thought he should start every session with five minutes of relaxed small talk, but wasn't very good at it. This particular morning, trying to be one of the boys, he asked David, 'Did you do any fornicating this weekend?' David observed, 'In endeavouring to be matey he got the word wrong. I mean lovers don't call themselves fornicators any more than freedom fighters call themselves terrorists.'

Annie Lennox sang on the show. In between takes I talked to her about her dad who worked in the Glasgow shipyards and died young. She said, 'When I was leaving to come to the show my youngest daughter asked where I was going and when I told her she said, "Would you ask Parky if he'll be my granddad."'

Not everyone was as fond of me as that. Writing in the *Sunday Telegraph*, Stephen Pile said the time was coming when I was going to nod off in the middle of an interview. And I thought I was more sprightly of late. But I couldn't quibble with his observation: 'Parkinson's work looks old-fashioned now. His deference, professional reserve and journalistic competence are out of keeping with the times.'

If that's what was wrong with me, then it was definitely time to go.

In show two the guests were Billie Piper, James McAvoy and Jennifer Lopez. Billie was starring in *Belle de Jour*, the internet blog that became a book and then a six-part TV series. Belle is a high-class call girl. Some said she didn't exist, that she was a creation of a group of writers out to make a quid or two. Billie claimed to have met her, and said Belle was confident, bright, beautiful and loved sex. I'm not sure Billie enjoyed the part. I think she was worried about the public reaction to Dr Who's girlfriend playing a prostitute – 'From Who to Whore', as one headline writer put it.

Inevitably, I asked the question about actors taking their clothes off, and sex scenes, and how far you go. James McAvoy, sitting next to Billie, volunteered the information that whenever he played a sex scene he hid his willy by tucking it between his legs and taping it down. That confession was edited from our interview but I think the public has a right to know.

According to the celeb mags, Jennifer Lopez was no longer J-Lo. The 'Demanding Diva' was a thing of the past. Well the entourage this time did seem smaller than the last time we met six years before but it was still about the size of the Russian army. The last time, at the BBC, her dressing rooms were draped with white damask and she was surrounded by bodyguards whose ancestors modelled for the Easter Island statues. When I went to visit my interviewee in her dressing room I was turned away on suspicion of being a deranged stalker. It was the same this time. A bodyguard asked my business. 'I am Michael Parkinson. Miss Lopez is on my show,' I said. Not a flicker. Fortunately, the tour manager intervened. When eventually you get to see her she is a pleasant, humorous and very beautiful woman. She was born of Puerto Rican immigrants in the Bronx and didn't so much live the American dream as create her own personal fantasy world far removed from the slums of New York.

In fact, what all three guests had in common was a childhood determination to be a success. This is not the same as wanting to be a celebrity. It is the difference between hard work and an appearance on *Big Brother*.

Later, in the Green Room scrum, James McAvoy looked at ease. He is going to be a big star. He connects with his audience in the same way Ewan McGregor does. Both have a composure, a self-confidence that is remarkable in men so young. Ewan's cousin, the actor Denis Lawson, defines the gift as being total concentration, enabled by a certainty as to who and what they are. 'As well as being a great gift for an actor, it also makes them very attractive to women. Women love men who concentrate,' he said.

The third show featured Colin Firth, Al Murray and Harry Connick Jnr. I had wanted to interview Firth ever since my wife fell in love with him as Mr Darcy in *Pride and Prejudice*. I was hoping he would turn out to be a puny man with a badly fitting hairpiece. In fact, he is tall and exceedingly handsome. What is more, he is charming and self-effacing. Damn him.

Al Murray was another newcomer to the show. It looked like

he'd be replacing me when I leave, with his talk show based around the persona of the pub landlord. In fact, of course, it's a comedy show based on the talk-show format, which seems to be the preferred choice of the people running television nowadays. Yet another jokey spoof chat show. Whatever happened to the art of conversation?

Murray insisted on doing the interview in character as the pub landlord – a mistake and I told him so. I pointed out that experience with Ali G and Frankie Howerd had proved beyond debate that the scripted, in-character interview did not work. Frankie Howerd, terrified of working without a script, had the entire interview on autocue. It was a disaster. Later, he admitted he had been wrong and the next interview he did without a script and was wonderful. Ali G also insisted on the entire encounter being scripted, with predictable results. We warned Murray's people but they were adamant. I wanted to debook him but the bosses regarded Murray as an ITV star of the future and were wary of upsetting him. We didn't script the interview but it was very carefully prepared and the result was that it didn't work. It looked and felt awkward and staged. The only artists who could be truly conversational in character were the glorious Dame Edna, the marvellous Lily Savage and the unpronounceable Cupid Stunt.

Michael Heseltine's Haymarket group of companies was celebrating its fiftieth anniversary and I was at the Grosvenor House to say a few words about the great man and introduce the cabaret. I almost never go to official dinners, first nights, cocktail parties or any such event. I don't like them, they don't suit me. So how come I was standing up in front of nine hundred well-heeled guests, thinking what the hell am I doing here? You could smell the money, and the reason I was sniffing it was because I had been having a rose named after me at the National Exhibition Centre in Birmingham when Michael Heseltine appeared out of a Japanese garden and reminded me of a time, forty-seven years ago, when I worked for him. His publishing empire, which included gardening magazines, was coming up fifty and would I help him out at the dinner?

That was why I was sitting at the top table at Grosvenor House surrounded by bankers and other friends of Michael's, including David Frost, John Major – looking ten years younger than when he was PM – Mary Quant and Stirling Moss. I introduced Shirley Bassey as the cabaret event, one of the few performers extant who could defeat the size and acoustic of the hall, which must have been built to house the Graf Zeppelin.

I started counting the ratio of bald heads to full heads of hair, which I normally do on these occasions if only to allow myself a slight feeling of superiority. I spotted a white-haired man on the next table who had fallen asleep. A picture of this with the caption 'The Man Who Fell Asleep During a Shirley Bassey Concert' would become a collector's item. Nothing woke him, not all of Shirley's anthems, until 'Something', when he jerked forward like a salmon at a fly. He was in fact attempting to rescue his front teeth, which had fallen from his slack mouth.

My mind wandered on from heads to haircuts. I have mine done by Leslie at Smile. I've been going there for nearly forty years. Same wife, same house, same job for all that time. Must be I don't like change or, more likely, recognise a good thing when I see it. Les has seen my hair go from dark brown to salt and pepper to white. There was a time when it went a most peculiar colour due to the sun.

Immediately rumours started that I had bleached it. The papers had their fun but then it became silly. One of the assistants in the salon told Les that she had been approached by a journalist who offered her a hundred quid if she could give them a lock of my hair so they might analyse it and tell the nation the awful truth. What we did was provide her with a snip of hair from a Pekingese of my acquaintance. We heard no more but I can only imagine the journalist's reaction to the analyst's report that Mr Parkinson did not dye his hair but, on the other hand, he *had* won a prize at Crufts.

Ricky Hatton, Paul Anka and Michael Winner were the stars of our fourth show. I first met Paul through Sammy Cahn, who took me to Vegas to see him in cabaret, a show that ranked as one of the very best I have ever seen. Anka talked about the heyday of Vegas and partying with Sinatra. He told the story of Sinatra getting drunk and belligerent one night at the Sands Hotel and having an argument in the Casino, which ended in the management sending for Carl Cohen, 'a mob guy', to calm him down.

Paul said, 'Sinatra pulled the tablecloth from Cohen's table, spilling hot coffee all over him. Cohen punched Sinatra in the mouth, sending his teeth flying all over the coffee shop.'

'What happened?' I asked.

'We never went back to the Sands again, is what happened,' said Paul.

Michael Winner talked about his recovery from a near-fatal illness. He said in hospital he was put in the Princess Margaret Room, provoking his reaction, 'Great, I thought, she died.'

I asked Ricky Hatton, who is such a funny, agreeable young man, how he squared his gentle, pleasant personality with his pitbull aggression in the ring. He said, 'It's nice to be nice before you beat someone up.' Great title for a book.

We booked an all-female show for our fifth. These always work well, partly because the women gang up on me in a game called 'Kill the Host', but mainly because women are better at relating to one another in that conversational gossipy way that works so well on the talk show. The guests were Sophie Dahl, Sharon Osbourne and Joan Rivers. I remember Sophie as a baby and look at her now – tall, willowy, beautiful. I knew her mum and her grannie and granddad, Roald Dahl and Patricia Neal, who were a fascinating couple. Looking at their granddaughter made me feel old.

Sharon Osbourne is a remarkable woman and I admire the way she has survived a turbulent life, making a virtue, nay a career, out of adversity.

You could say the same about Joan Rivers, who found comedy a better cure than pills or, indeed, suicide, as she had demonstrated on an earlier show, and in doing so created one of my all-time favourite comedy moments. She was sitting next to Cliff Richard and was describing how, at a particularly depressing moment in her life, she took a revolver and was about to blow her brains out when her pet dog jumped on her lap and nuzzled her. She paused in the telling, but I didn't fall for it. I had worked with enough comedians to know they can't keep a straight face for too long. Cliff, being nice, dear Cliff, offered her a reassuring hand, and asked sympathetically, 'What did you do?' 'I shot the dog,' said Ms Rivers. Indicating her fur collar, she added, 'Look, I'm wearing him now.'

Our next guests were the remarkable Attenboroughs. Dickie told me about his lifelong fascination with Gandhi and his first sighting of him in a cinema newsreel with his father in the 1930s. Dickie said Gandhi was dressed in his familiar dhoti and the audience laughed and jeered at his appearance. His father told him, 'My son, the loud laugh bespeaks the empty mind. This is a truly great man.' Later, when he was planning his film about Gandhi, he was particularly impressed by a story of Gandhi walking down a street and having to step into the gutter to make way for two white men. Gandhi said to his companion, 'It amazes me that men should feel honoured by the humiliation of fellow human beings.' Dickie Attenborough has made a singular contribution to British cultural life and history will judge him as one of the great nurturing guardians of the British film industry.

Sir David Attenborough is the greatest broadcaster of our time. His documentaries have entertained and informed countless millions, and no one has done more to explain the planet we occupy. The most damning condemnation of television today is that in the unlikely event of another David Attenborough turning up, the bosses wouldn't know what to do with him. He is irreplaceable and why he is not a Nobel Laureate is one of life's great mysteries.

Similarly, Bobby Charlton, the third guest on the same show, occupies a special place in our hearts. Not only was he one of the greatest footballers of all time, and certainly assured of his place in any England team of any era, but his gentle, modest way and the dignity of his bearing make him a role model for any sportsman. That many of the modern players choose to ignore his example (although, it's possible most of them don't know who he is) is both their loss, and their shame.

With the lovely Joanna Lumley I fronted the sixtieth anniversary of BAFTA at the New London Theatre. There was the usual crowd of autograph-hunters outside. Nowadays, they constitute two different categories – those who do it for love and those who do it for money. The latter is the largest category – by far. These are the people who sell the autograph on eBay, the ones who ask you to sign single sheets of paper or a photo without a dedication. Autograph books are rare. One eBay woman, with a child aged about twelve, gave me a page to sign. 'Look who it is,' she said to her son. 'Who is he?' he said. 'Parkinson,' she explained. 'What's his first name?' he asked. 'Don't know,' she said. I signed Britney Parkinson.

Miss Piggy was the first star guest on the BAFTA evening. I wanted to revive our relationship, to talk to her to see if the magic still existed. Sadly, the producers gave the job to Sharon Osbourne, which was a serious piece of miscasting. Fact is, Miss Piggy is a man-eater, a predatory female. All the humour stems from her relationship with men. The sexual tension, the source of her humour, is lost playing opposite a woman. 'Leave us now, we have woman's talk,' Sharon said to me. 'You have much in common,' I replied.

Sharon and the pig were OK, but the Kumars meeting Sir Ben Kingsley was awkward. It seemed like a great idea at the time – the Kumars meeting Gandhi is irresistible – but it suffered because Sir Ben seemed to be unaware that *The Kumars at 42* is a spoof chat show. The dynamic of the Kumars is the conflict between the son – the splendid Sanjeev Bhaskar – and his ambition to be a talk-show host, and his feisty grandma – the sublime Meera Syal – who thinks he is an idiot, and who has the hots for some of the male guests. The guest is simply the poor sap caught in the crossfire of their relationship, the victim of their confusion. When I did the show she called me 'a silver-haired mongoose'. There's an ancient twinkle in her eye, like a snowflake on a tombstone.

When I left the theatre the autograph-hunters were still there. The woman and her son hadn't moved from the front row. Behind them a man lifted up his book and asked me to sign. I reached out to take his book over the head of the boy who looked up at my armpit and he cried, 'Oh look, mam, he's got a big hole in his jumper.'

Daniel Radcliffe, the young actor made into an international star by playing Harry Potter, is a shiny person. Everything about him gleams from his highly polished shoes to his open, friendly face. He was on our seventh show to talk about his role in a TV drama called *My Boy Jack*, the tragic story of the death of Rudyard Kipling's son in the First World War. The story has a particular poignancy because Rudyard Kipling was the country's foremost advocate of war against Germany and encouraged his boy to enlist, even though he had failed a medical board. The ensuing tragedy resulted in Kipling writing bitter poetry about the war, including the chilling couplet:

> If any question why we died,
> Tell them because our fathers lied.

I was especially interested in the interview because of my fascination with the First World War and its poets. In fact, the day before I met Daniel I had bought a first edition of Wilfred Owen's war poems, which included a letter from his mother to a neighbour saying: 'Wilfred would have wanted you to have this book.'

Owen's observations of the horrors of war, of the bravery of soldiers, of the discrepancy between those who send men to war and those who fight them on their behalf, are as true and meaningful today as they were when he wrote them in the trenches ninety years ago. And we thought, as we always do, it was the war to end all wars. We vowed never to forget them. But we did. And we are still doing it.

Daniel was on the show with Dawn French, Jennifer Saunders and Ray Winstone. The last time I interviewed Dawn and Jennifer was at the BBC with Tom Jones. Everything went according to plan until Tom's song spot when the girls thought they would enliven the end by throwing knickers at the singer. The crowd loved it, Tom didn't mind (it brought back memories) but his management team thought it a disgraceful slur on their artist's reputation, this, in spite of the fact that there was a time in Tom's life when women threw so many undergarments at him, the knicker factory in *Coronation Street* went into overtime.

One evening Mary and I went to see Patrick Stewart in *Macbeth*, a powerful, compelling production, which, along with his recent work in classical theatre, marks him as one of the most charismatic actors of his generation. When he returned from America and the *Star Trek* franchise, he set about using his celebrity and financial clout to do all the work he had longed to do since leaving Britain for the States. He was also involved in good work as Chancellor at Huddersfield University and, over dinner after the show, asked if I would accept an honorary degree. The ceremony, he said, would be at Barnsley Town Hall. That was the clincher.

I had Lewis Hamilton, the hottest young man in all of British sport, on the show. That first season he could do no wrong. He was a slight, attractive figure with a quiet manner and a nutcracker handshake. He talked about the feeling of serenity that sometimes sweeps over him in the cockpit when he is doing well and at one with the car. He said he relaxes so much he often hums to himself during a Grand Prix. It was one of the few times I got an interesting response to that hoary old question about what goes through the mind of an actor, musician, athlete – any performer – as they push themselves to their limits.

Frank Tyson, the England fast bowler, was said to recite poetry as he ran in to relax him and aid his concentration. Dickie Bird told me a marvellous story of playing against the great man at Scarborough and hitting him for three consecutive fours. According to Bird, as he delivered the fourth ball, what he heard from Tyson was not poetry, but the challenge, 'Hit that bugger for four.' They were, said Dickie, the last words he heard before he ended up in hospital with a broken jaw.

Another time, after I had introduced Kiri Te Kanawa at an open-air concert and she had sung a sublime version of 'Summertime', I asked her what was going through her mind as she created a sound of such purity and beauty. She said, 'Halfway through the song I saw three ducks flying across my line of vision and I thought, I wish I'd brought my gun.'

David Cameron was on the same show as Lewis Hamilton. He recounted how he had met Kate Moss at a charity do. He remembered she had a house in his constituency that had recently been flooded, so he said how sorry he was, particularly because the local pub had also been flooded and he knew how much she liked the pub, but it was going to be opened in six months, so anything he could do in the meantime? He was, in his own words, 'wittering'. She told him he seemed like a really useful guy and could she have his phone number. He went back to his table and announced, 'The good news is I met Kate Moss and she wanted my telephone number, the bad news is she thinks I'm something to do with drainage.'

With Lewis Hamilton and David Cameron we lined up Sir Ian McKellen whom I encountered again a couple of days later when he presented me with the Variety Club's Lifetime Achievement Award. I was particularly honoured that he dressed up in tuxedo and black tie for the event because the last time we were together at a formal occasion his choice of clothing was what you might call eccentric.

We were in Sydney and I was asked to invite him to the Sydney Cricket Ground to watch a day/night fixture. I told Ian that, although he was invited to a sporting event, it was quite formal and he would require a jacket and tie. He said he would dress appropriately.

I was in the box at the SCG talking to one of the bigwigs when I saw him look over my shoulder in horror. I turned to see my friend standing in the doorway wearing what looked like a white umpire's coat, a baseball cap and purple clogs. 'I thought I'd come as Dickie Bird,' said Sir Ian.

We did a music special towards the end of the series with Rod Stewart and Michael Bublé in the studio and a host of clips recalling the important part music had played on the show over the years. The range of guests was remarkable, everyone from Artur Rubinstein to Liberace, Pavarotti to Joe Cocker, Yehudi Menuhin to Stéphane Grappelli. We had paired the two great violinists on the show and the result was a long friendship and half a dozen albums.

Yehudi Menuhin had been booked to appear and the researcher reported that, while visiting him, she saw an album by Stéphane Grappelli on his desk. She enquired if he was a fan and Menuhin said he had been sent the album but was not aware of Grappelli's work. We called Stéphane, who was working in a club in Paris, and asked if he would appear on the show with Menuhin. He was uncertain. 'He is a maestro, I am a humble fiddle-player,' he said. We convinced him and he flew in to meet Menuhin who, by this time, had listened to Grappelli's album and was insisting that if they played together they must first rehearse at his house.

Stéphane arrived, straight from his stint in the nightclub, and was whisked off to meet Menuhin. He was very nervous. He returned three hours later, his face wreathed in smiles. We asked him how the rehearsal had been. Stéphane said, 'How did it go? I tell you. Five bars into "Lady be good" who is the maestro?' Menuhin was in awe of Grappelli's effortless improvising, something he found as impossible to achieve as it would have been for Stéphane to play the Brahms Violin Concerto.

It is hard to imagine two more diverse personalities – Menuhin, an infant prodigy, a protected species from childhood; Stéphane, a child of smoke-filled rooms, who never had a formal lesson in his life and created, along with Django Reinhardt and the Hot Club, a sound as enchanting and fresh as any in all of jazz.

He told me a wonderful story of the Hot Club being hired by a very wealthy man to play at a party in the South of France. The catch was the host said it was a nude event and they would have to play in the buff. Money overcame modesty and they agreed. Stark naked except for their instruments, they were placed on the bandstand behind a velvet curtain and could hear the babble of the guests in the ballroom. As they started to play the curtain parted to reveal the guests resplendent in tails and ballgowns. As Stéphane said, it was all right for Django because he was sitting with the guitar in his lap, but the nude violinist had no means of covering up.

What happened? 'It went very well. They asked me back to do a solo spot next year,' said Stéphane.

When we reached the very last talk show I imagined I ought to feel differently from the way I did, which was relieved. The last time I gave it up I always knew there would be a way back. Now there was no chance of that happening and I was somewhat content and fulfilled by the knowledge. I had also given up the Radio 2 show because I always saw it operating in conjunction with television and, in any case, after twelve years, it was enough. To publicise the show a photo shoot for a magazine had been arranged. When I got to the studio I found they had constructed a large wooden box and were suggesting I step into it, and I did feel that was a bit premature.

The line-up for the final TV show was Billy Connolly, Dame Judi Dench, Sir Richard Attenborough, Sir Michael Caine, Peter Kay, Dame Edna Everage and David Beckham. They all had their own particular place in the history of the show and had contributed greatly to its success and my enjoyment. Peter Kay decided to wear a tie for the occasion but didn't know how to tie a proper knot. I obliged with a large and flamboyant Windsor. Dame Judi sang me a song and Dame Edna seemed smitten by David Beckham. It was all very jolly, which is how it should be.

As to the inevitable questions about how I felt, I was reminded of Fred Trueman's reply to the same question when he took his 300th Test wicket. 'How do you feel, Fred?' they asked. 'Knackered,' said Fred.

I had one more appearance to do to wrap things up and that was to link a compilation programme featuring just a few of the great stars and moments from about eight hundred shows. When I walked on to the set I discovered that the backstage area where the guests relaxed before walking down the stairs had already been cleared of furniture and fittings. Even the photos on the walls had been removed. It was then I realised that this was the very last time I would stand at the top of those stairs and be blown on by the big band, and never again would I sit in that black leather chair and feel the energy of the audience. I remember thinking, as I sat down, I'm going to buy this chair, otherwise they'll sell it off along with everything else.

I felt oddly forlorn, and the job of reliving the moments with Ali, Welles, Ustinov, Billy Connolly, Woody Allen, Paul McCartney, John Lennon and the rest did nothing to lighten my mood. In the audience were people who had been significant to the show over the years – Mary, my family, John Webber and James Erskine, my wise agents and friends, Dabber Davies, another mate who never missed a show and who can be heard laughing on every one from Bob Hope to Peter Kay. Missing was Richard Drewett who helped create the show at the very beginning and who was a special friend. He had been suffering a debilitating illness for years, facing it with the same humour and determination he put into everything he did. We invited him to the show and, against all expectation, he said he would come. Entering the building he fell and fractured a hip and later died in hospital. At his funeral his son told of visiting him in hospital and asking if there was anything he could do for him. 'How about an upgrade?' said Richard.

Some time later I went up north and revisited the old haunts, including a working-men's club I used to frequent with my dad. There was a very old man in the corner whom I recognised. I went over and introduced myself. He seemed baffled. I said, 'You remember, Mike Parkinson, used to live down Darfield Road. Jack's lad.'

'Oh, I remember now,' he said. 'Jack's lad. Not seen you for a very long time. What you been up to?'

INDEX